Ethics and Criminal Justice

This book examines the main ethical questions that confront the criminal justice system – legislature, law enforcement, courts, and corrections – and those who work within that system, especially police officers, prosecutors, defense lawyers, judges, juries, and prison officers. John Kleinig sets the issues in the context of a liberal democratic society and its ethical and legislative underpinnings, and illustrates them with a wide and international range of real-life case studies. Topics covered include discretion, capital punishment, terrorism, restorative justice, and reentry. Kleinig's discussion is both philosophically acute and grounded in institutional realities, and will enable students to engage productively with the ethical questions which they encounter both now and in the future – whether as criminal justice professionals or as reflective citizens.

JOHN KLEINIG is Director of the Institute for Criminal Justice Ethics and Professor of Philosophy in the Department of Law and Police Science, John Jay College of Criminal Justice, and in the PhD Programs in Philosophy and Criminal Justice, City University of New York. He also holds the Charles Sturt University Chair of Policing Ethics in the Centre for Applied Philosophy and Public Ethics, Canberra.

Ethics and Criminal Justice

An Introduction

JOHN KLEINIG

John Jay College of Criminal Justice, CUNY
Centre for Applied Philosophy and Public Ethics, CSU

CAMBRIDGE
UNIVERSITY PRESS

CAMBRIDGE UNIVERSITY PRESS
Cambridge, New York, Melbourne, Madrid, Cape Town, Singapore, São Paulo, Delhi

Cambridge University Press
The Edinburgh Building, Cambridge CB2 8RU, UK

Published in the United States of America by Cambridge University Press, New York

www.cambridge.org
Information on this title: www.cambridge.org/9780521682831

© John Kleinig 2008

First published 2008

Printed in the United Kingdom at the University Press, Cambridge

A catalogue record for this publication is available from the British Library

ISBN 978-0-521-86420-6 hardback
ISBN 978-0-521-68283-1 paperback

For Tziporah

Contents

Acknowledgments

When Hilary Gaskin of Cambridge University Press approached me to write this volume she encountered several years of resistance to such a project, and suffered a few more. I appreciate her persistence and willingness to listen to my hesitations and expectations. I am also appreciative of the comments of those whom Cambridge approached to review the proposal – constructive, sometimes divergent, but always valuable. Their authors can take some credit for the form of the final version, even though my obduracy prevailed on a number of issues.

Teaching responsibilities help to adjust one's ear to student needs and to the development of class materials. And so I am grateful for the opportunities that John Jay College of Criminal Justice has provided over the years that I have been working in this area. It has enviable resources and through the Institute for Criminal Justice Ethics I have been able to organize conferences on a number of the topics covered here. But teaching and administrative responsibilities do not provide the extended time one needs to author a book. And so I am particularly appreciative of an arrangement between John Jay College and Charles Sturt University in Australia that has recently enabled my assignment for six months of the year to the Centre for Applied Philosophy and Public Ethics (an Australian Research Council funded Special Research Centre) at Charles Sturt University in Canberra. A genuine *sine qua non*, but not sufficient. Beyond the institutional provision, Margaret Leland Smith has, by assuming my administrative responsibilities in New York, enabled me to translate the possibility into reality.

Several people have looked over drafts or parts thereof: Andrew Alexandra, Simon Bronitt, Brandon del Pozo, Hilary Gaskin, William Heffernan, Tziporah Kasachkoff, Jess Maghan, Evan Mandery, Haim Marantz, Kevin McCarthy, Candace McCoy, and Adina Schwartz. In addition, students in a Fall 2006 class at John Jay College alerted me to a number of unclarities and missteps. I have, however, retained and no doubt exercised the right to make my own mistakes.

My greatest thanks go to Tziporah Kasachkoff, to whom I dedicate this volume. Apart from her loving support, she became my Harriet Taylor, clarifying my thoughts, questioning my arguments, and transforming my sparse prose into palatable English.

In writing this volume, I have sometimes drawn upon other work. Usually I have rewritten the material, but occasionally I have drawn more heavily on wordings used elsewhere. Included have been *The Ethics of Policing* (Cambridge: Cambridge University Press, 1996); "Introduction: Handling Discretion with Discretion," in *Handled With Discretion: Ethical Issues in Police Decision Making*, ed. John Kleinig (Lanham, MD: Rowman & Littlefield, 1996), 1–12; "Selective Enforcement and the Rule of Law," *Journal of Social Philosophy* 29, no. 1 (Spring, 1998): 117–31; "Torture and Political Morality," in *Politics and Ethics*, ed. Igor Primoratz (Basingstoke: Palgrave/Macmillan, 2007), ch. 12, pp. 209–27; "The Conscientious Advocate and Client Perjury," *Criminal Justice Ethics* 5 (Summer/Fall, 1986): 3–15; "Ethical Foundations of the American Criminal Jury," in *Jury Ethics: Juror Conduct and Jury Dynamics*, ed. John Kleinig and James P. Levine (Boulder, CO: Paradigm Publishers, 2006), 1–19 (with James P. Levine); "Punishment and Moral Seriousness," *Israel Law Review* 25, no. 3/4 (Summer–Autumn, 1991): 401–21; "The Hardness of Hard Treatment," in *Fundamentals of Sentencing Theory*, ed. Andrew Ashworth and Martin Wasik (Oxford: Clarendon, 1998), 273–98; "Professionalizing Incarceration," *Discretion, Community, and Correctional Ethics*, ed. John Kleinig and Margaret Leland Smith (Lanham, MD: Rowman & Littlefield, 2001), 1–15; and "Disenfranchising Felons," *Journal of Applied Philosophy* 22 (November, 2005): 217–39 (with Kevin Murtagh).

Introduction

For most of the past two centuries, the institutions of criminal justice have been predominantly agencies of or accountable to government (be it local, state, or national). That is not to deny or ignore the presence or influence of privatization. But because government is usually the main source of funding and oversight, how we conceive of governmental power influences how we view such institutions and their processes, and the resources upon which we draw when we seek to justify them. The justificatory framework for this volume is broadly "liberal democratic" – that is, it views the role of the institutions of criminal justice in terms of "social peacekeeping" rather than of "pacification." It sees, in other words, the institutions of criminal justice as securing public rather than merely state interests. But to say one takes a "liberal democratic" approach is to speak in fairly broad terms. There is no single way of being liberal and democratic, and the institutions and processes of criminal justice found in the United States, United Kingdom, Europe, and Australia differ in many and sometimes quite significant ways, though not necessarily in ways that diminish their liberal democratic claims. Their histories (and to some extent their geographies) are sufficiently different to have given rise to what are often quite distinctive ways of being liberal and democratic. As a result, it is not possible to engage in a relatively brief introductory discussion of a liberal democratic criminal justice ethics that applies accurately and equally to the traditions and institutions of all liberal democracies.

In this volume I focus most directly on the structures and processes of criminal justice in the United States. Apart from the need to simplify, there are at least three additional reasons for this concentration. First, it is the tradition in which most of my own thinking about such issues has occurred (even though it is not the tradition in which I grew up). Second, criminal justice institutions in the USA have tended to generate the liveliest and sometimes the most probing debate, and so the philosophical and ethical discussion is frequently better developed in relation to US institutions. And third, until recently, university-level discussions of criminal justice have been better integrated into the US curriculum than into the curricula of other liberal democratic societies. Despite these considerations, I have attempted to offer some comparative observations and also to treat problems in ways that allow for their relatively easy transposition to other English-speaking liberal democratic traditions. In the suggested additional reading, I have provided references to extended localized expositions. In the course of some of my comparative observations, I hope that alternative ways of thinking will be opened up for US readers (especially as much of the American debate is still disappointingly parochial).

A few comments on the title might be appropriate. My concern in the volume is with *ethics* in criminal justice. There is a substantial literature on the sociology, politics, and administration of criminal justice, and a great number of explanatory theories about the institutions of criminal justice have been offered. I have not tried to summarize or add to that literature. Although I draw on it from time to time, my main purpose is to direct attention to some of the broader ethical questions that are prompted by the system, its institutions, and its processes. Such questions are *fundamental* and *pervasive*. They are fundamental in two related senses: first, in the sense that they are concerned with the basic currency of human interaction. They are concerned with what we *are* in our relations with others – that is, not only with what we *do* or do not do to and for others, but also with our attitudes and reasons for acting as we do. Behaving well may fail ethically if it is prompted by unworthy reasons, a point often exploited in cases of whistle-blowing when defenders of an exposed organization attempt to divert attention from its failings by impugning the whistle-blower's motives. Second, they are fundamental because ethical standards constitute our most basic tool for the assessment of other social norms – for example, those generated by politics, economics, law, or custom. We do not normally consider it appropriate to judge ethical standards by reference to political, economic, or legal norms, but instead subject the latter to ethical scrutiny. If political decisions or economic policies or laws are criticizable on ethical or moral grounds, we have a strong reason for seeking to change them. If what is put forward as good business or good politics is bad ethics, we should reconsider the former rather than the latter. It is not that for ethical reasons we should encourage bad commercial or political practices. Our goal should be to develop business and political practices that are not only ethically good but also good commercially and politically.

The ethical discussion to be found in these pages is focused on *criminal justice*. I understand by that the institutions of criminal justice (most centrally, police, courts, and corrections) and their occupational players (police officers, sheriffs, marshals, prosecutors, defense lawyers, jurors, magistrates, judges, correctional officers, and so on). But the institutions and their players are embedded in a wider system of law, a significant amount of which is devoted to other matters – such as contracts, torts, business, divorce, labor, and international affairs – and though we should not overdo their differences, there tend to be different role expectations associated with the different branches. In focusing on criminal justice and its players I do not provide a comprehensive account of either the broad governmental institutions we have or the roles of those who work within them. The civil jury does not operate in the same way as a criminal jury and ethical problems confronted by tort lawyers will at best overlap with those of a criminal defense lawyer.

Finally, this volume is intended only as an *introduction*. It envisages the constraints of a course in criminal justice ethics and does not claim or attempt to provide a comprehensive coverage of even the main ethical issues that practitioners will encounter or thoughtful citizens will ponder. But I hope to have provided a sufficiently developed framework of understanding to enable readers to grapple with those issues and to stimulate and enable such readers to take the discussion further.

In conclusion, it needs to be emphasized that this volume does not seek to endorse criminal justice systems or institutions or processes *as they exist*. Indeed, insofar as it refers to the workings of actual criminal justice systems, it will often be to suggest that the system as we find it falls short in various ways. Its purpose, rather, is to offer a normative account of the institutions and processes of criminal justice, that is, one that indicates how such institutions and processes might be legitimately reconceived and improved.

Part I

Criminalization

The institutions of criminal justice – most particularly the police, courts, and corrections – do not exist in a moral, social, or political vacuum, but reflect important and often controversial assumptions. The three chapters that follow attempt to expose and reflect on some of those assumptions, not specifically to reject them but to enable us to hear the "accent" with which we speak when we consider the activities of police, courts, and corrections. Our accent is that of a liberal democratic tradition, with roots in Greek, Judaeo-Christian, and Enlightenment thinking, characterized by ideas of equality, dignity, freedom, and responsibility, but increasingly enriched and challenged by ideas from other traditions. It is within this increasingly diverse environment that the institutions of criminal justice must develop a voice that is not only faithful to their heritage but also sensitive to the legitimate expectations of those who have come within their reach.

1   Civil society: its institutions and major players

We never hear our own accent. But others do.

Because you are reading this, it is highly likely that you possess certain beliefs about yourself and other human beings – for example, that you are a rational being and that in virtue of that you possess a certain dignity and, by implication, have certain rights such as those to life and liberty. You are also likely to believe that you – and others – are generally responsible for what you do. But these beliefs have not always been held and even now are not universally held. Indeed, at different periods of human history and in different places, these beliefs would have seemed alien and unintelligible. You hold these beliefs now because you are part of a *tradition* – in this case a *liberal* tradition – that originated several centuries ago in response to and with the decline of feudalism.

It is worth pondering the fact that what you believe and who you take yourself to be is due in large part to your social and cultural history. You probably see yourself not as having been born into a fixed social order with a relatively predetermined social role (as was the case with those born into a feudal society), but rather as a unique human individual possessing the ability, within the limits of your capacities and preparation, to be many things. But you did not come to be this individual on your own, as a tree might "naturally" develop its distinctive characteristics, given only adequate physical sustenance. Your genetic endowment aside, you are the self-reflective and self-determining individual you are by virtue of a fairly long process of social nurture provided by your family, your friends, your school, and other influences to which you have been exposed. All of these have enabled you to become the person you now are. Had you been reared in a different kind of society you would have had a very different conception of yourself. And had you instead been reared in the wild by animals or without human contact, you would lack most of the personal qualities you almost certainly consider to be central to the person you now are.[1]

Of the many things you have learned in the course of your life, one of the most important is that your relations with others are – or at least should be – mediated by certain understandings, expectations, and norms or standards, much of which we include under the umbrella term "morality." Although moral standards differ somewhat from community to community and even from individual to individual, there is significant overlap between them because we share a fair degree of understanding about the things that are important for our human flourishing and therefore about what should constrain as well as what should direct our relations with others. For example, almost all of us believe that we should not maim or kill others, treat others as objects for our manipulation or deception, or steal from them. Probably we also think that – insofar as we are able – we should positively care for others. It is not that these expectations are without exception or that we will apply them in the same way. But we are all physically embodied in much the same way, and our mental and emotional capacities are sufficiently similar for us to have shared understandings about what compromises or jeopardizes the flourishing of creatures such as ourselves. Moreover, to the extent that our understanding of constraints and requirements is *not* shared, we have a problem, for then our relations with others will be beset by conflicting understandings. Fortunately, this problem is not always irresolvable because, as language-speakers, we can engage in rational discourse with one another, and thereby address our differences with a view to their resolution or at least mutual understanding. Of course, differences in our understanding about what makes for a good or flourishing life can make *initial* encounters problematic, a matter to which we will later return.

One question that arises is why, if we share a broadly congruent morality, those shared understandings of what is expected of us are not sufficient to govern the social interactions of our daily life without the intervention of other social institutions. Why is so much of our daily intercourse with others constrained or determined or mediated by law and the larger authoritative structures that we see as originating with "government" or "the state"? That

---

[1] For an account of this phenomenon, see Michael Newton, *Savage Girls and Wild Boys: A History of Feral Children* (New York: Faber & Faber, 2002).

is a question to which the adherents of what is known as "anarchism" offer a skeptical answer. They consider that our moral resources *are* adequate for the business of life and that governments will always oppressively exceed whatever authority they possess. But anarchism is a view that has not found general acceptance, mainly because most of us believe that our personal moral resources alone are collectively inadequate to the task of mediating our relations with others in the full range of cases we are likely to encounter. In a world of limited resources, varying insight, and conflicting claims, we are often unjustifiably self-interested or partial to those who are nearest and dearest to us. Though self-interest and partiality are not illegitimate in themselves, they easily cloud our judgment. We are, moreover, prone to self-deception, weakness of will, and even to nakedly evil tendencies. Such impediments to wise and fair decision-making and conduct toward others show a need for some "outside" governance such as is provided by the state and its agencies.

Moral foundations of liberal democracy

Nominating the state as an institution that may legitimately require – even by threat of force – its citizens to conduct themselves toward one another in certain ways is problematic. It was a chief worry of seventeenth- and eighteenth-century English liberal theorists such as John Locke (1632–1704), who saw the tension between, on the one hand, the establishment of governmental institutions with coercive powers against citizens, and, on the other hand, citizens who had begun to see themselves as free agents with their own rights of self-determination and governance. Locke – a philosopher, physician, and political activist – was fortunate enough to be writing at a period of social transition in England (the English Bill of Rights was promulgated in 1689). The replacement of an absolute monarch by a constitutional one and the ascendancy of an elected parliament as the supreme political institution provided him with the opportunity to offer his reflections upon this transition as well as a "solution" to the problem posed by governmental authority. Although he was only one of many to write on such issues, Locke's writings came to be greatly influential not only in England but also in the New World ferment that resulted, in 1776, in what became known as "the American experiment." If you read the Declaration of Independence, which was drafted by Thomas Jefferson, you could almost believe that it was based on the writings of Locke. The US Constitution, moreover, incorporates a number of the key provisions of the English Bill of Rights.

Chapter 9 of Locke's *Second Treatise of Civil Government* (1690) is particularly relevant to our discussion here. Locke poses for his readers the fundamental political challenge presented by the burgeoning perception – recognition, if you will – of persons as sovereign over their lives by virtue of their standing as rational beings: Why, Locke asks, would sovereign beings tolerate the transfer of some of that sovereignty to government? His answer is simple and elegant: Without the constraining power of government we would find the exercise of our sovereignty "uncertain," because of the absence of guarantees that others will always respect the moral boundaries required by our status as rational, independent, and therefore sovereign creatures. But Locke believes that there is an obvious way in which we can secure our fundamental interests, and that is to cede some of our powers to people whom we specifically charge to protect these interests and to vest in these people the authority to ensure we are protected. The authority that we vest in such representatives will be legitimate only so long as they continue to act in good faith and on our behalf.

By means of this elegant solution to the problem of government, Locke sought to effect two ends. First, he wanted to reconcile coercive governmental power with our fundamental sovereignty – for, by choosing those who will protect our rights, we *consent* to their governance. Second, he sought to limit governmental power, for our consent is given *only* for the purpose of securing our fundamental interests or rights, and not for other ends.

The Lockean solution, which we commonly refer to as the "social contract theory of governmental authority," has become the dominant theory of liberal democratic states. But it is not without its problems or its rivals. Against Locke's narrow account, it has been argued that the role of government is broader than the mere securing of limited rights from others who would violate them. We have rights to welfare as well as to protection. Moreover, voting in elections, which we recognize as one of the major strategies for registering our consent, does not really express our agreement to the outcome and to what is later done on our behalf. Voting is too thin and too "staged" to do the work that Locke's theory requires. Even thinner is Locke's fallback of a "tacit consent" registered by our remaining in the state and being beneficiaries of its efforts. However, we shall not pursue here various attempts to meet these challenges. Nor shall we explore alternative views of political authority, which are no less open to challenge, interesting and important though such inquiries are. The social contract account is probably as good as we have and in any case provides a widely held and helpful way of framing our discussion.

One of the most remarkable features of Chapter 9 of the *Second Treatise* is Locke's attempt to provide an institutional diagnosis of the failings of a society that lacks governmental institutions. He refers to such a society as existing in a "state of nature," which Locke views as a social order in which people's conduct is normatively governed only by their apprehension of the "law of nature" – principles of morality. These principles are made known to them through their nature as reasoning beings.[2] This pre-civil social order, he suggests, will lack three crucial institutions: a legislature, a judiciary, and an agency for enforcement. According to Locke, we need a legislature because people as we find them disagree about the terms under which their interactions with others are to be conducted. This may sometimes be attributable to their failure to think through situations carefully enough; at other times it may reflect a partiality that improperly discounts the interests of others. What is needed is an institution to which we can give responsibility for making societal-wide determinations of the standards that are to govern our public behavior. That is what a legislature is called to do, albeit after a public and sometimes contentious debate. Its determinations become *law*.

But having laws is not enough. The laws need to be interpreted and applied. Locke believes that problems similar to those concerning our discernment of basic moral norms also surface with respect to our understanding and application of laws that have been promulgated. What is called for is an interpretation and application of the law that is both expert and disinterested. What we need, therefore, is a judiciary, or, more broadly, a judicial order, whose primary practitioners – judges – are versed in the laws and pledged to interpret and apply them independently and impartially.

---

[2] Locke's own account is also embedded in certain theological presumptions, though there has been considerable debate as to whether these are crucial to his position. For a valuable and provocative defense of the view that Locke's commitment to human equality requires recourse to such presumptions, see Jeremy Waldron, *God, Locke, and Equality: Christian Foundations of Locke's Political Thought* (Cambridge: Cambridge University Press, 2002).

However, not even a legislature and judiciary will be sufficient to make good the deficiencies of the state of nature. We saw that (according to Locke) fundamental to the problem of existing in a state of nature was an inability to ensure that our rights could always be exercised without the interference of others. So Locke argues that a further tier of institutional authority is required – one that "executes" or enforces the law as legislated and interpreted by the judiciary. Locke himself did not specify police or corrections officers as the relevant groups – for they had not yet been socially differentiated in the manner in which we now find them. In addition, we would probably expand this third tier to include customs officers, tax agents, marshals, security personnel, and others. But police and corrections personnel are its most conspicuous institutional representatives.

Thus are all the major institutions of what we sometimes speak of as the criminal justice system neatly encapsulated within Locke's broad theory of liberal democracy. The existence and shape of these institutions are not mere happenstance; rather, they are intended to reflect certain fundamental ethical ideals as well as practical concerns – namely, that individual human beings possess a dignity that is correlated with certain expectations about the ways in which they may treat and be treated by others, and that our best chance of ensuring such treatment will require social institutions of the sort that are represented by a legislature, a judiciary, and agencies of enforcement.

The outline sketched here leaves a lot of details to be worked out concerning our criminal justice system, details that we will see are often highly controversial. Nevertheless, it also enables us to appreciate the way in which our criminal justice system reflects a liberal democratic heritage, and we may thus be able to discern the particular "accent" of our own heritage – something we usually fail to hear.

Role morality

Let us now turn to one of the important issues that connect directly with our criminal justice system and those who work within it – the moral principles that apply to those who occupy institutional roles such as those of police officer, judge, or corrections officer. By "role" I understand a set of prerogatives and responsibilities that attach to a member of a social institution by virtue of his or her membership in that institution. For example, by being a police officer, a judge, or a parent, one has a social role that carries with it certain privileges as well as certain expectations. Some roles are more "natural" or preconventional than others, because these roles emerge and develop naturally within social groups rather than being deliberately instituted. Thus, the role of parent is deeply embedded within what we often speak of as the "natural" institution of the family (though, as we are becoming increasingly aware, the form that families might take may vary considerably). On the other hand, serving as a sergeant in a police department or as a deputy warden in a correctional institution is associated with quite purposeful decisions about how an "artificial" or legislated social institution (such as the police or corrections) is best organized and who its role occupants should be. These decisions confer on the occupants responsibilities and prerogatives that do not develop naturally (as do those of parents) but are governed by rules and regulations that are sometimes referred to as "terms of office." Both natural and artificial roles may be scrutinized and, on scrutiny, the obligations and rights associated with them may come to be revised without the institution itself being called into question. We may, for example, wonder whether fathers should continue to have the authority they possess, or whether the role of police sergeants should be expanded, or whether the role of a juror should include making judgments about the law itself as well as about the facts of the case at hand. In each instance we can engage in these exercises without calling into question the legitimacy or desirability of the institutions of parenthood, police, or jury.

The liberal democratic framework we have outlined above provides a basis for examining and evaluating past as well as current social institutions. Against this framework, we can see that slavery, for example, though it was once a prominent and thriving social institution, is now justifiably outlawed in most liberal democracies, even if we sometimes argue about borderline situations (such as cases of indentured labor). We now no longer debate the role of slave-owners and slaves and their "legitimate" respective rights and responsibilities, but reject the institution of slavery altogether. On the other hand, some liberal democracies have perpetuated certain traditional institutions (such as the monarchy) while radically altering their powers. Monarchical rulership, for example, has been constitutionalized and the royal role has become largely ceremonial (again, with some argument about the monarch's residual powers). Another social role that has been rejected in most liberal democracies (though not in the United States) is that of executioner. And the torturer, once employed by governments, no longer has a place in liberal democratic polities (even though, as we shall see, the advent of terrorism has led to discussion about the reintroduction of torturers as interrogators).

Holders of social roles are usually accorded an authority or set of prerogatives that are denied to other citizens. Such authority frequently carries moral weight. We see this quite commonly in the case of roles within natural institutions such as families: parents are accorded certain rights (and responsibilities) with respect to their own children that others do not have. These include the right to impose discipline and make certain determinative decisions concerning their children's education and welfare. But although parents have rights with respect to their children that others do not, the legitimate exercise of these rights is not unlimited. In the United States, for example, Jehovah's Witnesses cannot lawfully interfere with their children's receiving medically necessary blood transfusions, even though they may refuse transfusions for themselves. Similar prerogatives that are possessed by occupants of roles within "artificial" social institutions – such as the right to carry weapons that is accorded to police officers but often not to ordinary citizens – also come with limits. Police officers may not draw, point, or use their weapons as they wish. With such rights there normally come significant responsibilities.

You may wonder whether there are multiple moralities at work here – one for private individuals and another for occupants of social roles. Or, to put it in a different way, you may wonder whether each of us is bound by multiple moralities, the specific moral principles that apply at any given time depending on the particular social or professional role each of us occupies at that specific time. It sometimes seems like that. We know that people vested with governmental authority sometimes act as though they need not obey the laws or other rules that govern the activities of ordinary citizens. They seem to act as though their role as "one in government" exempts them from the responsibilities they have as citizens. However, within liberal democratic institutions, no citizens, regardless of the roles they inhabit, are exempt from the "rule of law." Liberal democracies are founded on the understanding that all their members, including those with governing responsibility, are subject to socially sanctioned laws (even though those laws sometimes provide them with certain prerogatives or discretionary authority). Indeed, not only are their individual acts of discretionary authority subject to a

rational scrutiny in terms of their role, but their role must also be rationally scrutinized in relation to the institution of which they are a part,
and the institution itself has to be justifiable by reference to our underlying social values. If any link in this chain of justification is broken, a role
occupant's conduct will be ethically and morally questionable. A police officer who engages in a high-speed pursuit must have role authorization to
do so; high-speed pursuits must be sustained as reasonable and defensible
components of a law enforcement strategy; law enforcement must itself be
defensible as a liberal democratic institution; and a liberal democratic form
of social organization must be justified in terms of basic rights or other
moral values. There is – or at least should be – a chain of reasoning that
links the discretionary decisions of a role occupant with those of ordinary
morality.

What we can see from this is that criminal justice ethics, along with
the ethics of its constituent institutions and the conduct of those who work
within them, is not divorced from ordinary morality. Rather, criminal justice
ethics *is* ordinary morality applied to a very particular institutional setting.
It is ordinary morality as it governs the conduct of those who occupy particular social and institutional roles, roles that must themselves be subject
to the scrutiny of ordinary morality.

Admittedly, the twin expectations of a role and demands of ordinary
morality will sometimes create hard cases. It will appear that a social role
requires that we violate the constraints of ordinary morality – not because
the social role allows an exception to what is morally required or expected
but because doing what we believe the role rightly demands of us will lead us
to act contrary to ordinary moral expectations, leaving our hands stained.
Should the hostage negotiator promise safe passage to a hostage-taker in
order to free those who have been taken hostage? Should police violate the
law in order to trap those who would otherwise escape its reach? Later I
will provide additional illustrations of these situations, some of which have
become known in the literature as cases of "dirty hands"[3] (so called because
the achievement of some good state of affairs can be accomplished only
by morally dirtying one's hands). But although dirty hands often involve a

---

[3] From a 1948 play of that name by the French philosopher, Jean-Paul Sartre (1905–80). In
the criminal justice domain, it often goes under the name of the "Dirty Harry" problem,
from the Clint Eastwood film of that name. See Carl Klockars, "The Dirty Harry Problem,"
Annals of the American Academy of Political and Social Science 452 (November, 1980): 33–47.

clash between a role obligation and some more general moral requirement, similar cases can also arise in contexts that do not involve institutional roles. In a famous hypothetical, Jim, a field botanist in a volatile South American country, happens upon the site of a mass execution about to take place.[4] Too late to withdraw unnoticed, he is brought before the leader of the guerilla group staging the execution. It turns out that Pedro, the leader of the group, is an old college mate of Jim, and in celebration of their reunion, he tells Jim that he will let the nineteen of the twenty who would have been killed go free if Jim shoots one of them. Should Jim optimize the situation by reducing the causalties to one, or should he refuse to violate a deeply entrenched principle that forbids the deliberate taking of innocent life? Will either decision leave his hands unstained?

Coping with diversity

The liberal democratic tradition of which I have spoken permeates our think-ing, giving a liberal democratic "accent" to the claims that we make, affect-ing both their substance and their form. Because these assumptions are so pervasive in our thinking we may not be aware of them. We may not believe that we have an accent. Accents are what "others" have. *We* speak, so we think, without the accent of cultural or historical influence. How we say it is how it is to be said.

One salutary way of coming to hear our own accent – and to assess it – is to attend carefully to alternative voices that can be heard in our midst. Our increasing social diversity gives a visible face to alternative moral understandings and social constructions. So do some contemporary events, such as the rise of various forms of religious or political fundamentalism, which call for a moral and social reordering of our lives. How should we respond to such calls? Many religious and political traditions, at least in some of their variations, consider that the toleration that liberal societies purportedly show toward the moral and social lives of their members is not only ill-advised or wrong but positively evil. Such movements are not restricted to one religion – or rejection of religion – but are found across the spectrum of ideological commitment. Because they are convinced that

---

[4] See Bernard Williams, "A Critique of Utilitarianism," in J. J. C. Smart and Bernard Williams, *Utilitarianism: For and Against* (Cambridge: Cambridge University Press, 1973), 98ff.

the dominant social order is evil or corrupt, adherents of these traditions may attempt to secure a reordering of our social, political, and religious institutions so that the religious or political truth, as they see it, will be served. Should we tolerate the intolerant?

Sometimes the tools they will use to usher in the new order will be consistent with democratic processes. They will vote for representatives who are committed, once they have been elected into office, to the abolition of certain forms of social toleration. That is a risk of democratic process. Often, though, this will not be their way. Sometimes their efforts to exemplify such visions will be shown in social withdrawal, as was the case with the Branch Davidians (tragically decimated by law enforcement agents in Waco, Texas).[5] Again, this may not be something we can or should prevent. Sometimes, however, proponents of a narrow doctrine will seek some way of imposing their vision of a "saving truth" on a broader society. And in these cases we must ask whether there is a way of challenging such initiatives that is consistent with the preservation of liberal democratic ideals. Or must we be intolerant of illiberality?

It is a question that has no easy answer. On the one hand, we do not want to be guilty of illegitimately using intolerant measures against those who seek to enforce intolerant views on others. On the other hand, we recognize not only that there is no guarantee that every dispute can be resolved by means of discussion and argument, but also that it is not even the case that we can count on others to prefer argument and discussion over, say, divine revelation or other certitude, as a means of arriving at the social and political truths we should live by. Still, we must try to come to grips with the question of how – in a way that is consistent with our liberal ideals – we should deal with those who would attempt to refashion society along lines that controvert those ideals. It is important not only that we think through such issues, but also that those who are agents of criminal justice do so, for they will be in the forefront of such encounters.

A time-honored though not always successful strategy has been to try to show that our opponents' position is based on faulty inferences – for example, that claims they themselves accept are at variance with their intolerant position. For example, the attempt to establish a theocracy might be

---

[5] For a detailed account and review of the issues, see Stuart A. Wright (ed.), *Armageddon in Waco: Critical Perspectives on the Branch Davidian Conflict* (Chicago: University of Chicago Press, 1995).

challenged by making clear that those who wish to impose a theocratic government on unwilling others have overlooked strands of their own tradition
that forbid such an imposition. So, Osama bin Laden's claim that Muslims
have an individual duty to attack Christians and Jews may be challenged by
a (better attested) interpretation of Islamic law that any such jihad must be
collective and prosecuted by a leader that followers of the tradition generally
recognize.

A different strategy is to show fundamentalists that the assumptions they
must make in order to justify imposing their position on others are dubious
assumptions at best. For example, it is doubtful that (1) they are better placed
than the advocates of rival authoritarian traditions to make determinations
of truth, (2) they are in a position to show this without presupposing what
they need to show, (3) they are free from the liability to error that plagues
the rest of us, and (4) even as the (supposed) recipients of relevant insight or
revelation, their understanding of that insight or revelation is not marred
by the fact that it has been apprehended by a fallible human being with
imperfect understanding. And so on.

Unfortunately, showing that fundamentalist arguments rest on dubious
assumptions carries no assurance that those who advanced them will be
persuaded to relinquish them or even to be less sure of them. Still, we
cannot forgo the attempt to reason with those who would impose on us for
we do not want to succumb to the temptation to impose on them in the
way in which they would wish to impose their own views on us.

Our point in this discussion is not to claim that truth, moral and otherwise, does not exist, though there is indeed a relativistic liberal democratic
tradition that countenances multiple "truths" or, at least in the case of
moral assertions, denies that they can have any truth value. What is being
suggested is that we should be extremely cautious about identifying what
"we believe" – either individually or even as a group – as "the truth without
qualification" and thus fail to appreciate that we have an accent, an accent
that may distort our speaking in ways of which we are not aware. We must
listen to others and hear ourselves.

Conclusion

We have used this chapter to embed the subsequent discussion in a broader
framework of social and political understanding. Even though we tend to

take for granted our institutions of criminal justice and the social order that sanctions them, we need to step back and reflect on what it is that we are taking for granted. When our liberal democratic societies were more homogeneous and less multicultural than they now are, and our various societies were less "connected," it may have been easy to ignore the deeper challenges posed by diversity. But we can do so no longer. Diversity of belief, custom, and institutional construction has much to commend it as an expression of the many and very different ways in which human beings may flourish and live good and fulfilling lives. But such diversity also carries within it an implicit danger when some of its manifestations deny the toleration that has enabled their adherents to find – and sometimes even to raise – their voice in cultures other than their own. As the recent trials of Saddam Hussein and Zacarias Moussaoui have shown us, none of our institutions, including the institutions of criminal justice, can afford to ignore the challenges of diverse and competing traditions. How do we establish the legitimacy of our claim to try them? Those who exploitatively challenge our social order should not leave us speechless. But neither should they be allowed to reduce us to oppressors.

2   Crime and the limits of criminalization

> Actions receive their tincture from the times,
> And as they change are virtues made or crimes.[1]

The last chapter offered one possible ethical framework for a criminal justice system, namely, a set of three institutions consisting of a legislature, a judiciary, and various law enforcement operations that reasonable people might be expected to agree to if they were concerned to protect and advance their basic interests or rights. Of course, as with most frameworks, the theory is neater than the practice and the various institutions that actually comprise our criminal justice system do not perfectly exemplify what they profess to be and do.

What makes conduct criminal?

In this chapter we shall briefly turn our attention to the issues of crime and criminalization. Although it is clear that the criminal justice system exists to identify, process, and respond to criminal activity within the community, the initial question we must answer is: What makes activity *criminal* in the first place? A quick response, based on the social contract theory that we spelled out in the last chapter, might be that activities are criminal if they transgress the laws that govern our social interactions. Because the laws we have are those that we have "agreed" to have imposed on us, those who violate them are properly subject to criminal penalties. But though this answer captures some of what we think justifies punishing those who violate certain laws, we will see that it fails to answer the more fundamental

---

[1] Daniel Defoe, "A Hymn to the Pillory" (1703), in Daniel Defoe, *Satire, Fantasy and Writings on the Supernatural*, ed. W. R. Owens (London: Pickering and Chatto, 2003), vol. I, 239.

question of why breaking some laws is viewed as criminal whereas breaking others is not.

Social rules that we designate as laws are highly diverse, and what we designate as criminal law represents only one small segment of the laws that we might be said to have agreed to have imposed on us. Some laws, for example, are laws about other laws – they are laws about how laws are to be made, interpreted, changed, and revoked. (These laws are sometimes spoken of as "second order" laws, for they pertain not directly to conduct that falls under the law but to the laws themselves.) But even laws that bear directly on our day-to-day activities (thus, "first order" laws) are of many different kinds. For example, we have various *administrative* rules that set out procedures for achieving certain ends (such as voting or getting married or starting a business). We also have rules of *contract* that specify what people who want to engage in certain exchanges (such as buying a house or selling a car) must do in order for those transactions to have legal effect and thus protection. And additionally, we have what are known as *tort* laws that regulate privately pursued redress for wrongs or injuries that result from carelessness (such as incautious driving) or negligent workmanship (such as an unsafe appliance that caused injury). And then of course there is *criminal* law, which focuses on what are usually called public wrongs or crimes (such as fraud, theft, and assault), and against which "the state" initiates proceedings.

What makes fraud, theft, and assault public wrongs or crimes? Were we to review the whole range of activities that our law characterizes as criminal we might be tempted to throw up our hands and say (as indeed some theorists have done[2]), that what makes an activity criminal is that it has been deemed to be criminal by the law. Of course, it is true that an activity becomes criminal in the eyes of the law only when the law has classified it as such. But there must be something more to what makes an activity criminal other than that the law classifies it as criminal. There must (or should) be some rationale for criminalization. At least there should be if we are concerned about the *ethics* of the criminal justice system. Why? Because those who are convicted of *crimes* are normally *punished* or at least penalized or imposed on in some significant way, and if this is to be justified we need to be able to point to some substantive problem with the conduct

[2] See, for example, P. J. Fitzgerald, *Criminal Law and Punishment* (Oxford: Clarendon, 1962), 7.

for which someone is punished and not simply point to the fact that the conduct has been outlawed. We need to be able to point to good reasons for outlawing certain conduct and imposing censuring penalties for engaging in the outlawed conduct.[3]

Traditional approaches

Unfortunately, there is little agreement about why we should view some conduct as sufficiently undesirable to justify us in imposing legal punishment on those who engage in it. To help us sort out the issues relevant to this topic and see how answers to the questions we have asked will shed light on the processes of criminal justice, it is useful to start with some traditional legal distinctions.

Mala in se and mala prohibita

The first distinction on which we shall focus is one that is drawn between acts that are said to be evil in themselves (often referred to by the Latin phrase *mala in se*), and those that are said to be evil solely in virtue of their being prohibited (referred to as *mala prohibita*). Acts that we consider intrinsically or inherently evil are evil not because they lead to bad results (though they usually do) but because they are in and of themselves wrong. Some acts that we consider evil in this way are murder, assault, fraud, and theft. We do not usually have qualms about their criminalization – that is, about establishing laws that make the commission of these acts criminal activities that are legally punishable. But what about the second category of laws – those that are criminal because they are prohibited by law? Why should fishing without a license or carrying a concealed firearm be seen

---

[3] In focusing on conduct we are, of course, narrowing the scope of what has traditionally been regarded as criminal. Mere possession (of a firearm) for example, is sometimes punished as is having a certain status, such as "being without lawful means of support." Historically, even intentions could be criminalized ("encompassing the death of the king"). That something has been traditionally viewed as criminal does not make it appropriately so. But even if we limit ourselves to what we think should be considered criminal, we will not find a single set of necessary and sufficient conditions; more likely a cluster of conditions some number of which will be sufficient to justify the crime label.

as criminal offenses? Does this not leave us with the empty account we rejected earlier, namely, that they are criminal only because the law deems them so?[4] That judgment, however, would be premature. Instead of looking at the intrinsic features of acts that are *mala prohibita*, we are directed to look elsewhere to understand their criminalization. Consider the laws that make it a crime for a person to drive on the left-hand side of the road in the United States and on the right-hand side of the road in the United Kingdom. Clearly, there is nothing intrinsically evil about driving on one or another particular side of the road. It probably makes as much sense to drive on one side as on the other. What is important is that travel on the roads not be (too) hazardous, so that although it does not matter which side of the road one drives on, it very much matters that all those who are travelling in a particular direction drive on the same side of the road. The United States and the United Kingdom have designated the side of the road on which you must travel (though each has chosen different sides of the road as its "legal" side). Because those who disobey this law (in either country) *endanger* others, it is considered appropriate to penalize them.[5]

Therefore, in addition to an act's being either inherently evil or making such evil outcomes likely, we now have a second reason why we should penalize certain conduct, namely, that it is conduct that, although not intrinsically evil, is such as would – given the demands of social organization – jeopardize others or endanger things we socially value. But we have not yet satisfactorily resolved the issue of why some acts should be designated crimes and others not. To see why something more has been thought necessary for an act to be outlawed as "criminal," consider the following two cases. Case 1: I carelessly leave an upturned rake on my front lawn only to have a neighbor's child step on it and suffer serious injury, my negligence thereby producing an intrinsically bad outcome. Although my negligence

[4] Much more extensive and subtle discussions can be found in Stuart P. Green, "Why It's a Crime to Tear the Tag off a Mattress: Overcriminalization and the Moral Content of Regulatory Offenses," *Emory Law Journal* 46 (1997): 1533–1615; and Douglas N. Husak, "Malum Prohibitum and Retributivism," in *Defining Crimes: Essays on the Special Part of the Criminal Law*, ed. R. A. Duff and Stuart P. Green (Oxford: Oxford University Press, 2005), 65–90.

[5] Here as elsewhere there are exceptions. Some *mala prohibita* – such as driving without an up-to-date car registration – will not endanger others. It is useful here to distinguish "crimes" from mere "violations," as does the American Law Institute's *Model Penal Code*, §1.04.

might provide grounds for a legal suit against me, it is not viewed as "criminal."[6] Case 2: I promise a woman that I will marry her but change my mind on the day of the wedding and, without notice, leave her stranded at the church. My breach of promise might be viewed as intrinsically evil (quite apart from the suffering it presumably would cause) but, here again, what I have done would not usually be viewed as a crime. So the question we face is this: What, beyond the actual doing of something intrinsically evil or something that, given other circumstances, makes an evil outcome considerably more likely, is necessary for an act to be deemed criminal?

Actus reus and mens rea

Generally, jurists have considered that criminal acts have two components: they must be evil (referred to by the Latin phrase, *actus reus*), and they must reflect an evil or guilty mind (in Latin, *mens rea*). It is not a very adequate breakdown (at least for some of what we criminalize), but for present purposes it offers a helpful ladder that we can later throw away. The *mens rea* requirement is meant to ensure that conduct that is punishable as a crime is appropriately "connected" to the agent of the act, and is not, say, something that was accidentally done by the agent, or forced on the agent, or done without the agent's understanding of what he or she was doing. We want to be sure, that is, that if agents are to be punished by law for their conduct, then they engaged in the conduct "guiltily" – in central cases, knowingly and with malice. And so the *mens rea* requirement is usually introduced to ensure that the evil that was done was done as a result of the agent's intention to bring it about. This is one reason why the negligently upturned rake does not suffice for criminal charges.

We are not, however, out of the woods yet. The distinction between conduct that can be characterized as an *actus reus* done with *mens rea* and conduct that cannot be so characterized will not capture only and all cases of criminal conduct because some kinds of act that have been deemed criminal do not in fact fulfill the combined requirements of possessing an *actus reus* and *mens rea*. There are, for example, cases of criminal negligence (such as negligent homicide) and the large array of strict liability laws (such as

---

[6] We do, however, recognize an exception in the case of negligent homicide – if, for example, I drive my car carelessly and run over a pedestrian on a crosswalk.

statutory rape or using incorrectly calibrated weights and measures), in which a *mens rea* seems to be lacking, though in some cases an assumed failure of diligence may be thought to reflect a moral defect.[7] Furthermore, some intentional injuries – such as false imprisonment or invasion of privacy – are often not seen as criminal but are simply viewed as torts. Still, generally speaking, crimes tend to be distinguished from mere torts by the dual fact that (1) they are intended, and (2) they bring about evil outcomes that can be said not merely to disappoint private expectations but also to transgress *public* standards. Or, perhaps better, though not unexceptionably, crimes weaken the system of public trust on which we rely. Thus, criminal conduct may be viewed as wrongdoing that has a public dimension – we resist it not merely on our own behalf but also as a matter of public policy. This helps to explain why the jilted bride would have no criminal case and why, generally speaking, we no longer view adultery as a criminal offense.

Voluntariness and responsibility

The *actus reus / mens rea* distinction conceals a further important presumption of criminality. The criminal act must have been performed voluntarily; the performer must be able to be held responsible for what was done.[8] A young child may intend to take the chocolate from the candy store, but we may not consider it capable of appreciating the moral significance of what it is doing. The insane person may intend to shoot his victim, but the voices that are urging him on may relieve him from responsibility for it. In yet other cases, a person may be suffering from some defect of reason that merely diminishes rather than negates his capacity for making responsible decisions. When we denominate certain kinds of acts as crimes we presume not only an *actus reus* that transgresses public standards but also a responsible *mens rea*.

---

[7] Often, however, strict liability laws are used to enhance public safety in cases in which establishing *mens rea* would be difficult.

[8] There are, however, complexities here that we shall leave to one side – though some of them emerge in the debate about strict liability offenses, in which responsibility may be questionable by virtue of a person's ignorance or other inability.

Moral turpitude and moral failure

We are, however, still left with the question of what makes certain evils publicly condemnable via criminalization. Some have answered that we criminalize those evil acts that reflect moral turpitude on the part of those who commit them. This of course can provide only a presumptive reason for criminalization, because actual moral turpitude will require that we look at the circumstances under which the law was violated.[9]

Nevertheless, the presumption of moral failure offers both a plausible reason for the *stigma* that we tend to attach to criminal behavior and a prima facie justification for our *punishing* those who violate criminal laws (namely, they morally deserve it). But we have to remember that we do not believe that every act of moral turpitude is appropriately criminalized. Moral turpitude is at best a necessary condition for criminalization. We resist criminalizing conduct such as jilting one's bride or committing adultery even though we may consider them acts of moral dereliction. Furthermore, viewing moral turpitude as central to the criminalization of behavior is problematic given how much we differ among ourselves about what constitutes moral depravity, differences that are clearly on view in debates about sodomy or drug use. Therefore, rather than claim that we criminalize behavior that reflects moral turpitude, it may be more accurate to say that if moral failure is a consideration at all in our decision to criminalize behavior, it is only moral failure of a certain kind that we are concerned to criminalize, and not necessarily moral failure that rises to the level of moral turpitude. But though we may see some of the trees more clearly, we are still not out of the woods. Let us try a different path.

The harm principle

Classical liberals appreciated the problems of taking the presence of moral failure or turpitude as the central consideration in decisions concerning whether or not to criminalize certain acts. And this appreciation led them to posit a seemingly more straightforward and less ambiguous criterion for justifiable criminalization, namely, that behavior is appropriately criminalized

---

[9] This was to the forefront of the debate about whether compassionate euthanasia should be regarded as a form of murder.

only if it causes (or threatens) harm to others. This, coupled with the expanded *mens rea* requirement, also accommodates much of what is attractive in the idea that criminality reflects moral failure.

The most famous expression of the harm account is found in the writings of the nineteenth-century essayist and activist, John Stuart Mill (1806–73). In a well-known passage (that, unfortunately, demands closer scrutiny than we are able to give it here), Mill wrote:

> The sole end for which mankind are warranted, individually or collectively, in interfering with the liberty of action of any of their number, is self-protection. . . the only purpose for which power can be rightfully exercised over any member of a civilized community, against his will, is to prevent harm to others. His own good, either physical or moral, is not a sufficient warrant. He cannot rightfully be compelled to do or forbear because it will be better for him to do so, because it will make him happier, because, in the opinions of others, to do so would be wise, or even right. These are good reasons for remonstrating with him, or reasoning with him, or persuading him, or entreating him, but not for compelling him, or visiting him with any evil in case he do otherwise. To justify that, the conduct from which it is desired to deter him, must be calculated to produce evil to some one else. The only part of the conduct of any one, for which he is amenable to society, is that which concerns others. In the part which merely concerns himself, his independence is, of right, absolute. Over himself, over his own body and mind, the individual is sovereign.[10]

The criterion that Mill suggests in the above-quoted passage (a criterion that has come to be known as Mill's "harm principle") was intended by him to be a negative criterion; it does not set out the conditions under which it is recommended that we interfere with another (adult) person's behavior, but rather the conditions under which we may *not* interfere with that behavior. We may not interfere with others' conduct unless it is harmful to others. In addition, it is meant to be a completely general criterion: it is meant to apply not merely to law-makers in their attempt to set limits on lawful behavior, but to everyone in his or her dealings with other adult persons. "Harm to others" is thus, for Mill, necessary if we are to interfere with others' conduct, both within and outside the context of law.

---

[10] John Stuart Mill, *On Liberty* (1869), ch. 1. Immediately after the passage quoted, Mill offers a few qualifications. His essay is available on line.

Certainly, with respect to criminal law, it seems to make good sense that "harm to others" should be the focus, for it seems to capture what we want to proclaim in the criminalizing of a particular kind of act – namely, that the act in question (intentionally, or, perhaps, recklessly) harms or threatens harm to others and so constitutes a public wrong. (Mill himself controversially goes even further by suggesting that *only* such conduct qualifies as morally wrong.)

But, as with other suggestions we have reviewed regarding what lies "at the heart" of criminalization, here too the solution is problematic. First, we need to determine just what constitutes "harm to others." One well-known account speaks of harm to others as conduct that wrongfully "sets back" others' interests,[11] but this does not take us very far unless we can determine what qualify as relevant interests. Even the view that our interests include desires for our welfare or well-being will not be particularly helpful given Mill's insight that "there is no parity between . . . the desire of a thief to take a purse, and the desire of the right owner to keep it."[12] The interest that a thief has in stolen goods (even if he is starving) does not (normally) have the same standing as that of the person from whom these goods are taken. Harming another, then, cannot be understood (by the law) merely as the frustration of that other's desires for well-being, for the frustration of some desires may in fact be in the law's interests and so not merit the law's protection. In addition, we should keep in mind that Mill puts forward his principle only as a necessary condition for criminalization and not as sufficient. Some harms are too small to be dealt with by means of the heavy engine of criminal law (in the Latin phrase: *de minimis non curat lex*) and others are not suited to its formal processes (as we often reflect in our response to harms done by juveniles).

There are several other problems with the harm principle that we shall note but not pursue here. (1) The principle seems to rely on a causal relationship between what a person does and some harm that befalls another. We've already seen in passing that harm is not always brought about. Not every attempt succeeds, and yet we generally punish attempts as well as

---

[11] See Joel Feinberg, *Harm to Others* (New York: Oxford University Press, 1984), ch. 1. Feinberg of course does devote attention to the scope of "interests." I have attempted a slightly different account in "Crime and the Concept of Harm," *American Philosophical Quarterly* 15, no. 1 (1978): 27–36.

[12] *On Liberty*, ch. 2.

completed crimes. Mill is not altogether indifferent to the somewhat problematic connection between what a person does and the harm that befalls another person, for he allows that we may sometimes be punished for omissions (failing to save a drowning child or contribute to the common weal, for example), and though an argument can be provided to suggest that omissions are causally potent, they are not causally potent in quite the same way as commissions.[13] Moreover, sometimes our acts are remote from the harms that befall others but we are held criminally responsible (we supply the gun that another fires). (2) In addition, we need to consider who the others are who are harmed. Not all crimes directly impact on other individuals – we may harm public institutions when we seek to bribe public officials or commit perjury, or our conduct may (somewhat more problematically) upset a general interest in public order. (3) There is considerable contention about what constitutes the "wrongful" invasion of interests – in particular, whether consent to harm done might negate or deflect the charge of criminality. We allow something like that in business ventures, where a heavy loser in the competitive marketplace is not (usually) considered to have been criminally harmed. Here we adopt the principle involved in an ancient saying: to the one who consents no wrong is done (*volenti non fit injuria*). But we are often much less willing to accept this principle with respect to conduct that might otherwise be viewed as *mala in se*: sadomasochism, voluntary euthanasia, suicide, mutilation, and, more recently, voluntary cannibalism.[14]

In addition, as Mill himself makes clear, there are rival positions to the view that the harm principle is the only criterion to which we can appeal in deciding which acts to criminalize and which not, rival positions that may even be consistent (albeit controversially so) with the aspirations of a liberal democratic society. Mill's rejection of interventions for the individual's "own good" may, for example, rule out seatbelt laws as well as some other paternalistic interventions that our society endorses as consistent with its liberal democratic principles (claiming as grounds for intervention that certain

---

[13] It may be worth noting that whereas most European countries have so-called Good Samaritan criminal laws, countries in the Anglo-American tradition have tended to oppose them. See my "Good Samaritanism," *Philosophy & Public Affairs* 5, no. 4 (1976): 382–407.

[14] See, for example, Vera Bergelson, "The Right to be Hurt: Testing the Boundaries of Consent," *George Washington Law Review* 75, no. 2 (February, 2007): 165–236.

small sacrifices of individual liberty are a reasonable trade for considerably enhanced safety).[15] Indeed, even Mill draws the line at self-enslavement. And what about behavior that is not harmful but is grossly offensive, such as racist rantings or public defecation or what Mill also recoils at, public indecency? Some would argue that intervention in regard to non-harmful but nonetheless offensive behavior would be appropriate while others might disagree, or disagree with respect to the kind of intervention that is appropriate. No doubt there will be similar disagreements about how to respond to conduct that harms no one, but which, like flag-burning or polygamy, challenges deeply and widely felt sentiments. These examples bring home to us that human conduct in its great variety does not come neatly packaged into exclusive categories of "criminal" and "noncriminal," and that the question whether we should or should not punish behavior that is harmful to self (or others), or is grossly offensive or in violation of widely held standards of right conduct, must take into account a variety of factors. Though we will surely find that cases of "harm to others" are those that are easiest to deal with, not even they are always easy to deal with, and other cases may have a legitimate claim on our attention as objects of criminalization. Of course, as we move away from cases in which harm is done to others we will find that decisions to criminalize are increasingly difficult to make as well as increasingly controversial.

Who should decide?

Of course, the fact that criminalization is the outcome of a *decision* about what should and should not be subject to punishment raises an additional important question – much debated by sociologists of crime – of *who* decides or, more importantly, *should* decide which acts in which circumstances should be subject to criminal sanctions. In liberal societies, it is a legislature that decides, with the legislature taken to speak for "the people," as it has been voted in by the people, and – at least in theory – if the people do not like what the legislature decides, other decisions can be made by other legislators whom the people can choose to replace the previous decision-makers. (A change of legislators can come about during the next voting

---

[15] Of course, one might argue in favor of some paternalistic laws without at the same time arguing for criminalizing noncompliance with these laws.

season and in some places even sooner if public protests are loud enough.) Sometimes, however, it appears that law-makers do not truly speak for the people at large. To be sure, laws are cast in terms that are general and seemingly applicable to all citizens and in like manner: all must adhere to them, law-makers and other citizens alike. But although all are subject to the requirements of the law, some laws are more onerous on some people and on some groups than on others. Anatole France famously and sarcastically remarked that "the law, in its majestic equality, forbids the rich as well as the poor to sleep under bridges, to beg in the street, and to steal bread."[16] Such laws as France referred to clearly affected the poor much more than they did the rich. But critics of the criminal law have frequently complained that laws *generally* tend to serve the values and interests of only particular segments of society – the well-to-do, the social aristocracy, men, Caucasians, or some other group or groups possessing some special social and legislative leverage – rather than society as a whole. At best (according to the complaint) some laws serve one group of citizens whereas other laws serve other groups. If this complaint is valid, then we have reason to believe that there really exists no single "people" for whom "the law" speaks, but only diverse groups, each with a particular set of interests, and no single way in which the interests of all can be recognized. (Of course, it is an open question whether the interests of all *should* be recognized. If the answer is negative, then we must somehow determine which interests should be recognized by law and which need not.)

The challenge of diversity

The multicultural challenge

The "harm principle" that Mill advanced addresses, at least to some extent, the problems raised above. But it does not solve them altogether. There will inevitably be disagreements about what constitutes the harm that is said to trigger legitimate interference with a person's conduct. For example, some think that abortion involves a significant harm to others ("the unborn") whereas others think that it does not (since they disagree that fetuses constitute "others" in the requisite sense). As liberal democratic societies come

---

[16] Anatole France, *The Red Lily*, trans. Winifred Stevens (New York: Dodd, Mead, 1922), 95.

to be increasingly diverse culturally – through immigration as well as the fragmentation of longstanding traditions – it will be increasingly difficult, in an increasingly wider range of cases, to come up with a single and uncontroversial determination of when "harm to others" (or some other criterion of social intervention) appropriately calls for a response on the part of the criminal justice system. This is because in multicultural societies, behaviors that most often raise the question of intervention – be it betrothing children, subjecting young girls to clitoridectomy, engaging in cockfighting, participating in animal sacrifice, employing rituals that involve drug use, or practicing polygamy/polyandry – will be behaviors that are embedded in cultural traditions that, *generally speaking*, we would want to respect. We are thus faced with the question of whether the behaviors that raise the question of intervention are criminally actionable harms or only appear that way to us because we have simply been taught to believe them so.

Moral autonomy and the limits of private judgment

These are obviously important issues, and although criminal justice practitioners are not generally faced with having to make their own determinations of what the criminal law ought to be or whether to intervene in particular situations, they ought to be aware that their administration of the law (through enforcement, judicial determinations, or penal oversight) takes place against a background of sometimes quite controversial decisions. The system's practitioners are not mere functionaries: "doing one's job" is not an excuse, much less a justification, for doing what is morally unjustified. Recall, for example, that this was precisely what Adolf Eichmann sought to advance in his defense when tried for his role as a Nazi functionary during World War II. History has been fairly dismissive of such rationales. But it is also true that agents of the criminal justice system are not free simply to import their private judgments into every aspect of the workplace. Those who take on roles within certain institutions agree (albeit within limits) to accept others' determinations about what and how they are to fulfill those roles. Or, perhaps, more accurately, there will be expectations built into their institutional roles, and where those expectations conflict with those of a person who occupies a role, the role expectations should *normally* take precedence. In general, it is anticipated that where the role requires behavior that grates with the role occupant, there will be procedures by means of which that person may seek to have the terms of the role reviewed and changed. Should such procedures not be in place, or fail to produce the desired outcome, the occupant of that role may then have to consider leaving the position or, in certain extreme cases, engaging in some form of disobedience. We would probably sympathize with a police officer in National Socialist Germany who sought to avoid enforcing some of the anti-Semitic laws that had been passed. And the same might be said of a nineteenth-century police officer in the United States who was expected to enforce "fugitive slave" laws.

However, the need to make difficult decisions may arise in far less dramatic cases than the ones described above. Consider a recent case in which a police officer in a homeless outreach unit objected to the use of trespass and disorderly conduct laws to arrest a homeless person sleeping in a large private parking garage. The officer believed that, in the absence of warm and safe alternative shelters for the homeless, arrest was an inappropriate and heartless governmental response. He informed his supervisor that he had a principled objection to arresting the homeless unless they were acting in a manifestly disorderly manner, and so wished for a more discretionary use of the law and of his part in enforcing it. His request for a special dispensation was denied and the officer was later ordered to make a particular arrest. When he refused he was suspended from duty without pay and brought up on administrative charges.[17]

We should ask the following questions: Was the police officer right to refuse? Were his superiors justified in bringing charges against him for his refusal? Were there other options that his superiors should have pursued? Though police officers often regard their being required to do what they view as morally objectionable as one of the downsides of the job that they must accept (and perhaps could have foreseen) as part of their job, should this have been a case in which the police officer resigned from the force rather than do what he found morally odious? Should he have simply sought a transfer instead? Or should the officer have remained on the job and in the unit, knowing that there was nothing to stop him from campaigning, off duty, for legal change? If the officer viewed the plight of the homeless as

---

[17] In Australian and English and Welsh law, however, police officers are accorded an "original authority" that – in theory – gives them absolute discretion in such matters. See Joseph Carabetta, "Employment Status of the Police in Australia," *Melbourne University Law Review* 27 (April, 2003): 1–32.

such a blight on the community that he was prepared to accept the cost of doing something about it, would it have been strategically better for that "something" to have been an action that might have had broader effects than the effect on the lone homeless person in whose arrest he refused to engage (one who, in all likelihood, would be arrested by some other, more compliant officer – as indeed was the case)? Might a better tactic have been to drum up collective support (perhaps through the police union) for not arresting the homeless merely on the grounds of vagrancy (much as any interested party or occupational group might do to oppose particular governmental policies)?

The point to be made here is that in considering what the officer ought to have done we should keep in mind the options, other than either compliance on the one hand or refusal followed by resignation or penalization on the other, that might have been open to him. In suggesting these other options, I do not want to deny that the officer's supervisor should have been sympathetic and more flexible about ways of dealing with the situation, thus showing better leadership qualities. But neither am I suggesting that, given the situation as it was, it was not the officer's responsibility as an officer of the law to recognize the importance of a supervisory hierarchy in policing or the existence of established procedures for changing laws that are believed to be unjustified. After all, the officer had willingly and knowingly accepted a particular social role and therefore could be understood to have accepted that, as part of that role, it was not for him to determine what the rules should be.

But I am suggesting that, both in judging what the officer should have done and how his behavior might appropriately be responded to, one should relevantly consider the unfairness of the plight of the homeless (as perceived by the officer), the discretion that the supervisor almost certainly had with respect to how to deal with the particular homeless person that the officer in question was called upon to arrest, and the fact that prior to being assigned the officer had sought to avoid disruption by indicating his position. He might have explained his humanitarian reasons for joining the homeless outreach unit and asked that, if at all possible, other officers be directed to make the arrest when the supervisor felt one was called for.

Of course, the decision about how we should regard the officer's conduct and the institution's response to it may be made even more difficult if the officer's moral objections reflect wider social, religious, or political divisions within the community. Consider the case of devout Catholic police officers, deeply opposed to abortion, who are assigned to ensure that – in the face of pro-life protests – the clients of an abortion clinic are able to avail themselves of its services without harassment. Certainly the officers may request reassignment, but if this is either not granted or not possible, the officers have to consider the importance that they give to their role as police officers against their views about abortion, views that reflect deep religious, political, and ethical commitments in the wider community.

The difficulty with all decisions concerning role responsibilities, when these responsibilities come into seeming conflict with societal rules, is knowing where and how to draw the relevant lines, and knowing how much weight to assign to the various factors that fall on either side of the lines we draw. There are no easy answers concerning which issues are worth fighting about and which is the best way to conduct that fight. There are no moral algorithms – formulae that allow us to calculate the "right" conclusion – only moral judgments. In other words, our best means for determining answers to these questions is to seek to hear, understand, and be responsive to arguments and counterarguments for each of the various views that are relevant to the judgment that we must make. As inhabitants of an imperfect world, even our best decisions will be less than ideal, but we can reach some "best fit" between opposing considerations and so arrive – at least in and for our present circumstances – at what has been said to be a "reflective equilibrium" of the various contending points that bear on how to resolve the morally perplexing problem that is before us. And we must remain open to the possibility that what is a "best fit" now may not continue to be so as our experience is enriched and our circumstances change.

Conclusion

Our purpose in this chapter has been to indicate some of the ways in which what is viewed as "criminal" in our criminal justice system reflects presumptions that may escape the notice of those who work within the system and, having escaped their notice, will then not be reflected upon and, when necessary, become objects of social debate and improvement. We may not always have the luxury of leaving our moral resolutions in limbo, but we may always act with the humility of those who know that the truth may be other than we take it to be.

3 Constraints on governmental agents

Laws are silent when arms are taken up.[1]

In an ideal world, socially acceptable relations would come about through people's voluntary conformity with both social norms generally and the subset of norms that the criminal law seeks to secure. However, our world is not an ideal one and, given the failure of people's voluntary conformity with norms that specify desirable social behavior, the criminal law and its supporting cast of actors have become essential tools for identifying and securing acceptable public conduct. The criminal justice system is of course not the only or even our most important instrument for discouraging anti-social behavior. We may offer various public incentives for voluntary conformity (such as just distributions of social benefits, a responsiveness to social need, and better education) as well as various nonpunitive disincentives (such as situational crime prevention techniques that diminish opportunities for and temptations to crime). And there are of course important social disincentives – such as the influence of family, peers, friends, and other affiliational connections. Nevertheless, the promulgation and enforcement of criminal law plays a critical role in securing public order. It does this through clear identification of behavior deemed criminal, efforts to prevent criminal conduct, the investigation and prosecution of crimes, and the fashioning of appropriate social responses to those convicted (of which legal punishment is usually the most prominent).

Of course, the need to discourage certain kinds of conduct does not provide a blank check to those charged with using the criminal justice system to try to ensure appropriate conduct. Even good ends do not justify

---

[1] *Silent enim leges inter arma*: M. Tulli Ciceronis (c. 106–43 BCE), *Pro T. Annio Milone ad iudices oratio*, with introduction and commentary by Albert C. Clark (Oxford: Clarendon, 1885), 10.

whatever means might secure them. Or do they? (As the comedian Woody Allen is said to have jokingly remarked: "If the ends don't justify the means, I don't know what will.") Although many moralists have insisted that good ends – no matter how important – do not justify any and all means necessary to achieve those ends, in the real world of politics it is much more commonly claimed that important ends may indeed justify the problematic means by which they are pursued, a position often echoed within the very "pragmatic" world of policing. Police often claim that their job requires them to "get results," results that are deemed of sufficient importance – such as saving lives, preventing serious harm, and apprehending assailants – that they are justified in doing whatever has to be done to get those results. The tension between the views expressed by the process-oriented moralist and those expressed by the results-oriented pragmatist suggests a somewhat complicated relation between ends and means that is worth examining.

Let us start with two small but significant complications. First, we speak of ends and means as though they are quite separate from each other, but in fact some ends may serve as means to further ends and so what is characterized as an end may at the same time also be accurately characterized as a means (to another, further end). For example, the use of mace by a police officer may be a means to take control of an unruly person; taking control of that person may itself be a means to a further end, namely, of maintaining social order; maintaining social order may be a means to yet some further end such as ensuring citizens the capacity to enjoy certain rights which in turn can be a means to (and an ingredient of) a still further end, that of human well-being and flourishing.

Philosophers have sometimes distinguished "intermediate" from "final" or "ultimate" ends, the latter being defined as ends that are valuable because of what they are and not because of what they lead to. (Examples of ends that have been regarded as final or ultimate are justice, human well-being, or the glory of God.) On the other hand, intermediate ends are ends that are valuable as effective means to other ends. That is a bit oversimplified, but it will do here.[2] The view that ends may sometimes justify the means used

---

[2] Some of the complications are discussed in Harry Frankfurt, "On the Usefulness of Final Ends," reprinted in Harry G. Frankfurt, *Necessity, Volition, and Love* (Cambridge: Cambridge University Press, 1999), 82–94.

to achieve them gets its plausibility from thinking of the justifying ends as ultimate or inherently good and therefore as providing a justification for whatever is necessary to produce them.

Secondly, as will become clear, even intrinsically good outcomes do not automatically provide good reasons for engaging in actions that lead to those outcomes. For some means that are adopted to produce good outcomes will be such as to subvert the very ends to which they are directed.

Suppose, for example, that a person's spiritual salvation is taken to be the all-important end of life. Suppose, furthermore, that faith is taken to be necessary for such salvation. Given these suppositions, the use of inquisitorial means to secure a profession of faith so that salvation will be achieved will undermine the very end that is sought. This is because the means employed (coercion) subverts that very element (namely, voluntariness) that is crucial to the connection between one's faith and one's salvation. Voluntary commitment is critical to genuine faith. Analogously, police who engage in certain forms of coercion in order to elicit confessions that can then be used in court will, if their coercive attempts are successful, end up with "confessions" that fail to be admissible in court because the prerequisite of their admissibility, namely, voluntariness, has failed to be met.

Different considerations will have to be appealed to in different circumstances to determine whether, in seeking to secure certain ends, particular means employed to bring those ends about are or are not justified. Consider the following cases of means and ends: (1) introducing plea-bargaining in order to free up the court system and increase convictions; (2) using cyber-surveillance technology to get information about terrorist plots; (3) mounting closed circuit television (CCTV) cameras to deter crime and identify criminals; (4) using undercover police officers to infiltrate criminal gangs in order to break them up; (5) using stun belts to maintain control of prisoners while they are away from their cells; (6) constructing "supermax" prisons to control "the worst of the worst"; and (7) sending suspected terrorists to foreign countries ("extraordinary rendition") knowing that harsher interrogation techniques than are permissible in one's own country may be used on them. These are all cases in which particular means are used to secure ends that are thought to be either valuable-in-themselves or closely connected to ends that are valuable-in-themselves. By what criteria shall we judge whether the means used to achieve these various ends are morally justifiable?

Given the variety of ends we may seek, the variety of means that may be employed to secure our ends, and the variety of circumstances in which we must operate, it is not surprising that there is no single and simple formula that will enable us to judge the legitimacy of using particular means to secure desired and desirable ends. Moral argument does not generally work like that. But in trying to judge the legitimacy of a course of action involving means and ends, there are several important questions we should raise regarding the ends in question and any means that are contemplated or used. Each of these questions needs to be answered satisfactorily if the means–end relationship is to pass ethical muster.

Are the ends good or good enough?

As we noted earlier, some ends are simply means to further ends. However, the only ends that will serve to justify means are those that are not merely directed to further ends: they must be valuable-in-themselves. But even with respect to ends that are valuable-in-themselves, we need to be assured that they are valuable enough (both in-themselves and because of any additional values that they serve) to support the use of the particular means. This point may be illustrated by the following. Suppose a police officer aims at securing the legal conviction of someone he believes guilty of a crime and decides, as police sometimes do, that he will "shade" his testimony to ensure that that person will be convicted. Securing that conviction cannot be a final and therefore justificatory end unless the person believed to be guilty really is guilty (and even then of course it does not follow that any means will do). Furthermore, the conduct of which the person is believed to be guilty must be conduct that is legitimately criminalized (within, say, a liberal democracy). If, for example, one believes that the personal use of marijuana should not be criminalized, then one might think that obtaining the legal conviction of a person guilty of using the drug is not an end that would justify what it takes to bring about that conviction (though that may not be a matter for an individual police officer to determine). But even if the offense *is* one that should be criminalized, it might still be questioned whether the offense is important enough to justify the use of the particular means used to bring about conviction for that offense. The resources required to ensure a conviction might be better employed elsewhere. Thus we might question whether police should be giving out summonses for jaywalking if more serious problems on the streets are thereby being neglected.

Are the means proportionate to the end?

Although we may effectively get rid of a pesky fly with a shotgun, it is clear that in doing so we would be using means that are disproportionate to the task. The shotgun is a disproportionate means to our end because there are so many easy, less costly, and less dramatic but just as effective alternatives for achieving our aim. But the proportionality requirement runs deeper than this. Often when we speak of disproportionality between means and ends we have in mind a notion of unfairness, the lack of a "moral matching" or fitness of means and end. The means are morally too extreme relative to the ends for which they are employed. Using wiretaps – a drastic invasion of privacy – to catch an occasional petty thief, for example, would be disproportionate in this sense. So might be the construction of an elaborate sting operation that police have sometimes used (say, sending letters falsely notifying people of lottery wins in order to lure them into custody), if employed simply to catch those who have failed to pay their parking fines. No doubt some offenses warrant imaginative investigative strategies, but if these strategies are also used to catch those who are delinquent only in regard to parking fines, the means will almost certainly be excessive. Our reactions may be moderated, however, if the scofflaws have each ignored thousands of dollars' worth of fines and the sting operation is designed to catch hundreds of such people at a time.

Can the ends be secured in a less invasive manner?

People sometimes refer to a principle of the least restrictive alternative. In a liberal democracy, we place a premium on minimizing the extent to which people's freedom is compromised (sometimes referred to as a principle of parsimony). We may sometimes achieve ends in more than one way, though one means will be less costly (socially and individually) than others. Other things being equal, we should try to secure ends in the least restrictive way, even if an alternative way would not be disproportionate to the ends being secured. Suppose that a large demonstration is being planned and the police are concerned that it will get out of hand. They could turn out in great force, with riot gear, in an effort to deter trouble from elements within the demonstration. Alternatively, they might meet with the organizers of the demonstration prior to its taking place in order to work out a *modus vivendi*. The demonstrators want to make their point and the police must ensure an orderly gathering. The police and organizers may be able to come to some prior understanding about how the rally will be organized – whether arrests are desired, how they will be handled, and so on. The latter strategy may be the less restrictive and therefore be the more acceptable.[3]

Will the means secure the ends?

The use of particular means in an attempt to secure valuable ends is rendered quite problematic if the means chosen are known – or should have been known – to be unlikely to secure those ends. (The Keystone Kops display both ineptitude and misjudgment in their attempts to secure their law enforcement ends – so much so that we regard their efforts as "antics.") In the real world of practical decision-making, whether or not we will be successful in achieving our ends by use of particular means is almost always a matter of probabilities, and sometimes it will be difficult to determine in advance what the probabilities of success will be. In addition, depending on the importance of the ends, we may adjust our judgment of what degree of probability should be required before we are justified in proceeding. The more important our ends, the more we may be justified in proceeding with means that are less than certain to achieve their ends. The greater the goods that we aim at, the more we may be willing to risk in achieving them.

Some people argue that unless the end *is* achieved the use of a particular means is not justified. But that would be a very high demand, for it would require that we wait until the means have been employed and we know the outcome of their use before we can pass any judgment on their justifiability. However, usually we want to know not only whether what we *have done was justified* but also whether we would be *justified in going ahead* with some

---

[3] The difference between the proportionality and least-restrictive-alternative requirements can be illustrated by means of the following hypothetical: I am being pursued by a gunman who wants to kill me. I would be justified in shooting him in self-defense (proportionality); on the other hand, I could slip through a doorway and could prevent him from following me (a less invasive means). I should pursue the latter option.

strategy, and this means making a judgment prior to our proceeding and therefore prior to our knowing the outcome.

It might be argued that sometimes, even if we know (or have good reason to believe) that we will not be able to achieve what we are after, we are nonetheless justified in proceeding with our attempts.[4] Where a small country is attacked by a larger one and fighting back is unlikely to be successful, it may be that fighting back is still called for: rather than cave in (even to a hopeless situation), which would be degrading, it may be a matter of moral dignity to stand and fight a battle even if one knows one cannot win it. Or consider a case in which the search for a killer will consume vast resources with little likelihood of success: one might argue that out of respect for the victim and victim's family one should do whatever one can to try to find the killer, even if little is likely to be yielded by one's efforts to do so.

Is there something intrinsically problematic about the means?

Sometimes means may be chosen that, though effective in achieving the ends that we are after, are nonetheless morally unacceptable-in-themselves. Consider the following two examples, in which the end sought is unquestionably valuable, but the means employed remain at best morally questionable and, most likely, morally unacceptable. (1) A police undercover officer, to gain information about an underworld figure, becomes intimate with a woman who has close connections with the person being investigated. The officer leads her to believe that he is in love with her and, in the course of the relationship, impregnates her. However, once he has exploited the relationship for whatever information he can get, he vanishes from her life. We might consider this an intrinsically unacceptable means to achieve the end of information-gathering, for we believe that exploiting intimate relations, and particularly those that are likely to involve not only the abuse of intimacy but also long-term costs, is not to be countenanced for information-gathering purposes. (2) Government agents torture or otherwise treat inhumanely those whom they believe to have terrorist connections in order to gain information related to "the war on terrorism." Or, in the same context,

---

[4] The traditional theory of war says that one is not justified in fighting back unless there is some likelihood of success. This is questionable, though whether we might have a duty to resist is also unclear.

government agents secretly and without court warrant subject citizens to comprehensive surveillance in order to obtain information that might be useful to them in their investigations. Since we consider torture and warrantless surveillance to be incompatible with our endorsement of the moral values of a liberal society, we will generally find these to be morally condemnable means.

We will return to such cases. The general point to notice, though, is that means are frequently not "morally neutral," that is, given value only by the ends to which they are directed. They often have a value in and of themselves, and in using them to secure some end we must take any intrinsic disvalue they have into account. The tendency to treat means as morally neutral has been a common failure in much political debate, where particular tactics (terror tactics) are seen as unacceptable if "they" use them, since they are pursuing evil ends, but such tactics (counter-terror tactics) are acceptable if "we" use them because we are pursuing good ends. This is also a pervasive challenge in policing, where deceptive and coercive means are frequently employed. May police, in order to catch drug distributors, illegally import drugs on behalf of a distributor they are trying to apprehend?[5]

Cicero's famous dictum, quoted at the beginning of this chapter, has been the subject of ongoing debate, most recently since the events of September 11, 2001. For Cicero, the end of winning a war overrode the constraints of law. Such has been the attitude of those who, since those terrorist attacks, have wished to argue that the hands of the US President, as Commander in Chief, cannot be bound. And yet this has created a great deal of uneasiness about the detention and treatment of people who are claimed to have terrorist connections. Are the laws silent? Or if not silent, may they be overridden or speak with a different voice? Before 9/11, but with terrorism already in focus, the late Chief Justice of the United States, William Rehnquist, wrote that "the laws will not be silent in time of war, but . . . they will speak with a somewhat different voice."[6] His point was that in time of war, civil liberties may have to be constrained, a point that we may acknowledge, though his account leaves it unclear how different that voice

[5] This was a problem in an Australian case, *Ridgeway v. The Queen*, (1995) 184 C.L.R. 19. The legislature subsequently responded by making an exception of government agents in sting operations.

[6] William H. Rehnquist, *All the Laws but One: Civil Liberties in Wartime* (New York: Alfred A. Knopf, 1998), 221.

may legitimately be. Does it allow detention without trial, the suspension of habeas corpus, detention without the protections of Common Article 3 of the Geneva Conventions, the use of military tribunals? Does it allow warrantless interception of communications? Does it allow torture, or, if not torture, then treatment that would otherwise be considered "cruel, inhuman and degrading"? A slightly different gloss on Cicero was offered during World War II in a British case: "Amid the clash of arms, the laws are not silent, they may be changed, but they speak the same language in war as in peace."[7] This suggests that the laws may not speak with a different voice (we may not reinterpret the prohibition against torture to allow treatment that would previously been covered by it), though we may institute special laws during a time of war that we would not consider appropriate during a time of peace. Once again, we may accept that special constraints may be necessary during times of war. But it does not help us to understand what those constraints may be or, indeed, whether there are some constraints that we may not impose.

The latter point is particularly important. In addition to the question of whether or not some means are of a kind that will need particularly important ends to justify their use, there is the question of whether some means are completely beyond the pale – that is, may never be used, no matter what the ends. Are there some means that are absolutely and unconditionally wrong and not merely defeasibly wrong (that is, wrong but able to be overridden in certain cases)?

Most liberal democracies formally condemn torture. At the same time they think that it may sometimes be a useful tool. And, when that is believed to be the case, efforts are made to characterize harsh interrogatory tactics as something other than torture. From 1987 until 1999, when its High Court forbade the practice, Israel's security forces were officially permitted to use "moderate physical pressure" against those suspected of terrorist involvement (the law speaking with a "somewhat different voice"). The major purpose was not to get confessions or aid convictions but to develop informational resources that would head off terrorist activity before it became lethal. Whatever we want to say about "moderate physical pressure," Israel's High Court eventually determined that it was not sufficiently distinguishable from torture and it was therefore outlawed. As torture, it

---

[7] Lord Atkin, *Liversidge v. Anderson* [1941] 2 All E.R. 612.

was impermissible, even as a counter to terrorism. But absolutely so? That is the voice with which most international conventions speak: "No exceptional circumstances whatsoever, whether a state of war or a threat of war, internal political instability or any other public emergency, may be invoked as a justification of torture."[8] Though international conventions typically allow killing or even war in self-defense, they draw the line at torture, and that is because torture crosses a fundamental moral boundary. We deny the dignity of others in a fundamental way. If torture is permitted, then *anything* we do to any other will be permitted as a means – at least when we believe that the ends are important enough (say, the possibility of saving a thousand lives, or the protection of national security). The point at which we sanction torture is seen as the point at which we move outside the constraints of morality. As a civilized society, we cannot make this move.[9]

But some have argued to the contrary, claiming that were a bomb to be set to go off in a crowded metropolis with no time left to evacuate the city, it would indeed be morally acceptable to torture someone who is withholding information that would enable the defusing of the bomb. This is a seductive argument, but we should be wary of its temptations. The main thing to notice is how much knowledge appeals to the "ticking bomb" example presuppose that we possess: that there is indeed a ticking bomb; that, if not defused, it will go off; that, if we are to get the necessary information, there is no alternative but to engage in torture; that torture will in fact yield the truth about the bomb's location; and that we will be in time and be able to defuse the bomb. In real life, we hardly ever meet all of these conditions when faced with a so-called ticking bomb threat. What is even more troubling is that those who appeal to the ticking bomb argument are almost always looking to use the permission they seek for torture in circumstances that are far less stringent than those of real ticking bombs in unknown locations.[10]

---

[8] UN Convention Against Torture and Other Cruel, Inhuman, or Degrading Treatment or Punishment (1985), art. 2.1. Israel's High Court, it might be noted, left the door to torture slightly ajar.

[9] Unfortunately, in a climate of *Realpolitik*, we try to do so – by characterizing what we do as something other than torture (or by getting or allowing others to do it for us).

[10] True, the mere fact that particular tactics are misused does not thereby show them to be illegitimate; but I am suggesting that misuse is endemic to the ticking bomb scenario.

The point of appeals to ticking bomb scenarios is often not merely to show that in certain extreme situations torture could be justifiable but, more generally, to provide a license for those who wish for greater flexibility in fighting terrorism. However, given our experience of the frequent misapplication and even corruption of authoritative license, we should be extremely wary of countenancing torture either morally or legally. If someone resorts to torture on ticking bomb grounds, we may – if sufficiently persuaded by the details of the case – perhaps forgive or excuse that person's resort to torture in the particular instance, but we should always stop short of countenancing "advance directives" for its use.[11]

The issue that we have been discussing – the use of morally problematic means to achieve what are recognizably valuable ends – has come to be generally referred to as the issue of "dirty hands." As we noted in Chapter 1, the issue of dirty hands often arises in connection with the claim that those who hold public office can sometimes fulfill the public expectations of their office (and so do what is in the public good) only if they act in ways that transgress ordinary moral expectations. So, for example, it has been claimed that although torture is indeed morally reprehensible, its use by those charged with the public's welfare may sometimes be necessary to secure that welfare. In doing what is ultimately required by their office, public officials may sometimes, regrettably but unavoidably, have to get their hands dirty. Or take the following example, in which officials were caught in circumstances in which their performance of an unexceptionable public obligation could be accomplished only by their violating a clear moral duty. It is often said that during World War II the British authorities decided not to warn the people of Coventry about an impending German air raid because the British had learned about the raid through the cracking of the Enigma Code and it was critical to the British war effort that the fact that they had cracked the Code be kept secret from the Germans. So, for the ultimate good of winning the war, the welfare and the lives of the people of Coventry were jeopardized, indeed sacrificed. Of course, the issue of dirty hands does not always arise in such extreme forms as these.

---

[11] Although I am suggesting a stronger moral case against torture, there is an interesting and related jurisprudential discussion about the defense of "necessity," which, if successful, functions to justify what would otherwise be prohibited. But an important element in that discussion is the recognition that the defense of necessity must be considered on a case-by-case basis.

It is not always clear what we should say – or indeed how we should think – about such cases as the above. Some who discuss the issue of dirty hands have claimed that such cases are cases in which it is "right to do wrong." This paradoxical way of putting the point reflects a deep division between so-called consequentialist considerations that point to the importance of maximizing good and minimizing evil and considerations that constitute certain kinds of acts as inherently wrong, that is, condemnable apart from any consequences they may have. It is a division that has no easy resolution. But the problem with much of the dirty hands debate, and particularly with the formulation just suggested, is that it tends to open the door to opportunism and may disincline one to give due weight to the moral principles that govern our conduct. It may be best simply to acknowledge that human decision-making is sometimes less than ideal and that occasions can arise in which there is no way to behave that will be unequivocally morally right. No doubt this is unfortunate, but, as part of the human condition, the most we may be able to hope for when we cannot but get our hands dirty in the process of trying to do what is best is to make the right decision about how to deal with the stain that our conduct leaves on our hands.

In a liberal democracy there is an additional dimension to these problems when those we have elected to office dirty their hands on our behalf. In judging them, we must also judge ourselves. No doubt this is one of the reasons why, when we think they have got their hands filthy, and not merely dirty, we feel not only angry at the way they have violated what we stand for but also guilty and ashamed at what has been perpetrated on our behalf.

Will the means have deleterious consequences that would make their use inappropriate?

An effective and otherwise acceptable means might run into difficulties if it has unintended and undesirable consequences. Racial profiling can provide a salient example. If members of a particular ethnic group are judged to be more heavily involved than other groups in drug-running, it might seem a prudent use of resources to surveil and investigate members of that group more intensively just because they are members of the group predominantly involved in that activity. But doing so may have serious deleterious side effects. Because only a minority of members of the minority group is likely to be involved in drug-running, it is therefore highly probable that a significant number of those investigated will be innocent of any involvement. If we add – as we usually can – that the group in question has been historically subject to social discrimination, then the profiling will tend to exacerbate their unfortunate social situation. Such was the experience of African Americans who felt themselves accused of and harassed for "Driving While Black": they found themselves subject to suspicion that they were up to no good just because their skin color associated them with a group presumed to be more likely to be involved in criminal activity.

In sum, the argument that the ends justify the means must make a number of assumptions about both the ends and the means if it is to pass ethical muster. Though the view that an end never justifies the means may underrate the significance that valuable ends may have for the justified use of particular means, the practical danger in the world of criminal justice (as in the world generally) is that ends will too easily be taken to justify whatever means are deemed necessary (and sometimes only especially convenient) for bringing about those desired ends. Ends must be constrained by means, and criminal justice is pervaded by moral challenges concerning the matching of means with ends.

Part II

Policing

We begin our discussion of the major institutions of criminal justice by considering its "executive," law enforcement, or policing dimension. Classic liberal democratic theory saw the policing role simply as one of ensuring that those who violated rights were called to answer for what they had done. But contemporary policing is much less clearly defined. Here we review the scope of the police role and the limits of police discretion in fulfilling that role, and then consider two of the important strategic powers that enable police to fulfill their role: coercion and deception. For obvious reasons these present great moral challenges.

4   Tensions within the police role

Police are occupied with peacekeeping – but preoccupied
with crime fighting.[1]

Evolution of the police role

Classical liberals had a clear but rather simple view of the police role. According to that view police were "enforcers" who (along with those who were
needed to oversee the decisions of the courts) were to ensure that those who
violated the rights of others answered for their wrongdoing. But already
when the police organizations with which we are now familiar came into
being in the nineteenth century, the emphasis was on crime prevention
rather than mere law enforcement: crime represented a failure in policing rather than just the occasion for it.[2] Our current understanding of the
police role is rather less clear and police are now frequently conflicted about
it themselves, some finding their role, at times, more accurately describable
as "crisis management" than as "law enforcement" or even as "crime prevention." And what is termed and now frequently fostered as "community
policing" is sometimes seen as less or other than "real" policing.

To shed light on what the current social role of police is and how this
contrasts with the way in which the police role was theoretically conceived
by classical theorists of individual rights and dignity, we would do well
to remember that their understanding flowed from their view of the limited role of government: governmental structures were instituted to secure

[1] Jesse Rubin, "Police Identity and the Police Role," in *The Police and the Community*, ed.
Robert F. Steadman (Baltimore: Johns Hopkins University Press, 1972), 25.
[2] See Col. Charles Rowan and Sir Richard Mayne, *General Instructions* (London: Metropolitan
Police, 1829), 1, where crime prevention rather than law enforcement is seen as primary.

individual rights against interference by others – the "others" being not only individuals but also institutions such as the monarchy and the church. In this view, the function of the police was merely to ensure that the purposes of government in securing individual rights were in fact carried out. Those who violated others' rights were to be tracked down by the police, brought to court, and convicted. But this view of government and so of that arm of it that police represented changed with the view of what needed to be secured for the well-being of citizens. Although classical liberals viewed government as concerned primarily with ensuring that individuals not be interfered with unjustifiably, the current liberal conception of the proper province of government is much broader. Along with that broader understanding of government's province has also gone a broader understanding of the police role.

To be sure, the view that policing's sole purpose is to catch crooks and put them away is still a major part of the popular mythology of policing. It focuses on a critical function of policing that is not to be disparaged or dismissed. But it is a view that, in the end, fails to capture all that we now believe government not only may but ought to do on behalf of its citizens (and through its policing services). Our view of what it is that police should do for citizens is intimately connected to our view of what it is that government is about, because most public policing is done under the auspices of government and as part of governmental authority. Police, indeed, are often at the interface of applications of governmental policy, ensuring their orderly implementation. Any change in our conception of governmental functions will, therefore, almost inevitably have an impact on the way in which we conceive of and experience police functions.[3]

For liberal democrats, although policing is a governmental function, the purpose of policing is to secure not *general* governmental interests but mainly those interests that are directed to the protection of the individual human rights of those who fall within their jurisdiction. Contrast this with the role of police in totalitarian states. Police in such states, as in democracies, also operate under the auspices of government, but

---

[3] The growth of private policing is generally supplemental – usually providing security for private associations that cannot obtain the level of policing presence they desire through the public purse or wish for greater control over the policing function within their jurisdictions.

their role is directed not to serving the interests of citizens as holders of individual rights but rather to serving the narrower interests of
those in power. Even benevolent dictatorships impose a conception of general well-being that has been constructed out of the interests of those in
power.

The question we must answer, however, is what it means to serve the
interests or protect the rights of individual citizens. As we noted, classical
liberals viewed the protection of human rights as restricted to the protection
of citizens against the illegitimate interference of others, where the chief
"others" were taken to be the governing powers, the church, and other
individuals. And the interests or rights that were taken to be in need of
protection were an individual's life, liberty, and property. Originally, these
were construed in negative terms as interests that were to be left alone.
More recently there has been a tendency to interpret them positively in
ways that merge into what we now think of as welfare interests, which
include not merely the requisites of survival and noninterference but the
wherewithal to make something of life and liberty. And so, in the view
of many who deliberate on human rights, what needs to be ensured or
secured by government is better reflected in statements such as the United
Nations Universal Declaration of Human Rights (1948). According to that
Declaration, human rights should be considered not only as protections
against the encroachment of others – institutional and individual – but also
as giving individuals the opportunity to make the best of themselves, often
thought of as the ability and opportunity to formulate and execute long-
range plans for themselves. Recognized, therefore, are rights to welfare as
well as rights to protection, and rights to education and healthcare as well
as rights to liberty and security. Ensuring both kinds of rights may fall partly
to government and its agents. This expanded view of rights has come about,
at least in part, as a response to the rise of capitalism, which has made
individuals much more vulnerable than before to market forces, such that
some safety net (in the form of social welfare programs) must be provided
if individuals generally are to be able to attain even a minimum level of
well-being. We are also more sensitive now to the vulnerability of – and
therefore the need for security against – exploitation in the labor market.
Such security has been seen as a right that has found expression in both
child labor laws and minimum wage laws.

Enforcers?

The change in our view of what counts as a human right and therefore of what counts as its violation has inevitably affected what is believed to be the proper province of government in its executive function. No longer is government seen merely as the protector of individual life, liberty, and property but, in addition, as the securer and preserver of some minimum level of individual economic and social well-being. The arm of government that is represented by the police is therefore no longer to be seen as having the sole function of making sure that others do not interfere with an individual's life, liberty, and property – that is, as "enforcers" – but, as well, as an agency of government that can fulfill various social service functions, functions that may generally be described as those of crisis management and order maintenance. These functions are pursued by police in a variety of ways, and sometimes by police agencies forming partnerships with other groups or agencies that serve the broader welfare interests of the community. So we find police sometimes working with groups that focus on the needs of the homeless, of drug-misusers, of runaways, of the domestically abused, and with units that provide social, psychological, and medical emergency services. (Sometimes relations between police and these other service-providers are strained on account of their different modes of response and also by there being no obvious "natural" division of responsibility. Such divisions as exist may owe as much to local resources and politics as to some "rational division of labor" and, under such conditions, failures in coordination of services may be inevitable.)

One reason why law enforcement as classically conceived cannot be taken as the sole concern of today's police has to do with our current recognition of the interconnectedness of human life and its problems. What looks like a lost child might turn out to be a case of criminal neglect. What appears to be a private spat might in fact be a case of criminal assault. What looks like disorderly conduct may be the behavior of someone having an epileptic fit or a mental breakdown. What appears to have been a mugging may have been the desperate action of someone who has become delusional, and what appears to have been a case of reckless driving may be the reactions of someone having a heart attack. A socially threatening situation – say, a man shouting and swinging a baseball bat on a public street – may be brought about through a failure to take medication. Human life and human interactions are complex phenomena, and when acts are rapidly interpreted without much by way of background information, they may turn out to be other than what they initially appear to be.[4] Oftentimes, situations that present themselves may require the involvement not only of police but also of other social or medical personnel. Addressing situations in a manner that is sensitive to their full scope may thus need the input not merely of those whose purpose it is to enforce the law but also of others who represent a variety of other interests, be they social, psychological, or medical. For better *and* worse we have divided up our social responses to human problems so that we can provide more specialized assistance for particular needs. In doing so, however, we are often led to neglect other dimensions of those situations that equally deserve our consideration. One of the important social contributions of police is to take control of socially disruptive situations in a way that enables other groups and agencies to provide appropriate responses. But this means that the police officer's role as a law-enforcer should be moderated by a sensitivity to the social, psychological, medical, and welfare needs of those to whose behavior the officer is called upon to respond. (Later I shall suggest that pressures for professionalization have sometimes contributed to the failure of police to provide adequate responses to certain social problems they encounter.)

Notwithstanding that we now recognize the social service role of police along with that of law-enforcer – indeed, that to be effective enforcers of the law police must also be effective as social aides – the idea that police should be law-enforcers first and foremost retains a strong hold on the public, and even on the police, imagination. No doubt it is the law enforcement dimension of police work that contributes most significantly to the glamor and mystique of police work, a glamor and mystique reflected in most police shows on television (even if recent more "reality-based" TV police series offer a modulated version of the "law and order" paradigm). This view of police work as essentially a matter of enforcement and coercion is reinforced by many of the appurtenances of policing – the batons and other weaponry that are on prominent display (at least in the United States); patrol cars with blaring sirens; and various paramilitary practices (such as a rank structure, roll

---

[4] That is the common experience of police on patrol and, particularly in times of heightened concern about terrorism, the temporal window for decision-making may be experienced as very narrow.

calls, and inspections). Given that we accord a general law enforcement role to police that we do not expect of people generally, why should this not constitute both the core and the periphery of the police role?

Some writers have offered what appears to be a compromise position. They recognize that police are now expected to deal with a wider range of issues than law enforcement, but nevertheless wish to accommodate this expanded role in a way that retains the powers that contribute to its mystique. This position has been championed by Egon Bittner, who suggests that "the role of police is to address all sorts of human problems when and insofar as the problems' solutions may require the use of force at the point of their occurrence."[5] According to Bittner, then, police are legitimately called upon to maintain order and provide certain social services (such as responding to domestic disturbance calls), because effectively dealing with such situations might require the coercive power of the police.

Although this account of the connection between policing and the provision of certain social services has its attractions – for example, it presents police activities as all characterizable in some uniform way, a way that is likely to resonate with police themselves and that fits well with the fact that it is the police who are the major repositories of societal force – it nevertheless presents a perspective on policing that skews it in a troubling direction. For it casts the use of force as a *critical* strategic option ("when and insofar as") and not merely as *one* of the various strategic options that police have at their disposal for doing their work. This may seem to have been reinforced by the recent upsurge of urban and fundamentalist terrorism. But the use of force is not the police officer's only or even main recourse, a fact more easily recognized in the United Kingdom, where police are not, as they are in the United States, armed with deadly weapons on prominent display and where force, though sanctioned, is used more as a last resort than as a *modus operandi*.[6] Though Bittner claims only that police concerns are ones in which police "may," rather than must, resort to force, the focus is too much on coercion as a means of which police may avail themselves, rather than on the ends – whether coercive or not – of police activity. And where the focus

[5] Egon Bittner, "The Capacity to Use Force as the Core of the Police Role," in *Moral Issues in Police Work*, ed. Frederick A. Elliston and Michael Feldberg (Totowa, NJ: Rowman & Allanheld, 1985), 21.

[6] In actual fact, US police departments advocate the use of (deadly) force only as a last resort, though a culture of "coming on strong" is deeply ingrained.

is on means that are coercive, force will tend to be resorted to rather more easily than might otherwise be the case.

Furthermore, focusing on a strategic means that police may use suggests a limit to the scope of police work that is unrealistic and undesirable. Many of the things that police do – and might appropriately be expected to do – have no direct connection with their use of force. Whether running an after-school athletic league (and thus having a negative impact on juvenile crime), directing traffic, informing the next of kin of someone's death, or giving lectures on public safety, police perform valuable public services that it is reasonable to expect from them, even though the activities in question are unlikely to involve any resort to force. There are also many other services that fall to the police – such as giving directions, providing dispatching services for emergency response, and offering advice on urgently needed assistance – that are of great importance to social well-being and should not be removed from the scope of the police role just because they are most unlikely to involve any use of force. True, the fact that police are socially entrusted with the use of force may give some of their other activities a cachet that others may not have, but this is a more subtle connection than is encompassed by Bittner's characterization.

Social peacekeepers

It is best to see police not simply as possessing the coercive power to get things done but as vested with public *authority* to further the end of social peacekeeping. That is, they are given authority to direct, organize, control, respond to, and investigate situations so that social peace may be maintained or restored. Included in that authority, though one that should be resorted to only when other strategies fail or are inappropriate, is the authority to use force and, when faced with situations that are disruptive of social peace, the use of initiatives to involve the participation of other agencies.

Our contemporary concerns with the management of crowds, with traffic control, and with being able to conduct our lives in an environment that is free from fear – in short, with the general maintenance of social order – are not concerns that have an automatic resolution. Rather, we first and foremost think of police as "on call" when a breakdown of social peace occurs and some measured response to critical incidents is called for. Of course, police are not the only people to respond to crises. Firefighters, emergency service personnel, social workers – to take but a few examples – also offer specialized response services and, indeed, often have resources at their disposal that are not available to the police. As has happened with other divisions of labor in our society, police may find that some parts of their work will be shared or gradually hived off to more specialized others. Nevertheless, there will and should remain certain basic peacekeeping responsibilities for which the police are specially trained, and even where more specialized services are also needed, police may have a crucial coordinating or other peacekeeping role.

The idea of social peacekeeping is not a new one. Even before the present era of professional policing, some were tasked with keeping the King's Peace – a zone of tranquillity surrounding the King and later expanding to include the realm. Embedded in an ancient household police power, the need for social peacekeeping has remained, even if its role has generally become less moralistic.[7] Nevertheless, the notion of "keeping the peace" is not a precisely defined concept, though certain dimensions of it may be articulated in a reasonably clear manner. It generally includes, but is not exhausted by, the attempt to prevent social conflict that takes destructive forms. In a liberal society, preventing social conflict that is likely to conduce to violence (and thus a violation of rights) will be accomplished mainly through an emphasis on and implementation of the rule of law. An attempt is made to ensure that constitutionally accepted rules not only set the standard by which behavior is judged and regulated but are also seen by the public as setting that standard. In this way not only crime but the fear of crime will be minimized. In an increasingly populous and complex society, this will involve the work of agencies – most notably, the police – that can coordinate public life in a way that minimizes intrusion into individual liberty but can do so without at the same time unacceptably sacrificing public security. Thus, for example, a police agency will allow and even enable demonstrations to take place, but seek to structure them in ways that minimize social disruption. To some extent, then, one might say that in doing what they need to do to ensure that social life runs smoothly, the police should function *inter alia* as social umpires. Their role – in large part, and

---

[7] For a provocative discussion of its development, see Markus Dirk Dubber, *The Police Power: Patriarchy and the Foundations of American Government* (New York: Columbia University Press, 2005).

with qualifications to be noted in the next section – is to broker responses to social situations in ways that will be conducive to an environment in which human flourishing can occur. In a liberal democratic society that is likely to be marked by a diversity of interests and even contestation about the importance and even desirability of some of these interests, peaceful social interchange will be secured only through the sensitive adoption of various constitutionally sanctioned forms of tolerance. For example, police will often try to negotiate rather than forcibly intervene, intervene judiciously rather than heavy-handedly, and act preventively rather than intrusively.

We should not underestimate the challenge for police that is involved in the task described above. In liberal democratic societies that are multicultural and multiracial, especially those in which there has been a history of conflict and discrimination, some segments of the broader society will have a strong inclination to interpret "social peace" exclusively rather than inclusively. Police officers are drawn from that broader society and may be infected by that history and its attitudes and so may be resistant to the requirement that they ensure an environment in which the rights of all are secured and fostered and the needs of all are taken into account. In such situations, asking – as is often done – that police first and foremost be repositories of social common sense may not amount to as much as we would like.

But whatever the efforts required of police (and others) to ensure social peace, there is no doubt of its importance in both the educative and the nurturing processes of society. Peacekeeping provides a powerful account of the purpose of policing. Social peace is an important element in the flourishing of human life because we are communal beings who find many of our aspirations and fulfillments in joint and cooperative activities, and this inevitably involves reliance on the benefits of a social environment in which people can, without undue cost in terms of security and other fundamental interests, make diverse contributions. Without social peace, our very well-being will be threatened. It is not to overstate the case, therefore, to say that our welfare depends on social peace, and social peace depends, to a significant extent, on an effective and well-meaning police service.

As we have noted, the effectiveness of the police depends, in turn, on public recognition – that is, on their *authority*. Authority is a social relation in which we recognize the *competence* of others to act. Although it is formally conferred by the award of a badge (what is sometimes known as de jure authority), there is a presumption – if the authority is socially recognized (what is referred to as de facto authority) – that those who possess it are competent to do what they are authorized to do (that is, that they possess expert authority). It is because police have been trained to do what we expect of them that we accord them the authority to keep the peace. To the extent that they fail in this task, their authority is weakened and we demand that more is done to prepare them for their role. If they lose their authority, they become no more than thugs, or thugs for the powers that be.

Community policing

Although the term "community policing" is of relatively recent origin, the idea is much older, and its introduction as a limited or specialized style of policing has been unfortunate. At a certain level policing has always been community policing. Police have always been embedded in the community they serve. That is, they are usually drawn from the community in which they serve, and they are expected to ensure that its public operations (traffic, gatherings, etc.) function smoothly and that disruptions to communal peace (such as crime and accidents) are addressed. It almost goes without saying that for their social functions to be successfully fulfilled, police require the support and cooperation of the community.

All of this sounds unexceptionable if we assume that there is a clear background understanding of "community." Unfortunately, however, there is a lack of clarity about the notion of community: what we sometimes glibly refer to as "the community" often comprises multiple communities. The term suggests a population with shared or at least compatible aspirations and values, but often this cannot be said of groups that are thought of or said to constitute the same community, despite their geographical proximity. Indeed, members of the same "community" or society may be divided in a number of ways, with antagonisms arising along the lines of these divisions. The lines of division – and so of antagonisms – may be ethnic (think of some of the hostility expressed within some populations toward Vietnamese or Mexican or Turkish immigrants who have settled in their midst); religious (think of the antagonism between some Protestants and Catholics or Muslims and Orthodox Jews who inhabit the same society); racial (think of the racial slurs and discriminatory behavior one sometimes witnesses toward African-American or Asian members of a society); sexual (think of the disparaging remarks and offensive treatment of homosexuals by some members of the society in which gays live); gender-based (think of the continuing discrimination against or exploitation of women); economic (think of the disdain with which some members of economic ghettos are viewed by other members of the society); or some combination of these.

The notion of community is therefore not a straightforward and simple one, and for that reason the notion of community policing does not have a straightforward application. Police may be drawn from subgroups within a society, and it may be wondered whether they can empathize adequately with other subgroups at the same time that they represent and express the concerns of their own community within the larger group. It is understandable, then, that sometimes relations between police and the communities they serve deteriorate into "us–them" attitudes on the part of both police and various members of the larger society. In some communities, police have even come to be viewed by some of their members as an occupying army, with an agenda and values that are at variance with those of most of the communities' members, while police, for their part, have sometimes developed cynical attitudes toward the communities they serve, viewing them with suspicion and even disdain.

It would seem, then, that despite the good intentions behind community policing, its implementation – especially in multicultural urban societies – is fraught with difficulties. A further source of these difficulties, only obliquely referred to above, is that when police are called upon to respond to incidents that require their attention, it is expected that they will try to deal with these incidents in a way that shows appreciation of their communal context – that is, in a way that takes into account the history, customs, and social understandings of the community in which these incidents have taken place and not treat the incidents as having occurred in a vacuum, isolated from their communal environment.

But this policy has opponents on "both" sides of the police/community divide, both groups seeing it as an unnecessary distraction from the main role of police as crime fighters and rights protectors and a diversion instead into the role – disparaged when engaged in by police – of social workers and social activists. However, as we have already suggested when discussing the police peacekeeping role, police cannot be effective as crime fighters if they do not also engage with the social dimensions of crime, an observation, admittedly, that does not determine how deeply their involvement with such dimensions should be.

Efforts have of course been made to address these issues. One of them, the attempt to have a police organization quantitatively reflect the composition of the larger society, is at best a rough and ready – even crudely political – solution. What is also called community policing is sometimes an effort to get police to identify with the neighborhoods in which they work. Moreover, crime is not simply a violation of social rules for which punishment is seen as an appropriate response. Crime is also embedded in a social environment, and in some sense it is a reaction to or, at the very least, a reflection of the environment in which it takes place. Some crime is situational, in the sense that it is features of the social environment that provide opportunities and temptations for criminal conduct. Some crime is cultural, in the sense that there exist social forces within the community that foster criminal behavior. Some crime is structural, in the sense that discriminatory policies operate to encourage or reflexively engender criminal responses. Some crime is economic, in the sense that limited resources, coupled with the presence of social expectations and demands that stigmatize these limitations, tend to loosen the restraints of rule following, especially when following the rules is economically costly. (The economic factors that may be at work here need not be restricted to what we regard as poverty, but may include the "comparative deprivation" that can be felt by middle and upper as well as lower economic classes.)

This is not to suggest that the environmental factors listed here negate individual responsibility for crime. But they do help us to understand criminal conduct within the larger social setting in which it occurs and why responding to crime may involve responding to elements within the larger social order. Seeing crime in the context of a larger social setting also enables us to see the connections between the criminal activity that takes place in a society and the social problems to which so-called community policing is often said to be directed. In an important sense, as we have said, all policing should be seen as community policing. Otherwise crime fighting merely offers topical relief and protection from crime without engaging with its underlying causes.

Of course, as we have seen, the underlying causes of crime cannot be dealt with by police alone. But because police are – or should be – out on the streets, they often gain a pretty good sense of the social dynamics and needs of the society in which crime takes place. And because of their role, the way in which their role is perceived, and their social know-how, police are institutionally well placed to press for socially productive responses to these needs and therefore (albeit perhaps sometimes indirectly) to crime itself.

As noted above, however, exerting pressure for social change within a community is not without risks for the police. To the extent that police involve themselves in broader social issues (even if the involvement is restricted only to issues that bear on crime), it is perhaps inevitable that the police will be seen as intruding on matters that have partisan political significance and so create animosities among those who are not positively disposed to the changes that they seek to bring about. At worst, their impartiality as officers of the law will be called into question. As a result, they are likely to be told to stay out of politics. But, in line with the argument presented above, it is well to remember that there is no way in which police work can be completely divorced from local sociopolitical issues. Though their work is distinguishable from politics, it is not separable from it. To illustrate by means of fairly non-contentious examples: police often have discretion with respect to whether to enforce a law that is socially outdated but still on the books, and they also have discretion with respect to enforcement of some laws rather than others when both cannot be practicably enforced at once. Their decisions in one or other direction in each of these cases will be partly sociopolitical, for the decision to catalyze change within the community or to maintain the status quo will inevitably have sociopolitical ramifications. The partisan links are seen more starkly in US mayoral races, which are often fought on law and order or similar grounds. When that is so, mayors, who are frequently responsible for the appointment of their police commissioners, will influence the ways in which a police department carries out its law enforcement function, and they will do so in conformity with their partisan agenda.

We have argued that social peacekeeping is not only compatible with law enforcement and crime fighting, but that law enforcement and crime fighting are indispensable and critical, albeit not exclusive, aspects of peacekeeping. Moreover, they represent aspects of peacekeeping for which police are especially well trained. (To be sure, we do have legal provision for arrests by citizens, known as "citizens' arrest," but for the most part ordinary citizens are not well equipped to effect an arrest, and when they do avail themselves of this power, it is usually mandated that they transfer it to the police as soon as possible. So the power of arrest, and of this aspect of crime fighting, is for practical purposes largely left to the police.)

Responding to tensions

Police cannot always fulfill their peacekeeping role without experiencing tensions among its various elements. Consider the following scenario: A street fight has broken out and a large crowd has gathered. The police arrive. From what is visible to them, they have ample reason to arrest some of the street-fighting participants. But the crowd is highly engaged in the outcome of the fight and would resent any intervention by the officers. The police might choose to ignore the signs that any intervention on their part is likely to inflame the situation, and defend their view with the claim that law enforcement is not a popularity contest and so their intervention's not being welcomed by the community is not relevant to the proper fulfillment of their role. But a larger peacekeeping concern might counsel caution at this point on the grounds that any "enforcement-style" intervention would probably serve only to escalate the situation and would therefore be inopportune and inappropriate. The police may judge that it would be better to leave any arrests for a later time and that their role would be better served by seeking other ways of defusing the situation. Obviously the scenarios can be reconfigured in various ways, and in some variants the police may have to take their chances. The point, though, is that peacekeeping involves good judgment rather than the simple application of an enforcement algorithm.

But tensions for the police role may also have larger dimensions and be precipitated by pressures outside it. Soon after the events of September 11, 2001, police in the United States and elsewhere were put on a "high alert" in relation to (potential) terrorist activity. Either on their own initiative, or, quite often, at the behest of federal authorities, police were asked to conduct searches, engage in surveillance, and detain people who might pose a danger to others even though evidence of any such danger was slight.[8] The stakes were high. For pragmatic reasons, and in the fervor and nervousness that

---

[8] In England, after the July 7, 2005, bombings, what are popularly called shoot-to-kill orders were instituted, with tragic results. The lesson here, perhaps, is not that

characterized the aftermath of September 11, security was allowed to trump liberty.

Some police departments resisted, and rightly so, for they correctly grasped that the social peace to be sought is also embedded in a set of constraints on governmental intrusion – basically, liberal democratic principles. As we know from the distinction between "pacification" and "peacekeeping," not every kind of peace is worth having.

Even so, it was commonly argued in the wake of the events of 9/11 that "the [US] Constitution is not a suicide pact"[9] and that the stakes constituted by terrorism warranted some compromise of liberal democratic principles by the agents of law enforcement. But the reference to "suicide" in justifications of the compromise of liberal principles as they apply both to individuals and to the nation does not reflect what is now usually meant by the allusion to the Constitution not being a "suicide pact." It is not ordinarily intended to indicate that, in the face of threat, Constitutional protections may be relaxed, but rather that the Constitution has been crafted in such a way that it is protective rather than self-destructive. It has stood the test of time. Admittedly, there is nothing sacrosanct about the clauses – and particular interpretations – of the Constitution. But since the writing of the Constitution – and despite what those in authority have sometimes maintained – no occasion has arisen that has provided a sufficient reason for the justified compromise of the liberal principles that the US Constitution was designed to protect.

In the end, despite this potential for internal tensions, the idea of social peacekeeping provides a valuable and workable reference point for discussions about the police role. It is not as abstract as the notion of "human flourishing" (to which the maintenance of social peace is ultimately directed, and for which social peace provides an important context), nor is it restricted to crime fighting, even though crime fighting is a critical police function.

---

shoot-to-kill orders should not have been instituted, but that when instituted they should been implemented only with stringent safeguards.

[9] The phrase comes originally from Justice Jackson's dissent in *Terminiello* v. *City of Chicago*, 337 US 1 (1949), but it has been cited with a different import in several other cases since then. See, e.g., *Kennedy* v. *Mendoza-Martinez*, 372 US 144 (1963); and *Aptheker* v. *Secretary of State*, 378 US 500 (1964). It echoes the questioning of Abraham Lincoln: "Was it possible to lose the nation, and yet preserve the constitution?" (Letter to Albert G. Hodges), <www.loc.gov/exhibits/treasures/trt027.html>.

Social peacekeeping and professionalism

There is no "philosopher's stone" to resolve once and for all every debate about limits and tradeoffs and interpretation. We might however, wonder how well the broad idea of social peacekeeping meshes with aspirations for police professionalism. I shall argue that though the positive understanding of policing conveyed by the idea of social peacekeeping stands in some tension with aspirations for increased police professionalization, it is fully compatible with police professionalism.

For the past seventy years, police literature has spoken of policing as an occupation in transition to a profession. In what follows we shall look at what this aspiration for professional recognition entails and why it should be thought that their social peacekeeping role is in some tension with this. As part of this discussion it will be helpful to compare policing with nursing.

Both the police and nurses provide something of a first port of call to those in distress. Police are called to deal with crises of various sorts and are often responsible for decisions about how the crisis is to be handled, be it calling for an ambulance, for a fire truck, for psychiatric help, or for others in the (broadly speaking) "helping professions." Furthermore, it is police who are most often responsible for overseeing the "cleanup" of catastrophes, mishaps, and accidents. (Think, for example, of the need for police to protect crime scenes or to ensure that a stalled, abandoned, or crashed vehicle is taken away so that the roads are made safe for traffic.) Nurses, too, in many situations, but most notably in emergency or triage situations, must determine how different patients are to be allocated to various hospital departments or members of the healthcare staff, and which of the various patients who are in need of attention should receive that attention first. And after the immediate healthcare crisis or need is met, it is again members of the nursing staff who must provide whatever after-care is called for, be it counseling, distribution of medicine, advice on hygiene or nutrition, or recommendations for various preventive health-care measures. Both police and nurses usually work in shifts, they deal with messy and stressful situations, and regularly encounter intense expressions of emotion. It is not surprising, therefore, that police and nurses share a close understanding of each other's work and the difficulties that that work involves.

Until about thirty years ago, nurses were said to "extend[ ] the hand of the physician,"[10] a description that reflected the way in which nurses were perceived not only by the physicians under whom they worked but also by the nurses themselves and the public at large. Increasingly, however, it was not a description that was well suited either to nurses' training and their accreditation as competent practitioners or to the multiple and independent responsibilities that they assumed on the job. It also failed to reflect their de facto on-the-job autonomy. (It was not uncommon for nurses to assume myriad professional duties – sometimes even including the intubation of patients – during night-time shifts when physicians were in short supply, duties that were assumed to be beyond the nurses' capabilities and authority once the morning shift of physicians arrived!) Not surprisingly, nurses sought public and professional recognition of the work that they actually did and the responsibilities that they actually shouldered, a recognition conferred through professionalization. The professionalization of nurses has come to be expressed through various forms of training and certification, a clearly set out definition of their responsibilities, better pay and control over their work conditions, and not only greater but explicitly recognized autonomy in decision-making.

No doubt there has been improvement in nursing competence as a result of all of these changes. But the professionalization of nurses (at least in larger hospitals in the United States) has also had a significant cost in terms of patient relations and, to that extent, patient care. It is now common to find nurses less engaged in "hands-on" patient care and more involved with monitors that track vital signs and with other electronic assessment machines. To be sure, from time to time nurses do check on patients, change intravenous drips and urine collection bags, take blood pressure, and perform other more or less technical tasks. Nurses still remain responsible for patient care but – according to some critics and certainly in some hospitals more than in others – there has been a significant shift (as there was with many doctors before them) from viewing patients as persons to viewing patients as repositories of "ailing organs." The complaint is that the personal touch traditionally associated with nursing care – attending to basic bodily comfort, talking with the patient, offering counseling and even (when needed) solace – has been sacrificed on the altar of a patient care that is

---

[10] From a statement of the American Medical Association, Committee on Nursing, 1970.

increasingly driven by the desire to deal with patients in ways that are amenable to measurement, and to assessments that can be "objectively" documented.

But patients are persons first of all, with social and emotional as well as physical needs. They are or may feel vulnerable, are often lonely, are often forced to lie in uncomfortable positions, and may be in need of changed linen or help to the bathroom. Many of these important dimensions of hospital care – important not only for the physical comfort and health of the patient but also for the emotional support that they offer – have now tended to become the responsibility of nursing aides or, if patients are wealthy enough, of private nurses whom they hire to stay with them on a per diem or even hourly basis.[11]

Police frequently look to nursing as the model for their own professionalization. Part of that professionalization is construed in terms of advanced training and certification, by obtaining college degrees, having their departments accredited by an organization such as CALEA,[12] and so forth. Part of their professionalization is construed in quantitative, technical terms – faster response times, computerized data and communication systems, high-powered vehicles, advanced weaponry and tools for the application of intermediate force, and more sophisticated surveillance technology. However, as more of their energy and innovation goes into the production and use of the technical trappings of law enforcement activity, it is easier for less attention to be devoted to improving what are seen as the more humdrum activities of policing, namely, simple crisis management or being in places where and when people need someone to talk to in cases of social distress (whether it is about directions or the availability of certain social services). No doubt, police in patrol cars are able to respond more quickly than officers "on the beat" (and that is often a good thing), but if they are no longer easily accessible on the street, an important dimension of their role as constables will have been lost. For there is often no trusted other out there who can

---

[11] Some may find this characterization unfair and at variance with professional codes and exhortations. And no doubt it does not capture the whole picture. But I think it picks up on a growing tendency that is more than (though not less than) a commercialization and a depersonalization of public life. Professional condescension is an endemic problem.

[12] Commission on Accreditation for Law Enforcement Agencies, formed in 1979, <www.calea.org>.

answer to the needs that the officer on the beat has traditionally served. The generally low regard for community policing initiatives is reflective of this.

It is time to make more explicit the important distinction between professionalization and professionalism. *Professionalization* is a formal social process whereby members of a particular occupation organize so as to achieve recognition and greater social standing, coming thereby to be regarded as a *profession*. Though they may attempt to do so, groups cannot simply and successfully announce to the world that they are a profession. They strive to be accepted as such, by means of formal training that qualifies them to do their jobs independently and, perhaps most important, by meeting the standards of competence set by those who are seen as authorities in the field. (Stress is often placed on the uniqueness of the service provided in terms of training and certification, the hope being that the public will regard them as exclusively entitled to provide the service they offer and, moreover, as entitled to govern themselves autonomously through the oversight of experts in their own field.) The professionalization of an occupation is therefore an (implicit) announcement to the public – a promise, if you will – that it can trust the work that is performed as not only worthy of professional respect but also as uncompromising of the public interest. For this reason, the development of a formal code of ethics for the occupation or organization is seen as an essential part of professionalization.

The professionalization of an occupation says little about the actual quality of the service that is provided, though one presumes or at least hopes that such professionalization of service-providers will result in improved service to the community. Still, one may be a member of a professionalized occupation without at the same time displaying professionalism. *Professionalism* refers to a level of competence and commitment in which service-providers show themselves to be dedicated to the ends or purposes of the activities for which the organization stands as well as to the enhancement of the quality of their engagement in those activities. It is a stance (a reflective commitment to quality) rather than a social categorization or strategy. Professionalism is not dependent on professional status: one does not have to be a member of a profession to act professionally. The nature of what it means to be a professional in police work is nicely encapsulated in the revised International Association of Chiefs of Police (IACP) Law Enforcement Code of Ethics, which states: "I know that I alone am responsible for my own standard of professional performance and will take every reasonable opportunity to enhance and improve my level of knowledge and competence."

Professionalism should be a necessary precondition for gaining professional status, just as love should precede the formality of marriage. Nevertheless, love does not always precede the formality of marriage and professional status sometimes gets detached from professionalism. As we have suggested in our consideration of the police role, many of its primary functions are such that professionalization might well detract from its broadly construed social value. All police should be encouraged to act professionally and enhance their professionalism. Professionalization should be seen as a secondary concern – seen at best as providing better environmental conditions for professionalism.

This attempt to refocus attention on professionalism rather than on professionalization should not be seen as an attack on an educated, highly trained, well-equipped, and efficient police service or even, to some extent, on raising the bar for entry and promotion within policing organizations. But it is easy to confuse ends, such as education and certification, such as professionalism and professionalization.

Conclusion

We see, then, that the police role is describable, in its most general terms, as social peacekeeping, and cannot, without loss, be reduced to a simple set of functions independent of it. It comprises a wide range of activities that may sometimes come into conflict and will need prioritization. At their most fundamental level, however, these activities will contribute critically to the maintenance of a social environment in which humans can flourish individually and collectively – where this is not restricted to the flourishing of a privileged social group. And police will do their work best where their primary commitment is to the internal goals of their role rather than to tasks that become detached from that role.

5   The burdens of discretion

> Discretion without a criterion for its exercise is authorization
> of arbitrariness.[1]

In pursuing their peacekeeping tasks, police are governed by the rule of law which, as we have already noted, is crucial to any liberal democratic order. The time-honored counsel that we should prefer a government "of laws, not men," reflects the awareness that there is always a potential for tyranny and arbitrariness – a potential that often comes to expression – when social decisions are placed in the hands of individuals who are not governed by rules that also apply to them.

Yet the idea of a rule of law needs more clarification than we have given it so far. Minimally, the rule of law is government by means of firm and pre-announced formal rules, rules that are expressed clearly enough to enable their application to be predicted with reasonable certainty. But rules that fulfill this requirement may still be rules that are oppressive and discriminatory, as they were, for example, in National Socialist Germany and Stalinist Russia. To guard against their oppressive and discriminatory use, laws within a liberal democratic framework must also meet certain normative (including moral) requirements – once catalogued by the legal philosopher Michael Moore as the separation of powers, equality and formal justice, liberty and notice, procedural and substantive fairness, and efficient administration.[2] In other words, laws must conform to broad substantive requirements such as these if the resulting order is to be characterized as one of the rule of law. It is not enough that there are laws; the laws themselves must be applied uniformly and meet certain broad moral expectations.

---

[1] *Brown* v. *Allen*, 244 US 443 (1953) (Frankfurter, J).

[2] Michael S. Moore, "A Natural Law Theory of Interpretation," *Southern California Law Review* 58 (1985): 313–18.

But exactly what does the rule of law amount to in practice? Does it require that whenever police observe the law being violated they *must* move to arrest or summons the violator? May they exercise no discretion about which laws to enforce and when? Does the exercise of discretion signify a return to "the rule of men (and, now, women)"? Or is it, rather, an important dimension of the rule of law?

In this chapter we will explore some of the complexities underlying the use of discretion in police work, though much of what we say here about discretion will also be applicable to those who work in other institutions of criminal justice, namely, courts and correctional facilities.

What is discretion?

Broadly speaking, one can be said to exercise decision-making discretion when one's decision is grounded in one's own personal (or, better, professional) judgment. But not every appeal to one's own judgment counts as using one's discretion. Although some writers have argued that the ability to use one's own judgment about some matter is enough to qualify a decision as discretionary, this position mistakenly removes the normative underpinnings from the idea of discretion and reduces it to behavior that one is free to engage in.[3] In other words, to say of someone that she had discretion to act in one way or another is to say more than that she was *able* to act on her own understanding and assessment of the situation – that is, that she was unhindered in her ability to decide. It is to say not only that she was able to act on her own judgment but that she had *authority* to act on such a basis. Exercises of discretion are exercises of recognized authority, not merely of available capacity.

Since the *Terry* decision, a US police officer who stops and frisks a passerby simply because he believes that the person is carrying contraband, or because he wants to harass that person, is not using his discretion (well or badly) in such a situation.[4] He has no discretion so to act: stopping and frisking may be undertaken only in certain relatively narrow circumstances,

---

[3] In a much-quoted characterization, Kenneth Culp Davis says that "a public officer has discretion whenever the effective limits on his power leave him free to make a choice among possible courses of action or inaction." *Discretionary Justice: A Preliminary Inquiry* (Baton Rouge, LA: Louisiana State University Press, 1969), 4.

[4] *Terry* v. *Ohio*, 392 US 1 (1968).

and certainly not whenever an officer is able to do it with impunity. The fact that "the effective limits on his power leave him free" to act as he chooses does not constitute what he does as an act of discretion. On the other hand, a police officer may indeed have discretion to enter private premises if he suspects that a burglary is in progress, or discretion to fire a Taser at a threatening individual who refuses to halt his advance on him. That is because these activities in those contexts are understood as prerogatives of his role as a police officer. Discretionary actions, then, are actions whose determinations lie within the actor's rightful authority. To say this is not to say that one always acts rightly whenever one acts within the bounds of one's rightful authority. For one may use one's authority wisely or foolishly, correctly or inappropriately, with integrity or shamefully. We need to distinguish discretion as a sphere of authority in which we may exercise our own judgment from particular exercises of that authority.

We will now turn to the important question of the range of police discretionary authority and how we should morally assess the discretion that is professionally accorded them.

Types of discretion

In policing, the need for discretion may arise at a number of points. Here we distinguish four discretionary contexts – those of scope, interpretation, priority, and tactics.

Scope

The need for discretion may arise when a judgment is called for concerning the scope of police authority, that is, concerning the question of whether a particular issue that presents itself to police is one with which their involvement is appropriate. Suppose I lock my keys in the car and flag down the police for assistance. Is this a matter for them? It may be, but only to a limited extent, perhaps only to the extent of their assisting me to contact my automobile association. (Lacking the specialized skills and equipment of an automobile agency, the police may not be equipped to open car doors without damaging them, and so it may not be wise for them even to attempt to do so.) Or suppose a dog chases my cat up a tree and the cat cannot get down. A job for the police? Sometimes police may agree to help, but at other times they may consider that others are more appropriately placed to offer assistance. Decisions with respect to the proper scope of police functions can sometimes be quite difficult, especially if they involve matters that may be private rather than public. Disputes with a neighbor over an overhanging tree would not normally qualify as a police matter, but beating my wife will. The police must decide which matters are private and which are of public concern, though the criteria for distinguishing between the two are not always clear and therefore may be a source of problematic decision-making for the police.[5] Moreover, whether police get involved in some issues might require them to make a judgment not only about what the present situation is but also what, if not dealt with, it might become, as well as what alternatives other than police action are available to deal with the situation they are facing. All of these considerations must be taken into account in deciding whether a particular issue falls within the proper scope of police action both generally and at a particular point in time. A significant question will also concern the other demands that are being made on limited police services.

Interpretation

A second point at which discretion may be called for is when police officers must decide whether particular actions are in violation of the law. For example, does a rowdy street celebration violate disorderly conduct rules? Or, if motorized vehicles are banned from a public park, should it be seen as a violation if someone enters in a motorized wheelchair? Or yet again, does a friendly game of poker using only pennies violate an anti-gambling law? Literally speaking, yes; but how literally was the law intended? And was that flash in the hand the reflection off a knife or a harmless object? Two different kinds of interpretation. Interpretive discretion is necessary in police work because laws are not always formulated with the precision or foresight that is necessary for one to be able easily to determine whether a particular piece of conduct falls within their scope, and human conduct does not come neatly packaged, with its identity labeled. Police may need to decide

---

[5] For a robust discussion, see James J. Fyfe, "Structuring Police Discretion," in *Handled with Discretion: Ethical Issues in Police Decision Making*, ed. John Kleinig (Lanham, MD: Rowman & Littlefield, 1996), 183–205.

whether behavior they encounter might have been reasonably intended to be outlawed by a law that, if read strictly, would seem to exclude it. For example, the possession of marijuana may be formally outlawed, but police in an urban department may determine that when a person is found to possess only a small quantity for personal use and no other crime is involved, an arrest will not be made. The same may apply to speeding laws. The existence of a speed limit of 65mph may seem to require no interpretation, but, in the absence of unsafe driving and confronted with limited resources, police may interpret the restriction on travel speed liberally, and not give summonses to drivers until they register 70mph on their speedometers or radar cameras. This will also accommodate the possibility of a small degree of inaccuracy in their measuring instruments.

Although discretion is often exercised on an individual basis, some of the examples given indicate that discretionary judgments may be made on a department-wide basis, with the criminalization of particular conduct by state law being interpreted by local police departments in a way that is more liberal than a strict reading of the law would have it. Thus, in applying the law, police organizations apply their "interpretive" discretion in deciding what conduct the law was reasonably meant to cover when it seems to them that a literal or strict reading of the law would be socially inappropriate.

Priority

Discretion may also be called for when police need to make decisions about how to allocate their time and resources. Some matters will be given priority over others. Several years ago, New York's mayor pressured the police department into enforcing jaywalking rules. Members of the department were extremely reluctant to take such action, complaining that they had more important concerns. In certain cases they were willing to enforce them – when, for example, people jaywalked in ways that created a traffic hazard – but where no danger was involved they considered the issuing of tickets for jaywalking a waste of their resources.

Judgments of priority may sometimes be quite difficult. Consider the case in which a police officer happens upon a mugging in progress. The mugger roughly pushes his victim – a woman in late pregnancy – to the ground and begins to run away. The officer needs to make a decision about whether to stop and assist the woman or to chase after the mugger. Ideally, the officer can call for assistance from her colleagues, but this option may not always be available. No doubt a strong "law enforcement" approach to police work will be seen to favor chasing the mugger over helping his victim, but in a case such as this, the officer's discretion is probably better exercised in ensuring that the mugged woman has not been injured or, if injured, receives prompt medical attention either from the officer or emergency services that are summoned.

Tactics

Finally, and critically, police officers will need to make discretionary decisions about the tactics they employ in resolving the situations that confront them. In a hostage situation, for example, police will need to exercise discretion regarding the best strategy to use to secure the release of the hostage. They must decide whether to try to talk the hostage taker into surrendering; whether to make promises to the hostage taker; whether to engage the services of a sniper; and so forth. Or, to take another example, if called upon to police a demonstration, the police will probably have discretion to determine how best to act so as to prevent it from becoming disorderly and disruptive. Or, to take still another case, if detectives decide to set up a sting operation to expose an insurance fraud, they will have to determine how best to structure that operation so that innocents are not misled into purchasing ineffective insurance. Most police work is tactical, and police will need to take into account the various considerations advanced in Chapter 3 when discussing means and ends: the importance of the ends; the proportionality of means to ends; the likelihood of the means actually securing the ends that they seek; the intrinsic moral features of the means; and the possible downsides of using some means to ends rather than others. A great deal of police discretion is constrained by patrol guides that seek to provide guidance for many of the decision-making situations in which police will find themselves, but that will never exhaust its contingencies. Some patrol guides, indeed, indicate where and under what circumstances police may exercise their professional judgment.

Justifying discretion

Police work requires that officers use their judgment in various ways and on various occasions. They must interpret laws and situations. They must choose between competing demands. They must decide how best to respond to critical incidents. To the extent that they are authorized to use their judgment on these occasions, we speak of them as having discretion. For discretion is, as we saw, not merely the capacity to use one's judgment but the authority to use it. But what justifies our giving discretionary authority to the police in the first place?

Although it is tempting to respond that the use of discretion is legitimized by the regulations of one's organization or the directives of its supervisory personnel, in fact relatively few police organizations have explicit and specific provisions for the use of discretion by their members. It is much more likely that any "authorization" of police discretion with respect to certain of their activities will be implicit in the police department's culture and will reflect a general recognition that officers need to make adaptive decisions in going about their work. They must be adaptive because police (much like the rest of us) are aware that the exigencies of life sometimes place us in situations in which the expectation that we abide by the laws and rules that generally govern our behavior must be flexible enough to accommodate the complexities of the situations in which we find ourselves. They fail to speak with sufficient clarity or sensitivity to the situations in which decisions must be made. To illustrate, suppose I am rushing my child to hospital after her involvement in a serious bicycle accident and am pulled over for speeding. I was speeding – no doubt about it – and was far enough above the speed limit to attract the attention of a police officer who, in normal circumstances, would issue me a ticket. But I explain the situation to the officer, who can see the child's condition and, instead of ticketing me, he escorts me for the remainder of the journey. The officer has exercised his discretion by taking into account the exigencies of my situation and has determined that the best course of action is to "forgive" my breach of the traffic law and to offer assistance. The officer may do this because it is not incumbent on him as a police officer to issue a ticket to a speeding driver. He may use his discretion to decide that exceeding the speed limit was justified (or at least excusable) in this case and, further, that because of the need to get to the hospital as quickly as possible, he should escort me so as to ensure that public safety is not compromised by the speed at which it is necessary to travel there. But even in the standard case of speeding, that is, when there is no overriding reason that the driver has for exceeding the speed limit, an officer may choose to give a reprimand rather than a ticket. If, for example, the driver is apologetic, and even willing to accept a ticket as the price of his conduct, the officer may choose to let him off with a stern warning. Given that the driver was not so far over the speed limit that he constituted an obvious danger to others, this was probably a reasonable exercise of discretion. But consider a situation in which an officer decides to let a speeding but very attractive driver off because of her looks. The officer certainly has discretion not to ticket a speeder, and not ticketing this particular speeder may even be appropriate. But if the officer exercises his discretion in not issuing a ticket, that discretion must be exercised for relevant reasons. Not ticketing a speeding driver because of her attractiveness is not relevant and is unjustifiable even though the decision not to ticket could have been justified.

In serious matters, such discretion will be more problematic. Some years ago it was reported that British police officers, when called to situations in which fathers had almost certainly engaged in sexual abuse of one or more of their children, claimed to "exercise discretion" by deciding not to arrest the alleged abusers. Some police responded to the public outcry when this use of "discretion" was made public by arguing that the arrest of these fathers (and their almost certain subsequent imprisonment) would negatively affect the family, given that there was no one else in these families who could, in their absence, fulfill their role as breadwinner. The police concluded, and claimed in defense of their decision not to arrest these fathers that it was better, given the circumstances of the families of these men, to issue a stern warning to them that they cease their predatory activity and that, should there be any hint of its continuance, arrests would then be made.

We can sympathize with the officers' concern about the impact that arrests would have on family cohesion and we can appreciate that this concern was, for them, a relevant reason for exercising discretion regarding the making of arrests. But a relevant reason is not necessarily a sufficient reason, and the police in this case overlooked a consideration basic to an understanding of the limits of police discretionary authority: As officers of the law, the preeminent concern of the police should have been for the victims of crime. Given that serious victimization had almost certainly occurred – and, indeed, might continue – it was not within a legitimate use of police discretion to decide not to make an arrest that would succeed in removing the source of the victimization. Their failure to make arrests in these cases not only put those who were probably victimized at risk of being victimized again. It also dishonored these victims by failing to make the attempt (by means of making an arrest) to start the judicial process that might ensure that their victimizers answered for what they had done.

The police were right to have noted and to have appreciated the negative impact that arrest and its sequelae could have on the families that were involved. But, nonetheless, they ought to have engaged social workers (or worked in partnership with them) to address whatever immediate and longer-term needs arose as a result of their making the arrests that were called for rather than not make the arrests at all. In short, the discretion not to arrest was not theirs to exercise or, to the extent that it appeared to have been granted by whatever authority, it was exercised unwisely given the seriousness of the offense. Lesser abuses might have warranted a different response.

It is plausible that police officers may have considered the social welfare agencies relevant to the problem that they were called upon to deal with as inefficient and overburdened bureaucracies that would be unlikely to make the necessary interventions appropriate to the problem at hand. Nevertheless, except in manifestly extreme cases, taking professional social work decisions upon themselves was an illegitimate extension of the police officers' role into areas beyond the scope of their training and expertise. No doubt, where the police role ends and the social work role begins will not always be clear. We can grant that real-life situations are complex and messy and do not come neatly categorized, requiring that there is some interpenetration in the social division of labor. Appropriate responses will also be dependent on contingencies. We might think that in a case in which officers are confronted with a pregnant woman who has unexpectedly gone into labor, their intervention would be appropriate. If there is no time to call for and await medical help or for getting her to a hospital, it would not be improper for the officers to assist in delivering the child. Indeed, many officers receive training that enables them to provide emergency medical assistance where others are not yet available to provide it. Nevertheless, in the case of the sexually abused children the officers intruded too far into a domain that others should have overseen.

Our conclusion, then, is that whether and how much discretion should be available to officers on a particular occasion depends on the contingencies of that occasion: in part on the availability of others who may be more competent to respond to the crisis that the officers are facing at that time and in part on the harm that is threatened or perpetrated. It always needs to be asked whether, if the officers choose not to use the powers available to them, they would dishonor victims of others' acts.

Selective enforcement

So far we have glossed over an area of police discretionary authority that has proven particularly controversial, and that is selective enforcement of the law. Let us consider again the case of a speeding motorist who, apprehended, respectfully accepts that he was speeding and awaits a ticket that the officer then decides against issuing on grounds that good order will be adequately served by letting the motorist off with a stern warning. Or consider a case in which someone steals a coat from a store and later, having been overcome with guilt, returns it to the store-owner, who, to make good the warning pasted on his shop wall ("Shoplifters will be prosecuted to the full extent of the law"), calls the police. The owner and police officer confer and, believing that the shoplifter has (by the return of the coat) shown that he has not only regretted his action but acknowledged its wrongfulness, decide not to proceed with an arrest.

Should police have an option not to arrest or issue a summons to those who have violated the law? We have already considered circumstances under which it would be inappropriate to exercise discretion – where, for example, it would evidence a failure of appropriate regard for the victim of a crime. However, as the examples just provided indicate, not all failures to arrest or summons show such disregard. In the speeding case there is no identifiable victim, and in the shoplifting example the shop-owner himself consents to an informal response.

Notwithstanding the above cases and cases like them, a number of commentators have argued that when it comes to enforcement of the law police should have no discretion. The following arguments have been advanced in favor of this position.

Full enforcement requirements

Many states in the United States have promulgated what are called "full enforcement statutes," statutes that require police officers to enforce all the laws without exception. Such full enforcement statutes would seem to preclude any selective enforcement except, of course, in circumstances in which police must choose which of the various calls on their law enforcement service they must respond to when they cannot respond to all at once.

However, as with other laws, despite what full enforcement laws literally say, they are not always literally intended and, as we saw earlier, in these cases some interpretation is called for. Law is a rough engine, clear enough and comprehensive enough to limit what needs to be limited, but often not nuanced enough to justifiably exclude some forms of conduct or situations. The latitude or stringency with which these laws are interpreted will depend, understandably enough, on the interpretive discretion of the police officer (or agency). We noted an example of this earlier in the case of the motorized wheelchair. The law that excludes motorized vehicles from the public parks was designed to secure people's enjoyment of park grounds against engine noise and the danger that motorized vehicles would pose. But the statute is formulated in terms that are so broad that, taken literally, it also serves to exclude motorized wheelchairs. Sometimes we must look beyond the letter of the law in order to understand – and act in conformity with – its spirit. Of course, the issue of interpretation is often and properly a matter for the courts. If, for example, the vehicle is a Segway™ personal transporter, it may be best to have some more authoritative judgment. But a motorized wheelchair is unlikely to need the engine of judicial determination.

Of course, full enforcement statutes should be interpreted with sensitivity to their purpose. They are intended to ensure reasonable predictability of enforcement practices, a predictability that is clearly important for the orderliness and consistency in our social environment that is fundamental to our being able to flourish in that environment. None of us could do well, much less flourish, in a social environment in which police officers picked and chose when and what they would enforce.

But enforcement can be taken too far. In Victor Hugo's *Les Misérables*, Inspector Javert believes that, come what may, he must arrest Jean Valjean for violating the terms of his parole after Valjean has been released from prison, where he had been sent for having stolen bread to feed his starving family. Whether or not we sympathize with some of Valjean's conduct subsequent to his long imprisonment and the parole conditions placed on him, Hugo's complex, richly textured, and ironic account of the admirable person that Valjean later becomes makes it clear that Javert has gone overboard on enforcement. It is not just a matter of the best use of enforcement resources, but also of the point of ensuring that the law is enforced. The wisdom of enforcement must lie in its point, and in Hugo's story it appears that, given the circumstances of Valjean's later life – circumstances that are known to Javert – enforcement has little (or perhaps even no) point at all.

But still, full enforcement statutes are important, for they place an onus on police to ensure that laws do what they are intended to do, namely, provide not only clear and fair but also predictable guidelines for public behavior. But the predictability of the law depends on law-abiding citizens as well as violators of the law knowing that police have a defeasible obligation to enforce the law. That is, they have a binding obligation to enforce the law in the absence of some competing obligation. The considerations that will "defeat" such obligations will need to be of a kind that would not undermine the authority that we vest in those who are charged with enforcing it. That is why discretion is a form of authority and not merely an exercise of individual decision-making power.

Rule of law

Quite aside from the question of the legitimacy of police selectively enforcing the law in states with full enforcement statutes, there is the question of whether selective law enforcement contravenes the fundamental liberal democratic presumption that our public life is governed by law, not individuals. Do police who selectively enforce the law arrogate to themselves a role that, wisely, we have vested in others, namely, the legislature? Our liberal democratic forebears separated out the powers of legislation, application, and execution, precisely to provide a check against excessive concentrations of power. Is that check not eroded if police are permitted to exercise discretion in law enforcement?

Although this objection is important and deserves to be taken seriously, it ignores the fact that permissible selective law enforcement is not just police officers' choosing to detain or release a person merely because, in their personal (but professional) judgment, that would be an appropriate thing to do. Their discretion is exercised against a background of existing laws that are duly passed by the legislature, and for that reason, we may think of selective law enforcement decisions by police as reflecting their (permissible) use of discretion to act in accordance with their professionally sensitized interpretation of the law. Moreover, discretion to selectively enforce the law is likely to be limited. If, for example, a woman kills the husband who has abused her for years, an officer may not exercise discretion by refusing to arrest her. A serious harm has been done, and the officer has no discretion to refrain from booking her. Although the officer may be deeply sympathetic to the woman's plight, and may even have been familiar with the wretch who has at last been disposed of, nevertheless, the brutal husband, for all his obnoxiousness, possessed certain human rights, and it is not for the officer to determine whose rights should and should not be protected. (Of course, the officer may hope that the woman will be able to avoid the normal consequences of her act, but that is a matter for the court and not for the individual officer to determine.)

The case, however, is different when there has been no jeopardization of others' interests or – sometimes – when victims do not wish to press charges. In Hugo's *Les Misérables*, Bishop Myriel believes that there is redemptive potential for Valjean and therefore refuses even to acknowledge to the police that Valjean has *stolen* his silverware (a refusal tantamount to a refusal to press charges). Earlier we saw how, in the case of the coat shoplifter, arrest and prosecution were deemed unnecessary by the police after consultation with the store proprietor. But contrast these two cases with a case in which neighbors have called police to intervene in a violent domestic dispute. When they arrive, it is clear to the officers that the woman has been beaten by the man who is present. They move to arrest him, but she begs them not to take him away. It was all her fault, she says: she burnt his favorite dish and he had reason to be upset. Should the police desist? In times past, police were often permitted discretion in such matters, for an uncooperative victim in a situation without direct witnesses does not make for a strong case in court and there is usually little point in arresting someone on charges for which the police can later present no evidence. Moreover, they were inclined to view domestic violence as a private matter rather than something of public concern. But currently in many jurisdictions, if there is evidence of bodily assault the assailant *must* be arrested. Researchers have argued that in certain communities women are unlikely to cooperate with the processes of prosecution out of fear, or dependence, or cultural tradition, even though they might be glad of and thankful for the intervention. In a significant number of cases, officers' failure to intervene more strongly than they did resulted in further harm being done to the female victim by the person whom the police initially failed to arrest. In retrospect, permitting discretion at the point of initial intervention was seen to be unwise because too risky.[6]

We can conclude, then, that discretion legitimately "fine-tunes" the rule of law rather than compromises it and, at their best, exercises of discretion reflect a recognition that the rule of law is not about rigid enforcement of the law but about its appropriate application.

Vagueness and uncertainty

A further and different objection to allowing police to use discretion is that such use deprives the public of the clarity and certainty that give law its predictive value. We need to know, in our interactions with one another, not only what the law demands but also under what conditions these demands will be enforced. It is argued that allowing police to enforce the law selectively robs us of the ability to use the law as a clear guideline to what is and what is not legally permissible conduct.

This objection would indeed have a point were exercises of selective enforcement to result in imposing greater burdens than would otherwise be the case. But this is not usually the way that selective enforcement works, and it is certainly not the way that it should work. True, a police officer who might reasonably have chosen to arrest neither A nor B in a particular situation may decide to arrest A but not B, if A makes a nuisance of himself.[7] But the relevant discretion is shown primarily in the decision not to arrest, and not in the decision to go ahead with the arrest (given, of course, that the officer has reasonable cause for making that arrest).

We can conclude, then, that since selective enforcement diminishes rather than exacerbates burdens that might otherwise be imposed, the uncertainty of this "windfall" should not be seen as a defect of selective law enforcement and therefore as a reason for eliminating it.

[6] For a review of this research, see Christopher D. Maxwell, Joel H. Garner, and Jeffrey A. Fagan, "The Effects of Arrest on Intimate Partner Violence: New Evidence From the Spouse Assault Replication Program," *Research in Brief*, US Department of Justice Office of Justice Programs (Washington, D.C., National Institute of Justice, July 2001).

[7] See John Van Maanen, "The Asshole," in *Policing: A View from the Street*, ed. Peter K. Manning and John Van Maanen (Santa Monica, CA: Goodyear, 1978), 221–37.

Discrimination

One serious objection to selective enforcement still remains, and that is its potential for unfair, discriminatory use. The claim here is that selective law enforcement can be used to unfairly diminish the burdens of some but not others and so to operate as a tool for unfair discrimination between persons or groups. From the fact that officers have discretion it does not follow that they will use it for the right reasons. Indeed, appeals to such authority may be used to mask discrimination. This is particularly problematic in law enforcement because it tends to mark out the relevant group not merely as second class but also as criminal.

Unfortunately, there is some merit to this concern. In the United States, middle-class youths who have been found to have violated the law have often been allowed to get away with a warning, whereas African Americans in the same situation have been arrested, a disparity of treatment that also occurs in other countries in which there are economically depressed and marginalized minorities. Perhaps the minority person who is arrested when some others are not has no grounds for complaint if there is probable cause for her arrest and the officer is within her rights in choosing to enforce the relevant law. But there are certainly grounds for complaint when like cases are not treated alike, as is surely the case when race, ethnicity, or other arbitrary considerations serve as the sole reasons for differences in treatment. Here the legitimate complaint is that police behavior exhibits a lack of comparative fairness, and this complaint has force even when the discriminatory behavior is not intentional or conscious but due to prejudicial attitudes and judgments of which the police are unaware.

Outlawing selective enforcement might seem to offer a partial solution to unfair selective enforcement practices. But this strategy is best resisted because it is unlikely to accomplish what its advocates contend. If police are prepared to justify their deviation from discretionary guidelines with the claim that their discriminatory practices are simply the outcome of legitimate discretion, they will find alternative ways of acting discriminatorily under a full enforcement policy. Given the unsupervised nature of much police work, there may be little effective control over discriminatory enforcement practices. Bias will be reflected in police judgments of probable cause and police perceptions of reasonable suspicion. Of course, patterns of unfair discrimination in police summonses and arrests could be more easily detectable by better and more accurate record-keeping of those activities, but useful though such information would be in revealing unfair discriminatory practices, it would not, of course, offer any solution to the problem – except that, insofar as discrimination on the part of police is unintended (and/or subconscious), awareness of the pattern may itself heighten police sensitivity to the problem and so lead indirectly to changes in their practice.

We have seen that allowing police to use discretion in their work allows them to respond to individual cases with greater sensitivity and, therefore, to promote (where possible) general overall fairness in terms of enforcement of the law. For this reason, it is better that abuses of discretionary power by police be dealt with in ways other than by abolishing altogether the use of discretion.

Moreover, police professionalism is not likely to be fostered in an environment in which police are never permitted to rely on their own professional judgment, but are reduced simply to bureaucratic functionaries who must apply the rules without recognition that the rules by which we organize our lives are general and sometimes fail to speak with sufficient clarity or sensitivity to the situations in which decisions must be made, and without attention to the ways in which particular human situations may call for and best be dealt with by remedies that lie outside a strict and unbending imposition of the law.

One partial solution lies in encouraging and supporting a greater commitment on the part of police to professionalism in their work – not that such a commitment will eliminate all bad judgment. Nevertheless, to the extent that we are successful we will generate a commitment to making decisions on appropriate grounds and developing a sensitivity to and an awareness of the ways in which subconscious prejudices may insinuate themselves into decision-making. Although better record-keeping may enable police organizations to keep track of such efforts to counter discrimination, their use should be primarily diagnostic.

Constraining discretion

Police discretion is always circumscribed, sometimes stringently – for example, with regard to firearm use – and sometimes less so. Clearly, then, police discretion is a limited authority. But how should such limits be drawn and who should draw them?

It might be thought that we who vest police with their authority, and recognize that as part of that authority they should have some discretion about its use, should also determine what constraints should be placed on it. But this is one of those issues in which what may be true in theory may not be completely appropriate in practice. It is not generally practicable that we determine those constraints because it is the police themselves who – broadly speaking – possess the best grasp of the conditions under which they must make their decisions, and have the most informed understanding of the leeway needed to make good judgments. For this reason, determination of the limits of police discretionary authority is most effectively decided by those who are responsible for its exercise, namely the individual police offi- cers themselves and/or the organizations to which they are joined. However, though we would do well to give police the first say on such matters, should it turn out that they are inclined to use their discretion unwisely and make judgments that undermine the legitimacy of their authority (either by not employing discretion when they should or by claiming it when they should not), they can be pressured into reconsidering and – it is to be hoped – rethinking that authority, at least in those areas that are giving rise to problems. This pressure is needed because, although police are well placed to draw the lines of proper police conduct, they are also interested par- ties, and we should not be surprised if sometimes the way they draw the lines unreasonably favors their interests. This was certainly the case with respect to firearm use. Such pressure may be exerted in a number of ways: through implementation of the results of scholarly research (as has hap- pened, for example, in domestic disturbance cases), through media pressure (often effective, but somewhat more problematic), and through court deci- sions (as has happened with "stop and frisk" and "use of force" policies).[8]

Conclusion

The police are answerable to the community they serve, and this means that to the extent that it is legitimate, police use of discretion will be one expres- sion of the general authority that we as a community have vested in them, a vesting that implies – given that we are a liberal democratic community – our actual or (reasonably) presumed consent to be subject to the exercise

---

[8] See *Terry v. Ohio*, 392 US 1 (1968); *Tennessee v. Garner*, 471 US 1 (1985).

of that authority. Thus, ultimately, the legitimization of discretion lies in the foundational sources of police authority, namely, the consent of the governed. Of course, we give our consent to the police acting on their own discretion with respect to certain of their activities only because we believe that those making discretionary decisions are competent to make them. Our consent will, therefore, be seen to be justified only to the extent that the discretionary power that we have awarded the police is exercised by them in ways that are fair and legitimate. If it turns out to be otherwise and police discretion is regularly used unwisely, then the discretion we have awarded them will amount to a license on their part to exercise arbitrary power and this would be a reason to withdraw or limit that power. Past history bears this out: police discretionary authority has been expanded or contracted in response to determinations of the degree of wisdom that police have shown in their decision-making.

6   Coercion and deception

The police must obey the law while enforcing the law . . . in the end life and liberty can be as much endangered from illegal methods used to convict those thought to be criminals as from the actual criminals themselves.[1]

We authorize the police to keep our social peace. To enable them to do this we grant them the prerogatives of sometimes using coercion and deception, conduct that, generally speaking, calls for special justification. In this chapter we explore the ethical foundations for granting police the authority to use coercion and deception as well as the limits we place on their use.

It is a basic *ethical* presumption of our dealings with one another that we should not act coercively or deceptively without sufficient justification for doing so. The ethical treatment of others requires that we treat them as rational agents who are authors of their own decisions, and not as tools that we may use or manipulate as we like. Coercion and deception – each in its own way – diminishes (and sometimes eliminates altogether) the possibility that others' actions will result from their rational appreciation of the options that are, in point of fact, actually available to them. They constitute conditions for decision-making that, absent special justification, have no place in a liberal society.

Because coercion and deception deform the possibility of others acting in ways that reflect their status as rational agents, why, if at all, should we grant such prerogatives to police? We will review various forms of police coercive activity before reviewing some common deceptive strategies.

---

[1] *Spano* v. *New York*, 360 US 315, 320–1 (1959) (Warren, J.)

Coercion

The precise elements of coercion have been a matter of considerable debate.[2] In part that is because of a certain imprecision about the idea itself. Some have argued that, in addition to physical force, the notion of coercion encompasses certain kinds of moral and psychological pressure (such as that from peers) as well, perhaps, as certain kinds of "inner" psychological compulsions (such as obsessive handwashing). However, others have not wished to view the concept of coercion as referring both to various sorts of psychological pressures as well as to the use of force. They have argued, rather, that there is a conceptual distinction to be made between threats that affect someone's will – which they regard as a genuine form of coercion – and the imposition of physical force that makes the will irrelevant. Whatever the merits of making a conceptual distinction between coercion and force, in our discussion we shall use "coercion" to include both, because the ethical issue in each case concerns the legitimacy of interfering with an agent's voluntary and self-authored conduct and it is that legitimacy that will be the focus of our discussion.

At a certain level, we sanction the use of coercion by police just because we accept the legitimacy of the government under whose auspices they operate. Even though liberal democratic governments act by consented-to authority rather than by mere force, we authorize governments to use force in certain circumstances as part of the authority we vest in them, understanding that the police will constitute a major vehicle for that expression of governmental force. (We should, however, remember the importance, within our broad cultural tradition, of attempting to accomplish social ends by the more pacific means of persuading and educating citizens to behave in certain ways rather than trying to bring about those social results by resorts to threats and force. We should remain mindful of the statements of Mahatma [Mohandas K.] Gandhi [1869–1948] and Martin Luther King [1929–68] to the effect that force tends to dehumanize others and perpetuates – sometimes even escalates – conflict rather than resolving it.[3] Such statements are salutary reminders of the troubling dimensions of the use of force, but they do

---

[2] For a general review and valuable contribution to that debate, see Alan Wertheimer, *Coercion* (Princeton, NJ: Princeton University Press, 1987).

[3] See, for example, Michael J. Nojeim, *Gandhi and King: The Power of Nonviolent Resistance* (Westport, CT: Praeger, 2004).

not show that force is never justified. Although the use of force against another free agent always represents a compromise of values, it is a compromise that can sometimes be justified on defensive and perhaps also on punitive grounds.)

But why should the state's authority to coerce be vested in the police? In Chapter 1 we spelled out the grounds for such authority, namely, that the best guarantee of our rights generally is through specialized governmental institutions, and the best guarantee specifically of our right not to be interfered with by others is through governmental law enforcement agencies.

The presumption of course is that police (and especially street officers) will not merely be trained and employed to competently implement the coercive authority of government, but that they will succeed in protecting individuals better than individuals could protect themselves. It is additionally presumed that police will succeed in protecting *more* individuals better than associations privately set up for protection services. Remember that, according to the state-of-nature theory that we looked at in Chapter 1, in the absence of an established civil society, individuals have the natural right to avenge wrongdoing themselves. Therefore, if police cannot do better than individuals can to ensure safety and security, then the coercive authority that we vest in police will not be justified. It is, therefore, ethically incumbent on police organizations to ensure that, to the extent that their members have been granted formal authority to employ coercive force, they exercise it wisely, fairly, and well.

Police use of force is frequently differentiated into "intermediate" and "deadly" force, though there is some artificiality to the distinction, because the employment of what is viewed as intermediate force can sometimes result in death and the use of what is viewed as deadly force need not kill. Still, the distinction between these different forms of force recognizes that each is associated with different risks and that, generally speaking, each is associated with different intentions. For the most part, intermediate force has the limited goal of bringing a situation under control so that a person can be delivered (usually) to the criminal justice system, whereas deadly force (normally intended as a defensive measure) might be understood as risking the circumvention of the criminal justice system on account of the fact that, should the use of this force result in the death of the suspect, the suspect will be deprived of his day in court. We will, in what follows, consider the use of intermediate and deadly force separately.

Intermediate force

When police officers intervene in a situation in which public rights are being or have been violated, the authority of their presence or word may not be sufficient to bring the situation under control and stronger measures may be required. But how are police officers to determine the level of justifiable force in such situations?

Viewed simply as an ethical issue, we arrive at an answer to this question by considering the conditions for means–end reasoning that we discussed in Chapter 3. First, police should use force on others only to the extent that it is required and directed to some good – for example, the protection of human rights. Secondly, the force they use must be proportionate to the end they seek to secure. Thirdly, there must be some reasonable probability that coercive force will achieve the end that is sought. Fourthly, the means should not be inherently unacceptable. And finally, the means used should not be of a kind likely to have significant unwanted side effects.

All of these considerations should come into play in police use of inter-mediate force. There must be a determination that the end is important enough to justify the use of force, with no less restrictive means of con-trol being both available and practicable. (Jaywalking, for example, would not normally be an important enough violation to justify arrest or forcible intervention.) And even when the violation does justify forcible interven-tion, the forcible tactics must not be disproportionate to the ends they are intended to achieve. (Though police were justified in confronting those who protested at the export of veal calves from Sussex, England, to the Netherlands, the fact that many of the protesters were elderly persons made the police use of riot gear to confront them almost certainly dispro-portionate to the situation and therefore unjustified. So too is often the use of mace or batons to evict the homeless from railway or subway stations: in ordinary circumstances a firm grasp of shoulder and forearm may be all that is permitted.) Additionally, the means must be such as to be likely to achieve the ends to which they are directed. (Much of what is done as part of the "war against drugs" seems futile, with valuable police resources being deployed to remove a particular drug-dealer, only for another to fill his place.) And some means are either problematic on account of their effects (such as using racial profiling to guide "stop and frisk" searches, likely to have the additional effect of exacerbating racial tensions within a community) or are problematic in and of themselves (such as what the police did in a famous Californian case, in which they admitted a suspect to hospital so that his stomach could be pumped for the drug capsule that he had swallowed during a raid; given the radical invasion of the suspect's body, the court, not unreasonably, found such behavior "shocking to the conscience"[4]).

As a way of helping officers to use force wisely and only when necessary, many departments have sought to inculcate a "continuum-of-force" strategy that expresses itself by means of an ascending scale. In their attempt to bring a situation under control, police should first attempt to proceed solely by means of their authority conveyed through their uniformed presence. If this is not effective, they may progress to verbal command (or engage in verbal judo). If this does not obtain the wanted results, they may then move on to "passive control," in which only minimal physical contact is used. More aggressive physical contact, in which painful force may be applied (say, come-along holds or joint manipulation), may be used only when resistance is still encountered. Still more painful but generally noninjurious tactics (such as the use of a stun gun or pepper spray) may be appropriate if the resisting person fails to yield to lesser measures. And more severe tactics, generally involving potentially injurious force (such as the use of batons or kicks) may be used if these fail. Finally, and as a last resort, the police may make use of lethal force (such as firearms). It is thought that if officers can keep this continuum in mind they will be more careful about what level of force a particular situation requires. Unfortunately, however, a continuum-of-force strategy stands in tension with an equally common training norm, namely, that officers should move swiftly to take charge of a situation by "coming on strong." This has the effect of encouraging officers to enter the continuum at a fairly high level – indeed, one that may prove to be counterproductive. Clearly there are important ethical tradeoffs involved – between, on the one hand, the amount of risk to which officers can reasonably be expected to expose themselves in attempting to apprehend a suspect, and, on the other hand, the amount of force that can reasonably be imposed on resisting citizens.[5]

---

[4] *Rochin* v. *California*, 342 US 165, 172 (1952).

[5] This taps into a much larger debate about reasonable risk-taking in adversarial (both police and military) situations.

In recent years, considerable attention has been given to developing instruments of intermediate force that will maximize the possibilities for control and minimize the potential for injury. As alternatives to the use of "close encounter" weapons (such as batons) and high-risk ones (such as guns), a whole range of intermediate force strategies has been developed, including various sprays (such as mace and oleoresin capsicum), weapons that deliver electric shocks rather than bullets (such as Tasers and stun guns), Velcro restraints, and even rubber bullets. Although significant injury and even death have sometimes resulted from the use of these alternative measures, they have a better record in minimizing injury than traditional alternatives and are, for that reason, sometimes better adapted to the circumstances in which police find themselves. They help to accomplish the immediate police mission effectively and safely. No doubt even more effective and less risky equipment will be developed as time goes on and, as it is, police will be ethically obligated to use it.

Ironically enough, however, the use of less damaging alternative techniques of control – adopted to enable a more ethically nuanced treatment of suspects – has in some cases given rise to police behavior that raises its own ethical questions. What has been found is that the less injurious the coercive technique, the greater is the willingness on the part of police to use it – and so to use it unnecessarily.[6] Mace is used to clear an area when words could have sufficed; Tasers are used as "shortcuts" to get reluctant drivers out of their cars; stun guns are applied to the feet of persons who will not provide wanted information. These examples are not, unfortunately, imaginary. As serious injury – and so evidence of abusive force – has diminished through the use of less damaging methods of coercive control, there has been an increasing temptation to use abusive force with impunity. What we learn from this is that though resources may be developed to allow police officers to calibrate the amount of force necessary to do their job in an ethically responsible way, the ethical deployment of these resources depends, as does ethical conduct generally, on the integrity of the officers themselves.

Considerations of motive used to be critical in American law concerning the use of intermediate force. Until fairly recently, one well-established test

---

[6] In some respects, this is a version of the classic situation that Plato popularized by means of the myth of Gyges' Ring (*Republic*, Book II, 359b–360b). To test how moral a person is, see how he behaves if he can make himself invisible.

for the use of force considered not only whether the force was necessary and proportionate but also whether it was "applied in a good faith effort to maintain or restore discipline or maliciously and sadistically for the very purpose of causing harm."[7] But a drawback to applying this test was that it is not always easy to ascertain motives for behavior. Eventually, in 1989, the US Supreme Court resolved the issue by backing a test that made no reference to motivation. Taking as its cue the fourth amendment to the US Constitution, which affirms the right of individuals to be "secure in their persons . . . against unreasonable . . . seizures," the Court argued that the use of intermediate force was justified only if it passed a "reasonableness test" – one in which the state's interest in bringing a situation under control must be "balanced" against the interest that individuals have in not being subject to forcible intervention. What this means is that the interest of the state in bringing a situation under control is not automatically to be given a greater weight than is given to the interest of individuals to be free from the forcible interventions necessary to bring the situation under control. However, this determination is to be made not with the benefit of "the 20/20 vision of hindsight" but from the perspective of "a reasonable officer on the scene." Such an officer must make an assessment of "the severity of the crime, whether the suspect poses an immediate threat to the safety of the officers or others, and whether he is actively resisting arrest or attempting to evade arrest by flight."[8]

This latter qualification was particularly germane in the court case whose decision established the test for justifiable use of intermediate force. In that case, the diabetic complainant, Dethorne Graham, feeling the onset of an insulin reaction, asked a friend to drive him to a convenience store for orange juice. Graham ran into the store but, seeing a long line at the check-out, ran out again and asked to be taken elsewhere. A police officer, noticing his rapid entrance and exit, followed the car, made an investigative stop and, although told about the problem, decided first to check whether there had been some trouble at the store. Graham got out of the car, rapidly circled it a couple of times, sat down on the curb, and passed out. When he came to, police backup cars had arrived on the scene and Graham was handcuffed firmly behind his back. Both the friend's and Graham's attempted

---

[7] *Johnson* v. *Glick*, 481 F. 2d 1028, at 1033 (2nd Cir), *cert. denied*, 414 US 1033 (1973).
[8] *Graham* v. *Connor*, 490 US 306; 109 S. Ct. 1865 (1989).

explanations were rebuffed, and when another of Graham's friends arrived with orange juice the police refused to allow it to be given to him. Only after satisfying themselves that there had been no problem at the store did they take Graham home, allow him to have juice, remove the handcuffs, and leave. However, in the course of his encounter with the police, Graham sustained a broken foot (when he was dropped), cuts and bruises, injury to his shoulder, and probably the onset of tinnitus – though there is no indication that these injuries were deliberately inflicted. The Supreme Court did not pass judgment on the reasonableness of the force but did uphold the right of Graham to press a civil suit against the police – a suit that lower courts had ruled against on the grounds that, despite Graham's injuries, the officers had not acted with malicious intent.

The *Graham* case illustrates several points. First, it indicates how the law, though rightly judged by moral criteria, may not, in its own reasoning, mirror those criteria. For example, were we to make an ethical assessment of the officers' behavior, we would want to take account not only of what the officers did or did not do with respect to Graham but also of the attitudes and motivations with which they conducted themselves. Perhaps the officers were not acting maliciously and sadistically when they dismissed Graham's and his friend's attempts to offer explanations for behavior that may have seemed to them suspicious, but surely such dismissal betokens callous unreceptiveness to the possibility of there being a feasible, acceptable explanation for what they witnessed. The case also illustrates how tempting it is to resort to force when it is easily available and confirms the importance of training officers to make nuanced assessments even when under pressure. Officers may have good reason to be risk-averse, but they do not have good reason to view – and therefore respond to – every situation as though it were a worst-case scenario.

There is, therefore, a potentially complicated but nevertheless manageable judgment to be made. Citizens ordinarily have a right to be free from uses of force against them. Police, acting on behalf of society, have a responsibility to bring hazardous situations under control. Individual police officers must make imprecise judgments about threats to their own and others' safety when deciding to intervene in a situation. Unlike other citizens, police officers may not opt out; and, in determining that they ought to intervene, they must do so on the basis of uncertainty about what may have occurred or be occurring and about what level of risk they may expose themselves and others. How to respond fairly and responsibly under conditions of uncertainty is an important challenge for those charged with preparing police for their peacekeeping role.

Deadly force

We use "deadly force" to characterize police practices that carry a very substantial risk of serious injury or death, and for this reason "use of deadly force" generally refers to the use of firearms, though strong arguments have been advanced to include the use of chokeholds and the engagement in high-speed pursuits, given the lethal consequences that may easily result from them.

The use of deadly force raises ethical issues additional to those associated with the use of intermediate force because causing someone's death constitutes a more serious invasion of the individual than other coercive bodily interventions (except perhaps the use of torture). Furthermore, if the victim of deadly force is in fact killed, he will have no day in court either to plead guilty or to make his defense, and this will result in the circumvention of the criminal justice process for which the police are held to be gatekeepers. The ethical bar for the use of deadly force should thus be raised very high.

Questions concerning the ethical use of deadly force have arisen most critically and consistently in the United States, where police are armed as a matter of course, though recent events in England, where, in response to terrorist attacks, police were given what amounted to "shoot-to-kill" orders, have given rise to many similar ethical concerns.[9]

Traditionally, police in the United States were permitted to use deadly force in two circumstances: when it was necessary to defend themselves or others against grave injury or threats to life, and when it was necessary to apprehend a fleeing felon. Killing in self-defense or in defense of others has never been viewed as especially controversial, though this is not to say that it is always and unconditionally justifiable. Moreover, there are significant controversies about its limits and underlying rationale – controversies about whether the perception of threat was in the circumstances a reasonable one; whether the threat was to life or something integral to life (such as one's

---

[9] Similar permissions were given when widespread looting occurred after Hurricane Katrina devastated New Orleans in 2005.

limbs or eyes); whether the threat was imminent (or planned to take place later, so that other measures might have been taken to avert it); whether measures short of homicide might have been successful in thwarting the threat; whether the person posing the threat was intentionally threatening (and not, say, a child who did not appreciate the lethal implications of what he was doing); and whether the aggressor forfeits his right to life or simply has it overridden. These are just some of the many considerations that are at the heart of the substantial philosophical and jurisprudential literature that addresses the question of the justifiability of defensive homicide.[10]

But more problematic than the defense-of-life ground for the use of deadly force has been the fleeing felon rule – an old common-law provision that was incorporated into the American legal system. The fleeing felon rule allowed that where alleged felons sought to escape apprehension, deadly force could be used if there were no other means of stopping them. That someone sought to flee the processes of justice was seen, moreover, as an aggravating factor.[11] Nevertheless, one of the problems that generated ongoing concern with the fleeing felon rule was that were the felon to be killed then the normal processes of the criminal justice system would be circumvented, a fact made especially troubling given that in current jurisprudence "felons" are (most often) those who have committed offenses for which the penalty is longer than a year in prison rather than (as felons were originally regarded) those who were most likely to be subject to the death penalty.

Despite ongoing debate and concessions by a few police departments, national change came only with the 1985 Supreme Court case of *Tennessee* v. *Garner*,[12] which mandated limits to the use of deadly force in fleeing felon cases. Given that the use of deadly force was one of those issues about which many police were reluctant to limit their discretion, that discretion, the Court decided, needed to be limited externally. The Court's reasoning prefigured *Graham*, and indeed provided some of its impetus. The Court determined that in fourth amendment terms shootings constituted

---

[10] For an overview of many of these issues, see Suzanne Uniacke, *Permissible Killing: The Self-Defence Justification of Homicide* (Cambridge: Cambridge University Press, 1994).

[11] And, less commendably, as disrespect for police authority, evidenced in the roughing up that often follows a chase.

[12] *Tennessee* v. *Garner*, 471 US 1 (1985). Some have argued that an earlier impetus for change was the decision in *Monell* v. *New York City Dept. of Social Services*, 436 US 658 (1978), which made police departments (*inter alia*) liable for the wrongful actions of their employees under 42 U.S.C. Sect. 1983.

"seizures" that needed to pass its reasonableness test – which, as we saw, required a "balancing" of the government's interest in apprehending fleeing felons against the fleeing felons' own human interests, in particular their interest in life. The Court determined that this latter interest was so strong that only if a fleeing person had posed or continued to pose a grievous threat to others would the use of deadly force be justified. In effect, then, the Court's decision collapsed the fleeing felon rule into the defense-of-life standard.

The *Garner* decision has had a profound effect on American law enforcement. Despite predictions that it would make policing impossible or more dangerous, it has probably had the opposite effect. By tightening up the conditions under which deadly force may be used, it has tended to ratchet down the use of force, not only by police but also by those whom they police. Furthermore, television police programs notwithstanding, for most police it has diminished the pressure to take action that is more often experienced by officers as traumatic than as triumphant.[13]

Deception and lying

In times past, the use of intermediate force played a larger role in police work than it now does, as it was employed not only to bring situations under control but also to extract confessions at a time when confessions played a more significant role in the judicial process than they currently do. Now, however, greater oversight has come to be exercised over the voluntariness of confessions (resulting in diminished use of "third degree" coercive forms of interrogation) and the production of corroborating evidence has increased in importance. As a result, the use of force as a fact-finding device has lost much of its value and police investigators have to secure evidence in ways other than through resort to force.[14] Since those involved in criminal activity do not normally choose to turn themselves in, evidence may not

---

[13] It has also reduced peer pressure to use as much force as is permissible rather than only as much force as is necessary.

[14] This last point might seem to be counterindicated by what is occurring in the so-called war on terror. But we must keep separate the issues of fact-finding for the purpose of conviction and fact-finding for the purpose of avoiding terrorist attacks. The point about the latter is that any information coercively gained to avert a terrorist attack cannot legitimately be presented in a court of law (though attempts to circumvent that have been made).

easily be gained without the use of deceptive practices. In relatively minor use in early policing, but currently a major tool of criminal investigation, deception is employed through use of undercover officers and paid informants, and by means of hidden surveillance devices, unmarked police cars, and plainclothes officers. All these strategies and devices are intended to mislead people about their freedom from governmental scrutiny.

Use of deception by police, like use of deception generally, demands careful examination because, as part of our shared moral understanding, we consider truthfulness in human relations to be an important value, and deception represents a troubling challenge to if not an undermining of that value. In what follows we shall look at why truthfulness is important, under what circumstances deception is justified, and whether deception by police represents a permissible exception.

In being truthful we acknowledge the rational agency of others, recognizing that our dealings with them are with beings capable of rational appraisal and decision-making. When we deal with others truthfully we display the respect for them that is due to choosers – as those who not only can but ought to be permitted to make their own assessments and choices regarding their actions. Moreover, to the extent that our relations with others are based on truthfulness, we are able to engage with others in many of the associative activities and relationships (such as cooperative ventures and friendships) that we value for their own sakes. Of course, truthfulness or honesty has other values as well: it helps us to make plans that are advantageous to ourselves and others for whom they are made because, although honesty does not guarantee the truth of what we say (for, although sincere, we may still be mistaken in what we say), a general commitment to truthtelling makes it more likely that we and others will be able to make good decisions based on the actual facts.[15]

We practice deception when we say or do something with the intention to produce a false belief in others.[16] The fundamental ethical problem with intentional deception lies in its manipulativeness. When we intentionally deceive others, either by lying or otherwise (lying being distinguished from

---

[15] As we will see, this does not mean that we could not carve out certain classes of exceptions. Police deception, for example, is often oriented to the discovery of truth.

[16] Though we may not succeed in misleading through our intentional deception, and one may be misled without anyone intending it, we shall leave these complications aside.

other forms of intentional deception by the fact that it is *verbally* communicated), we seek to subvert the rational agency of those whom we deceive and use them to further ends of our own determining. Because of this, deception undermines social trust, an important precondition of much that is constitutive of our flourishing.

The philosopher Immanuel Kant (1724–1804) believed that lying was always wrong – among other reasons, because it treats the person lied to as a means to an end other than that person's own. For Kant, the prohibition against lying was absolute and unconditional: we are not even permitted to lie to a murderer who asks us whether or not we are hiding an innocent person (to whom we have in fact given refuge).[17] Admittedly, that is not quite the same as being required to inform the murderer where his quarry is concealed. But however much we agree with Kant's principle that we should not use others for purposes independent of their own ends, and however important truthfulness is, and destructive as deception may sometimes be, it does not follow that we are absolutely prohibited from engaging in deception. For just as the duty to refrain from using coercive force may be overridden by considerations of defense of self or others, so may the duty to tell the truth be overridden by the same considerations. We have obligations not to cause harm, to prevent (where we can) harm being caused by others, and to bring to justice those who intentionally cause others harm. In certain circumstances, these important obligations may override our obligation to be truthful. The difficult ethical question will be to determine just what these circumstances are, and the conditions under which deception would be justified. As with all ethical judgments, here too we will need to make various assessments, taking into account the necessity of engaging in deception as a means to achieve our ends, the importance of these ends, the moral cost of engaging in the deception, and of course the wider impact that our deception may have.

Let us now apply these considerations to the policing context. "Intelligence-driven" policing, which seeks to base the deployment of police resources on a knowledgeable grasp of what is going on in the social domain,

---

[17] Immanuel Kant, "On a Supposed Right to Lie from Altruistic Motives," in *A Critique of Practical Reason and Other Writings in Moral Philosophy*, trans. Lewis White Beck (Chicago: Chicago University Press, 1949). For an engaging and subtle attempt to reconstruct Kant's argument, see Christine Korsgaard, "The Right to Lie: Kant on Dealing with Evil," *Philosophy and Public Affairs* 15 (Fall, 1986): 325–49.

may use a variety of deceptive techniques to garner relevant information. The investigation of criminal activity often makes use of deceptive techniques such as wiretapping, bugging, and other forms of surveillance, the use of paid informants or undercover officers, and interviews and interrogations that involve deceptive withholding of information – a list that is not, of course, exhaustive. In its response to terrorism, the United States government has conducted various deceptive searches of telephonic and digital communications and financial transactions.[18] All such strategies are meant to mislead others about the conditions under which they are acting. For police and other government agents, as for people generally, the key questions will be: Should particular deceptive techniques be employed and, if so, what constraints should be observed on their use? Although we will focus on the second question in what follows, the two are not unconnected, because some of the factors that will constrain the use of deception will also serve to outlaw the use of certain techniques.

Jerome Skolnick, a pioneering sociologist of police culture, has usefully distinguished three contexts in which police may find deception useful in the course of their work.[19] There is a broad *investigatory* context, in which police act preventively, seek clues to the commission of crimes, or seek information about someone suspected of engaging in criminal activity. There is an *interrogatory* context, in which someone in custody is being questioned by police or their agents. And finally there is a *testimonial* context, in which police are examined or cross-examined under oath. For each context there are constraints on the legitimate use of deception, though in some contexts the constraints are more stringent than others.

Investigation

When police seek to prevent crime or to track those who have committed crimes, they are given a fair degree of latitude in their use of deception.

---

[18] True, a government may claim that what it does falls within the scope of existing law and therefore that there is no deception (only ignorance) involved. But if most people think that the law prohibits such eavesdropping, this disavowal will not carry too much weight. But even if government agents remain within the scope of what is legally permissible, that does not stop it from being deceptive: unmarked police cars are legal but deceptive.

[19] Jerome Skolnick, "Deception by Police," *Criminal Justice Ethics* 1, no. 2 (Summer/Fall, 1982): 41–2.

Although we may grumble about the use of unmarked cars and speed traps
as deterrents to dangerous driving and means of snaring speeding drivers,
we generally accept these tactics as being necessary. However, we are less
accepting of such police tactics when the traps are set in order to, say,
raise local revenues. For we all recognize that in the latter case the means
are not appropriately suited to the end. Similarly, we accept (at least to
some degree) the use of decoy and sting operations when such operations
are used to identify those involved in prevalent crime. Such strategies can
offer an effective and (from the public's perspective) relatively safe way of
detecting those involved in the criminal behavior: better that a police officer
poses as a drunken target than that another hapless citizen falls victim. But
such operations become more problematic when the dangers and costs –
to police, public, *and* offenders – are disproportionate to the supposedly
justifying ends. It is not surprising therefore that we are less sanguine about
the (often sexist) deployment of women police officers as decoy prostitutes
out to catch unwitting male customers, given the risks and consequences
in relation to what, in the mind of many, is an objective that has little
constructive social purpose.[20]

Not only must we be careful that when deception is used, it is justified
by being necessary to our ends and by the ends themselves being warranted,
we must also be careful that the invasions suffered as a result of our decep-
tions are neither indiscriminate nor excessive. If surveillance technology is
used by police, that technology should be designed and utilized so that
innocents do not have their privacy unnecessarily invaded. And if police
infiltrate unpopular groups they must be certain that they are not infil-
trating them simply because they are unpopular, on the grounds that the
group only "might" be dangerous or in other ways up to no good. In a liberal
democratic society, privacy rights are important and should not be violated
on inadequate grounds. It is not merely that private information may be
misused – though that is *always* a concern – but that we must be assured
that as moral agents we have some control over our self-presentation to others. If we have no assurance of privacy, our capacity to relate to others on
our own terms – our autonomy – is seriously compromised. We have to be
especially mindful of this when we are dealing with those who are unlike
ourselves.

[20] See, for example, Thomas W. Nolan, "Galateas in Blue: Women Police as Decoy Sex
Workers," *Criminal Justice Ethics* 20, no. 2 (Summer/Fall, 2001): 2, 63–7.

There are other hazards associated with the use of deception in police work. Police who deceive (say, when working as undercover cops) may be at risk of exposure and, if exposed, at risk of injury or death – risks that may not be warranted by the ends (say, drug busts) that are pursued through the deception. Additionally, police informants are subject to serious risks when attempts are made to break up groups (such as drug rings) on whom information has been passed to the police.

The costs of deception in police work are often high, and we must ascertain what they are and whether they are worth the results. If they are not, then deception cannot be justified, both as a practical and as an ethical matter. Thus, because risky deception is often employed by police in connection with the identification and apprehension of sellers, buyers, and users of illegal drugs, we should not lose sight of the larger question about how, as a society, we should best address the issue of illicit drug use. Treatment alternatives to incarceration – an option now being offered via the use of drug courts – presents one of a range of social strategies that may respond to the problem more rationally (and effectively), and police organizations might want to argue collectively for such alternatives (notwithstanding that individual police are expected to be supportive of the drug laws currently in place). Furthermore, although there may be no way to fight the "war on drugs" without placing officers at risk, given the context of the drug problem as we currently find it, we should remember that the context in which we now have to operate to rid ourselves of the drug problem is one that is partly the result of previous (inappropriate) responses at the level of basic drug policy and so is to that extent of our own making. That is one reason why we should not compartmentalize the ethical questions facing police officers so that the questions we addressed in Part I are forgotten.

In the United States, though not in Canada, the United Kingdom, or Australia,[21] one form of investigative deception, known as entrapment, can be appealed to as a formal affirmative defense against conviction. Although there is some debate about how to characterize what entrapment must involve, the general idea is clear: a situation is set up that "invites" the commission of a crime and then the ensuing criminal conduct is used as grounds for arresting the individuals who fall into the trap. More than

---

[21] In the latter countries, it may sometimes lead to a stay of proceedings, but at other times it may simply result in certain evidence being excluded or a mitigation of sentence.

one ground for ethical concern has been advanced concerning the setting of such traps. Although some have argued that innocent people are actually being induced by the entrapment situation to commit crimes that they would not otherwise have been disposed to commit, others have argued that the problem is one of governmental excess: it is unseemly or even criminal to induce someone's violation of law (whether or not the person was otherwise so disposed). These two concerns are independent of one another, though they are often connected: it is because government agents ethically overreach in their deceptive activity that innocent people are lured into crime. United States law, however, focuses on a person's predisposition to crime rather than on the conduct of police in trapping him.

Some of the complexities to be found in entrapment cases are brought into relief by the 5–4 Supreme Court decision in *Jacobson* v. *United States*.[22] In that case, Keith Jacobson's name was retrieved from a mailing list obtained in a raid on a Californian pornography distributor following the tightening up of child pornography laws. Jacobson had previously purchased a pornographic magazine featuring underage boys. A series of sting operations was commenced, and over a period of two and a half years, Jacobson was approached eleven times in five different operations, the purpose being to induce him to violate the law. After the eleventh approach, Jacobson mailed away for a magazine, and was subsequently convicted of receiving child pornography through the mail. Jacobson appealed on the ground that he had been entrapped and his appeal eventually succeeded at the Supreme Court level. The minority opinion was that Jacobson had been "predisposed" to purchase child pornography through the mails, as evidenced by the fact of his earlier purchase and sometimes affirmative (but not illegal) responses to earlier sting contacts. Most of the majority judges felt that the government had gone too far in getting Jacobson to cross the line. However, because previous Supreme Court decisions had always been settled by reference to the predisposition of the trapped person rather than to the overreaching of the governmental agents in trapping him, this criticism of governmental behavior could not be used as grounds for granting Jacobson a successful appeal. So the majority had to adopt the different strategy of arguing that although Jacobson may indeed have been predisposed to purchase child pornography (as evidenced by his earlier purchase and ongoing expressions of interest

[22] *Jacobson* v. *United States*, 112 S. Ct. 1535 (1992).

in child pornography), it had not been shown that he was predisposed to purchase it in circumstances under which its mail order purchase would be illegal (as it had subsequently become). The disposition, then, had to be not merely to engage in a certain form of (*malum in se*) conduct, but to engage in that conduct *as illegal*.

The present entrapment defense is somewhat anomalous, for it is a defense available to someone only if the deception inherent in such cases is carried out by a person acting in a governmental role.[23] Were a friend to lure one into an illicit activity in which one would not otherwise have been inclined to engage, one could not advance an entrapment defense. The fact that it is only when the government practices this sort of deception that it can constitute a defense shows not only that the government should not be in the business of creating crimes but also the implicit importance we assign to government agents not overstepping proper boundaries.

Interrogation

For present purposes, interrogatory deception takes place when people can be said to be in custody. Ethically speaking, that occurs when they believe that they have no choice about the interrogation to which they are being subjected.[24] Usually they will be under arrest. The sense that one has no choice in the matter greatly increases a person's vulnerability to police power, and this must be taken into account in assessing the use of deceptive tactics.

In both the Anglo-American adversarial and the European inquisitorial systems, it is important that what police extract from those they question be voluntarily given. Although those questioned may end up unintentionally disclosing facts about themselves that they might have wished to keep

---

[23] In English law, however, though entrapment does not constitute a formal affirmative defense against conviction, the phenomenon of private entrapment is recognized. See K. Hofmeyr, "The Problem of Private Entrapment," *Criminal Law Review* (April, 2006): 319–36.

[24] Does the belief need to be a reasonable one? It does not have to be a correct belief. But there are subtleties involved because of the authority of police to coerce, and it may not be known whether that authority is being used coercively. For example, if the person submits to police questioning because the officer is wearing a uniform, does that make the situation coercive?

concealed, it is important that whatever they do say under questioning is freely said. There are various ways in which people who are custodially constrained may have this freedom jeopardized. First, they may feel unduly pressured to answer in certain ways, and this may result in what is said being neither voluntary nor truthful (a problem more likely to occur if interrogators use "third degree" measures or torture). Secondly, the interrogatory context may be corrupted by the disparity of power between the suspect and interrogators, a disparity of power that constitutes what is spoken of as fundamental unfairness. In a Florida case (*Florida v. Cayward*), police interrogators presented the suspect in a rape-murder case with "official" correspondence that "confirmed" the discovery of his DNA on the victim's clothing, correspondence that had been manufactured on a stationhouse computer with software that made it appear genuine.[25] Faced with this seemingly incontrovertible "evidence," the suspect chose to confess and was convicted. The conviction, however, was subsequently reversed by the Florida court of appeals on the grounds that the use of phony letters was grossly unfair to the defendant because their material authoritativeness left him in no position to question their legitimacy. The police held all the cards. (No doubt opinions will differ as to the legitimacy and appropriate grounds for such a reversal, but perhaps one can appreciate the arguments on both sides of the divide.) Whatever one thinks of the wisdom of the decision in *Cayward*, it is clear that the use of deception and trickery to get those in custody to incriminate themselves must be done with a good deal of sensitivity lest the disparity in power subvert voluntariness, produce unreliable responses, or prove to be unfairly exploitative.

Testimony

Police must often appear before judges or courts. When they seek search warrants or other permissions that require court approval, or when they are called upon to testify in a trial, they are sworn to "tell the truth, the whole truth, and nothing but the truth." But we might wonder why, if their roles as investigators and interrogators are compatible with the use of (some) deception, that is not also the case as givers of testimony. Why should they be inhibited by the oath they are required to swear? Why indeed? Police

---

[25] *Florida v. Cayward*, 552 So 2d 971 (Fla. App. 1989).

testimonial deception is a practice so well established and accepted (within police culture) that reference to it has acquired its own terminology. At one time testimonial deception in the New York City Police Department was cynically referred to as "testilying," but various cosmetic analogies are now used nationally and internationally to characterize deceptive testimony that "shapes," "massages," "tailors," or "shades" the truth. Though testimonial deception is sometimes engaged in for self-serving reasons (to avoid self-incrimination or to hide incompetence), it is often employed for much the same reasons that it is employed at earlier stages of the criminal justice process, namely, to ensure that those who have violated the conditions of social peace will answer for what they have done.[26] Because this is true, the question that naturally comes to mind is why, if deception is sometimes justified in the course of apprehending and interrogating a suspect, it can find no justification in the trial that will determine whether or not the suspect is found guilty.

The reason that the trial stage of the criminal justice process must be free from deception is that even though all deception has the potential to be socially subversive, this is especially so in the case of testimonial deception. Within liberal democratic societies, courts provide a critical context within which issues of fact regarding events that have occurred can be determined by means of rational processes, and deception at this stage of the criminal justice process undercuts a court's capacity to provide an accurate assessment of the competing accounts of the case.[27] In other words, during a police investigation and interrogation, in which the goal is to collect facts relevant to what has happened during the course of a crime, police are permitted to engage in certain deceptive practices. At trial and under oath the court is presented with conflicting accounts of what happened and how police came about their own account of the matter. The goal at trial is to assess those conflicting accounts, not only to establish the prosecution's case – if possible – beyond reasonable doubt, but also to provide assurances that rights were not violated in the process. The use of deception at trial

---

[26] Sometimes referred to as "noble cause corruption." See John Kleinig, "Rethinking Noble Cause Corruption," *International Journal of Police Science and Management* 4, no. 4 (2002): 287–314.

[27] Those processes operate somewhat differently in the adversarial Anglo-American and inquisitorial Continental traditions, but in each case the purpose is to reach conclusions based on evidence and the weight of the reasons presented.

undercuts the legitimacy of the criminal justice process not only in its fact-finding but also in its rights-protecting function.

It is certainly true – as police frequently claim – that determination of the facts in a criminal case is a somewhat flawed process in which the standard of proof of guilt is high, the rules of evidence sometimes obstruct the presentation of evidence of guilt, defense lawyers are sometimes overzealous, judges sometimes lack impartiality, and defendants are generally less than forthcoming. Nevertheless, it would aggravate and not alleviate the problems of the process were deception to be sanctioned as a corrective.[28] Not only does the court offer itself as a place in which important questions of truth may be rationally resolved, but it also functions as a check on the use of deceptive practices during investigation and interrogation. The court may decide that certain deceptive tactics used to obtain information were violative of one or more of the fundamental rights that it is pledged to uphold and therefore that "information" gained as a result of these tactics should not be admitted. If police are given room to engage in testimonial deception, this monitoring role of the court will be jeopardized.

Conclusion

We authorize police to protect and to some degree secure our lawful rights, and to enable them to do this effectively we permit them to engage in coercive and deceptive practices on our collective behalf (so to speak). Nevertheless, recognizing that uses of coercive force and deception are normally unacceptable, we constrain their employment by ensuring that they are appropriately targeted, proportionate to the tasks with which police are confronted, and crafted to minimize untoward consequences. As our agents, they must work within boundaries that we can morally justify to ourselves.

---

[28] To the extent that the court system is tiered and decisions can be appealed from a lower to a higher court, it has a built-in corrective of its own. Even if it is less than perfect, it may be better than the human alternatives that are available to us.

Part III

Courts

Once charges are laid, those charged come before "the court." This is not to be equated with a trial. Initially, a prosecutor will review the charges and determine whether to pursue the case or dismiss it. If the case is pursued, it is more likely – in the American context at least – that it will be plea-bargained rather than tried. If tried, it will go before either a judge or a jury for a determination of "guilt" and sometimes of "sentence." Here we look at the roles of prosecutor, defense lawyer, judge, and jury in the disposition of charges, and some of the major ethical challenges that confront their distinctive roles. Although we look at each "player" separately, their roles, though distinctive, are deeply intertwined. There is a division of labor within a formally integrated process comprising myriad rules but also significant discretion.

7 Prosecutors: seeking justice through truth?

Law enforcement officers have the obligation to convict the guilty and to make sure they do not convict the innocent. They must be dedicated to making the criminal trial a procedure for the ascertainment of the true facts surrounding the commission of the crime. To this extent, our so-called adversary system is not adversary at all; nor should it be.[1]

After an arrest is made, the suspect is booked and arraigned before a judge, who sets bail and asks how the defendant wishes to plead. The case then goes to the prosecutor's office to be reviewed and disposed of or referred elsewhere. The prosecution process differs quite significantly from one jurisdiction and country to another. In some places, for example, police retain a prosecutorial role, at least in regard to misdemeanors, though most prosecution services are separate from the police and function as independent arms of government. However, we should be mindful of the fact – and its implications – that in most states of the USA prosecutors are elected to office and in the remainder are political appointees. As we shall have occasion to notice later, each of these facts may affect the judicious discharge of a prosecutor's duties. Nor should we ignore the fact – though we cannot reflect it adequately here – that in the United States practices at the federal level often differ from those at a state or local level.

Notwithstanding the many ways in which prosecutors differ from jurisdiction to jurisdiction (for example, in how they come into office, in the range of their prosecutorial duties, and in their independence of or involvement with the police), they all have in common the responsibility for reviewing cases that are sent to them and for determining the most appropriate

[1] *US* v. *Wade*, 388 US 218, 256 (1967) (White, J., concurring and dissenting).

disposition of each.[2] After reviewing a particular case, a prosecutor may decide to dismiss the case altogether, revise the charges regarding it, or keep some of the charges and dismiss others. Prosecutors may do any of these before or after a formal hearing. They may also refer the case to a lower or magistrate's court, or (in the United States) send the case, if it is a serious one, to a grand jury, which will decide whether there is sufficient evidence for an indictment. In the event of an indictment, prosecutors may then either enter into a plea-bargaining arrangement or, if the case goes to trial, bring the government's case before the court. In the latter case, prosecutors may assist police by indicating what evidence is required to secure a conviction (though if police are not forthcoming with what, from the prosecutor's point of view, is necessary to establish the guilt of the defendant, the prosecutor may decide to abandon the case on the grounds that there is insufficient evidence for a successful prosecution).

Though the exact forms and limits of the prosecutorial role differ from place to place, we consider in this chapter several of the major ethical issues that commonly confront those who occupy a prosecutorial role.

The prosecutorial role

According to Justice Sutherland, a prosecutor "is the representative not of an ordinary party to a controversy, but of a sovereign whose obligation to govern impartially is as compelling as its obligation to govern at all; and whose interest, therefore, in a criminal prosecution is not that it shall win a case, but that justice shall be done."[3] Winning a case and doing justice are not necessarily opposed. Indeed, one might hope that justice will be done *through* winning a case. But justice will be done through successful prosecution only if the interest of the prosecutor is not merely in the conviction of the

---

[2] Not all prosecutors are reactive. Large (and ambitious) prosecutorial offices may also develop their own investigative divisions, often specializing in certain kinds of offenses (such as cybersex, corporate fraud, or official corruption).

[3] *Berger v. US.*, 295 US 78, 88 (1935) (Sutherland, J., for the Court). There is something of an ambiguity here between "just" as it applies to a trial conducted by means of fair processes and "just" as an assessment of the rightfulness of the outcome. One presumes that the former will result in the latter, though, unfortunately, this is not always the case. On the role of a prosecutor, see also the American Bar Association's *Standards of Criminal Justice Relating to the Prosecution Function*, <www.abanet.org/crimjust/standards/pfunc_blk.html>.

defendant but in the conviction of all and only guilty defendants. Justice Sutherland's statement reminds us not only of what is distinctive – and complicated – about the prosecutorial role but also of the principles that inform it.

Prosecutors are representatives of the "sovereign," which, in a liberal democracy, means the people themselves – people considered as possessors of rights – among which are included a right to the redress of wrongs that are done to them and the right to a fair trial if they are accused of wrongdoing. But not only do we possess such rights as sovereign, but we are also charged with the task of securing these rights for others through governmentally established institutions, of which the criminal justice system is one. The securing of our own and others' rights is possible, however, only if the prosecutors who represent us have as their objective not merely the obtaining of convictions but also the obtaining of them through a procedure that is likely to produce convictions exclusively of the guilty. To be true to their calling, therefore, prosecutors must have as their interest not the obtaining of convictions *per se*, but the obtaining of them through substantively and procedurally fair means.

That prosecutors may come to assume their role as representatives of the sovereign/people by being elected to that position or by being appointed to it by government need not, at least theoretically, be problematic. But in practice, the process by which one comes to inhabit the role of prosecutor may lead to a compromise of the integrity, impartiality, and even-handedness that we should expect from our prosecutorial representatives. Let us look first at the election process.

Those elected to any office in a liberal democracy are elected by a majority of those who vote. But, as John Stuart Mill noted, majorities may be tyrannous,[4] and for this reason a liberal democracy is a bounded democracy – bounded, in the United States, by a Constitution (and in many other countries, by common-law precedent). The Constitution is meant to constrain the actions of the majority so that minorities are not, by popular consensus, excluded from their full rights of citizenship. But in the case of election to a prosecutorship, constitutional protections are not sufficient to counter the dangers of naked majoritarianism. The process of election involves the public presentation of the candidates in a light that will garner the most votes

---

[4] John Stuart Mill, *On Liberty*, ch. 1.

from the greatest number of eligible voters. Unfortunately, in today's world, the public fear of crime can be an insidious force and makes campaigning on a platform of toughness a strategy more likely to put one in office than would a campaign on a platform of justice, even though presenting oneself as "tough on crime" often draws on and reinforces racial and other social and historical prejudices. True, any partisanship may subsequently be checked by the adversarial system itself. For, as Mill also maintained, truth is more likely to emerge from an adversarial process in which contending parties check each other's positions.[5] But the adversarial process does not work as well in practice as it does in theory: the contending parties, especially in the case of the most vulnerable, are often unevenly matched in skill and dedication.

The major alternative to electing a prosecutor, namely, appointment to office, can also be problematic. Because prosecutors possess enormous discretion in how they go about discharging their duties, it is easy for them to reflect the particular social values of those who appoint them, values that may have a decidedly partisan cast that will influence their understandings of the law and the way that justice is to be served. It is not that we require our prosecutors to be entirely neutral.[6] There are, after all, victims to be represented and liberal democratic values to be secured. It is rather that some forms of partisanship may distort the goals of the criminal justice system, and if they are manifested by those who are probably the system's most influential agents, a question mark is placed against its authority.

What is regarded as sufficient for police to make an arrest and for criminal charges to be filed may not be sufficient to meet the high standards that a court sets for conviction – namely, establishment of the facts relating to a charge "beyond reasonable doubt." Although, formally, prosecutors need no more than probable cause to proceed with a case, they should not minimize the significance of the higher standards with which the courts operate. Prosecutors therefore have the heavy public responsibilities of determining which charges (if any) it is appropriate to bring in a specific case, whether the available evidence is sufficient to go forward with that case and, if so, the best way to move forward with the case. Sometimes these determinations involve a weighing of the public interest against the intrinsic merits of a case. It may, for example, consume more resources than even a favorable

---

[5] Mill, *On Liberty*, ch. 2.
[6] In European courts, prosecutorial neutrality is more highly valued.

outcome would make worthwhile. If the prosecutor does decide to go for-ward with a particular case, a full trial will be one of the options, though prosecutors choose this option in only a small number of cases. Alternative responses may include the recommendation that the defendant be required to enter a treatment program or, more often, the attempt to secure a plea-bargain arrangement whereby a guilty plea is entered either for diminished charges or (as is sometimes allowed in some places in the United States and elsewhere) a lesser penalty for the same charge.[7]

Prosecutorial discretion

In order to fulfill their role and be responsive to the uniqueness of the cases that come before them, prosecutors are usually given considerable discretion with regard to how they handle the cases that come before them – a latitude of judgment that is most evident in the fact that it is for prosecutors to decide whether or not to prosecute at all. (Indeed, as many commentators have noted, prosecutors have more discretion than any other agent of the criminal justice system.) Formally, a prosecutor may proceed with a case if the evidence is such that she believes there was "probable cause," that is, if she believes that it is probable that the accused is in fact guilty of the crime for which he was arrested. But, given that the judgment as to whether there was or was not probable cause is not a highly demanding one, setting probable cause as the standard (rather than, say, a higher standard such as reasonable cause) may allow the prosecutor excessive latitude and may be used by her to gain improper leverage with respect to the defendant. For example, a prosecutor may use her authorization to proceed to trial on the basis of probable cause as a bargaining chip to get a defendant to accept a plea agreement, and in this way may get a defendant to compromise the presumption of her innocence for reasons that have little to do with the merits of the case.[8] But the trouble with probable cause is not merely

---

[7] Corresponding to the prosecutor's responsibility will also be the responsibility of the defense lawyer to ensure that the prosecution establishes its case beyond reasonable doubt or offers a plea agreement that does not improperly impinge on the defendant's rights. We will discuss defense responsibilities in the next chapter.

[8] Theoretically, a defense lawyer will be able to "smoke out" any attempt by a prosecutor to conceal a weak case behind a plea agreement, but theory does not always match practice. A defense lawyer may press a defendant to accept an agreement because the penalty in the event of a guilty verdict in a trial is likely to be much greater.

that it is too low a standard (for pursuing charges though perhaps not for investigation), but that it is a standard that is so elastic that its elements leave too much room for "creative" interpretation. (For this reason, it is often said that a prosecutor can take a grand jury wherever she likes.)

Prosecutorial discretion, like police discretion, is a bounded authority and, also like police discretion, prosecutorial discretion can be misused or abused. One must always bear in mind Justice Frankfurter's reminder that "discretion without a criterion for its exercise is authorization of arbitrariness."[9] If, for example, a prosecutor's exercise of discretion is determined by the goal of reelection – a common problem – it will be inappropriately determined, even if the decision made happens to be a good one. Prosecutorial decisions are primarily limited by considerations of fairness (albeit constrained by the availability of resources).[10]

Unfortunately the pressures on prosecutors to exceed the rightful or ethical boundaries of their discretionary authority are manifold. For one thing (not unlike police) prosecutors are often judged by the results that they achieve, and this puts them under institutional as well as public pressures to "deliver," pressures that can be especially burdensome for the many prosecutors who are career oriented and whose advancement within those careers is bound up with their success in achieving convictions. Additionally, for those prosecutors who see their prosecutorial role as a way station to better, higher, or more lucrative positions, it will be important that their reputation is such as to serve their interests in career advancement. Bonuses and promotions, even within prosecutorial work, often depend on prosecutors' "score" – a grade that reflects, at least generally speaking, prosecutorial "triumphs," that is, successes where the odds may not have been terribly strong or the case may have been given a great deal of public attention. Measures of success do not usually include cases that are later overturned on appeal.

The negative effects of these pressures may be especially significant when prosecutors, in response to such pressures, pursue their prosecutorial role in ways that are vindictive, "overzealous," or in other ways inappropriate and are then appointed or elected to the judiciary where their misconduct continues, but on a different and higher level. Sometimes, indeed, prosecutors

---

[9] *Brown v. Allen*, 344 US 443 (1953).

[10] For a valuable discussion of limits on prosecutorial discretion, see James Vorenberg, "Decent Restraint of Prosecutorial Power," *Harvard Law Review* 94 (May, 1981): 1521–73.

who have their trial decisions overturned by higher courts on grounds of misconduct have themselves become members of such courts of review.[11] Although there is an ascending process of criminal justice accountability, the effort and expense of engaging in an appeal often constitutes a deterrent. Appealability is not itself a corrective to what could later be established as prosecutorial misconduct.

Despite the above points, it is a mistake to think that prosecutorial decisions to take some cases and dismiss others or to plea-bargain some and take others to trial are made simply on grounds of winnability or publicity. Most prosecutors' offices complain that they are overburdened and so engage in a certain amount of triage that is based not merely on the merits of a case but also on the perceived need to reduce caseload as well as on the ways in which prosecutors' future ambitions will be best served. In the former case, caseload is reduced by short-circuiting the judicial process through plea-bargaining (a strategy often criticized as reflecting an inadequate concern for the merit of cases). In the latter case, a prosecutor's aspirations for reelection, promotion to a judgeship, appointment to a major law firm, or election to public office, may incline her to concentrate on those cases that have higher profiles. In both cases, unprofessional considerations can be concealed under the cloak of prosecutorial discretion.

Also under the cloak of prosecutorial discretion may be an illegitimate "innovative" use of laws to respond to political lobbying or public pressure, thus bending the rule of law. This was almost certainly the case with many of the "fetal endangerment" cases of the late 1980s and in the high-profile criminal prosecution of the oil giant Exxon. In the former cases, pregnant women who were drug-users were prosecuted using statutes dealing with child endangerment and delivery of drugs to a minor.[12] In the latter case,

---

[11] Not that misconduct is confined to trial decisions (it may be perpetrated in plea agreements) or that it always leads to overturned decisions (since the prosecutorial "errors" may be deemed "harmless"). The point is that the influence of bad prosecutors may be perpetuated into the judiciary. (It has, however, also been suggested that with the role change, such prosecutors subsequently show themselves to be more savvy about prosecutorial subterfuges and less likely to tolerate them.)

[12] In these cases, it was not merely a matter of creatively using the law, but also of the practical focus on (mostly poor minority) women who lacked *access* to treatment programs. The prosecutions took place against a background of hyped public concern about "crack babies." See Drew Humphries, *Crack Mothers: Pregnancy, Drugs, and the Media* (Columbus, OH: Ohio State University Press, 1999).

Exxon was prosecuted for the discharge, in 1989, of millions of gallons of crude oil into Prince William Sound, Alaska, after the Exxon *Valdez* ran aground. Here, prosecutors resorted to clauses of the Clean Water Act, the Refuse Act, and the Migratory Bird Treaty Act, whose application to what happened in the *Valdez* case required an overzealous – but popular – stretch of meaning of those statutes. Other innovative applications have involved the use of laws designed to combat international terrorism as weapons against domestic street gangs.[13] The point here is not that interpretations of laws should always be bound to the supposed original intent of the legislators or that laws should never be applied to circumstances unforeseen by their originators. It is rather that the interpretation of laws should not be contrived so as to accommodate political interests and/or public pressures and thus smell of prosecutorial ad hocery and/or political harassment. (Sometimes a clearly "manufactured" interpretation of the law cooked up for the purpose of securing an indictment will be met with a successful motion to dismiss that indictment, as was the case in some of the fetal endangerment prosecutions, but in some courts such motions will not succeed.) For the most part, the best protection against the bending of the law by prosecutors lies with the legislature's framing laws after a public debate about their wisdom.

Another unsavory prosecutorial practice engaged in for the purpose of obtaining convictions is sometimes to be found in cases involving more than one defendant when each is tried separately. For example, in cases in which two people involved in a murder are tried separately, the prosecutor may make claims in one trial that are inconsistent with those made in the other: a prosecutor may present one defendant as the trigger person in one case and the other may be presented as the trigger person in the other case. Since it may be in the interest of each defendant to implicate the other, this strategy – outlawed by some US states but permitted by others – has sometimes been a workable means of obtaining severe penalties for both defendants.[14]

---

[13] See Timothy Williams, "In Bronx Murder Case, Use of New Terrorism Statute Fuels Debate," *New York Times* (July 8, 2006): B1.

[14] See *Florida* v. *Gates*, <www.2dca.org/opinion/September%2027,%202002/2d02–1189.pdf>. More common, perhaps, is the situation in which the defense fails to get the severance it seeks in cases in which there is more than one defendant, and in which the prosecution can exploit a spillover effect from one defendant to the others, especially if defendants

Furthermore, to improve their prospects of success, prosecutors may choose to ignore police misconduct or perjurious testimony or may use questionable expertise or information. More critically, prosecutors may will-fully withhold or negligently fail to learn of exculpatory information that would bear on the defendant's guilt or on the penalty that might be appropriate – information to which the defense has a right. Such information, sometimes referred to in the United States as "Brady material,"[15] has been extended to material relating to the credibility of witnesses[16] (for example, whether they have been offered – and therefore might have been possibly compromised by – some benefit in return for testimony).

Some of the temptations that beset prosecutors in the execution of their duties are not only common and often succumbed to, but also so clearly corruptive of an impartial concern with truth, and hence with guilt and justice, that they have warranted inclusion in professional codes of pros-ecutorial conduct.[17]

Personal and professional reputation – the personal and professional esteem in which others hold us – both influences our self-esteem and (because in many social contexts a bad reputation will inhibit acceptance and advancement) affects our ability to relate to others on non-prejudicial terms. And this is true notwithstanding that our reputation, good or bad, may have little to do with our actual qualities. Prosecutors, like the rest of us, are not immune to finding it troubling if they are not held in good repute. As a consequence of this, the egos of prosecutors and their offices

point the finger at one another or at others. See Eric L. Muller, "The Hobgoblin of Little Minds? Our Foolish Law of Inconsistent Verdicts," *Harvard Law Review* 111 (January, 1998): 771–835. More generally, see Charles Nesson, "The Evidence or the Event? On Judicial Proof and the Acceptability of Verdicts," *Harvard Law Review* 98 (May, 1985): 1357–92.

[15] Based on the decision in *Brady* v. *Maryland*, 373 US 83 (1963). In that first-degree murder case, the prosecution withheld from Brady's defense a statement in which his compan-ion confessed to the killing.

[16] This was given a law enforcement focus in the murder trial of O. J. Simpson, when the defense managed to get access to information that undermined the testimony of Los Angeles detective Mark Fuhrman.

[17] See, for example, American Bar Association, Prosecution Function Standards, <www.abanet.org/crimjust/standards/pfunc_toc.html>; Crown Prosecution Service (UK), Code for Crown Prosecutors, <www.cps.gov.uk/victims_witnesses/code.html>; and Inter-national Association of Prosecutors, Standards of Professional Responsibility and Statement of the Essential Duties and Rights of Prosecutors (April 23, 1999), <www.iap.nl.com/stand2.htm>.

sometimes figure more than they should in their professional decisions, a problem that has been acute in cases in which a prosecutorial success in court has been reversed on appeal. The admission of mistake that reversal on appeal (or even challenge) signifies – with consequent loss of face for the prosecutor (or prosecutor's office) – is more than many prosecutors are willing to concede.

Plea-bargaining

The decision on the part of a prosecutor to seek or consider a plea agreement falls within the purview of his or her professional discretion and is, in fact, a major exercise of it. Essentially, a plea bargain is an agreement between a prosecutor and defendant in which the defendant agrees to plead guilty (and sometimes to provide prosecutorial assistance by testifying against others) in return for one or more of the following: a lowering of the charges, a drop-ping of some charges altogether, or a lighter sentence. Judges are not often involved in state plea negotiations, though judicial approval must be given to whatever agreements are reached between prosecutors and defendants. That approval usually requires establishing that the defendant's waiver of his rights to a trial and against self-incrimination is knowing and voluntary and that the prosecutor has an adequate factual basis for the charges to which the defendant is pleading guilty. Unfortunately, however, the estab-lishment of these important matters is often perfunctory.

Plea-bargaining is deeply entrenched in the American system, with over 90 percent of criminal cases being decided by plea agreement. European countries are much more cautious about the use of such agreements (though their reluctance is diminishing) and their use of them is more restrictive: when what amount to plea agreements are entered into they require much greater judicial participation and supervision and such agreements are gen-erally not entered into with respect to sentencing.

Although defenders of plea-bargaining regularly argue – though not always convincingly – that the American court system would collapse under the weight of its workload were plea-bargaining to be curbed, they also claim significant benefits that plea-bargaining has for the cause of justice: it assures a conviction that a trial, with its high standards of proof, may not secure, and it may ensure one defendant's testimony against others in cases in which there may be several defendants in a criminal enterprise. There are practical, economic, and social benefits as well: plea-bargaining helps prosecutors, judges, and public defenders manage their caseloads, personnel resources, and budgets; for the defendant it offers the prospect of conviction on a less serious charge, a lighter sentence, and diminished social impact (all of which may be quite significant should a felony charge be reduced to a misdemeanor). Moreover, for both the defendant and the government, plea-bargaining has the benefit of resolving charges in a way that is both speedier and less costly than resolution by trial.

Even so, both the offer and the acceptance of a plea bargain is fraught with ethical danger. A prosecutor who offers a plea bargain to a defendant and is rebuffed by the defendant who insists on going to trial may be tempted to make retaliatory (and even vindictive) threats to such a defendant, who, the prosecutor feels, has added to his prosecutorial burdens. In addition, a plea bargain may appear to flout the liberal democratic commitment to the presumption of innocence until guilt is proven – though prosecutors have argued that since acceptance of a plea bargain is completely voluntary, none but the factually guilty are likely to surrender their right to trial and their right against self-incrimination in return for the promise of a reduced charge and/or penalty. These latter claims, however, lose some of their plausibility when the initiative for a plea bargain comes not from the defendant but from prosecutors who may be motivated to pressure a defendant to accept a guilty plea. When this happens, serious questions arise about the voluntariness of a defendant's plea. This point is brought home by the fact that, in an effort to obtain a guilty plea, prosecutors frequently multiply charges beyond necessity (though not permissibility), and make it known to defendants that if they insist on going to trial they will "throw the book" at them.[18]

Not only has the latter happened, but in the United States it has also been sanctioned by the Supreme Court. The classic case in point is that of Paul Lewis Hayes, who was indicted for attempting to pass a forged check (for US$88.30).[19] The prosecutor sought a plea agreement that would have had Hayes go to prison for five years, but in the event of Hayes's unwillingness

---

[18] See, for example, Candace McCoy, "Plea Bargaining as Coercion: The Trial Penalty and Plea Bargaining Reform," *Criminal Law Quarterly* 50 (2005): 67–107.

[19] *Bordenkircher* v. *Hayes*, 434 US 357 (1978). A more extreme and more controversial case is *North Carolina* v. *Alford*, 400 US 25 (1970), in which the option (under North Carolina law) was to plead guilty and accept a life sentence or go to trial and risk the death

to accept the agreement, the prosecutor indicated that he would seek to have him declared a habitual criminal and sentenced to life imprisonment. Hayes nonetheless insisted on his right to a jury trial and the enhanced indictment was obtained. Hayes lost at trial and was sentenced to life. Even though the (discretionary) threat to seek to have Hayes declared a habitual criminal was simply made to deter him from going to trial, the Supreme Court upheld the decision 5:4 on the grounds of the general importance of plea-bargaining, the fact that Hayes's decision to take his chances was voluntarily made, and the judgment that the verdict reached at his trial was supported by the evidence.

Presuming he was guilty, Hayes may have been foolish, the prosecutor retaliatory, and the Court insensitive. Nevertheless, his case points to the considerable pressures under which defendants, innocent or not so innocent, may be placed to accept "guilt" in exchange for diminished charges or a lighter sentence. No doubt some would claim that the innocent would not plead guilty but would insist on going to trial because, knowing their innocence, they would be confident that proof of their guilt could not be demonstrated to the level required by the court for conviction. But such a response underestimates the sense of helplessness that a defendant may feel with respect to his ability to obtain good legal representation, the risks and uncertainty (even with good representation) of the outcome of jury deliberations, and, if guilty – though not as seriously as charged – the uncertainty of receiving a sentence commensurate with his guilt.[20] Furthermore, one could point to the vulnerability of defendants to questionable strategies sometimes available to – and, more importantly, sometimes employed by – prosecutors to convince juries of guilt: use of jailhouse informants, use of dubious "expert" witnesses, and withholding of potentially exculpatory information from the defense, to mention only a few. Such strategies – sometimes prohibited but got away with – may be sufficient to enable a zealous prosecutor to get an initial conviction.[21]

---

penalty. Alford claimed that he was innocent but feared the death penalty in the event that he was convicted by a jury.

[20] The great disparity that often exists between plea-bargained and trial sentences can exert a strong psychological pressure even on an innocent defendant.

[21] In addition, in cases of low seriousness innocent defendants are often urged to plead guilty so that they can be released from pretrial detention with a plea-bargained sentence of "time served."

Even more troubling with respect to prosecutorial offers of plea bargains are cases in which pleas are offered to persons who have already been convicted but whose convictions have been overturned on substantive grounds. Here a plea bargain may be offered in which the (considerable) time in prison that the accused has already served is proffered as a condition for release if he admits guilt rather than tries to clear his name through a re-trial. It is understandable that even innocent persons may reach a point at which their desire to avoid the ordeal of yet another trial may outweigh the desire to clear their name. This was the case, for example, with Kerry Cook, who had already spent twenty years on death row (in Texas), during which he had suffered through three trials. Just before the fourth trial, he was offered a plea agreement in which his freedom was made conditional upon his acceptance of guilt.[22] This offer might not have seemed a bad deal had he been guilty but, given the many flaws – prosecutorially created as well as substantive – that were involved in his prior trials, there was good reason to think him innocent. A plea agreement might well have looked attractive even to a person committed to affirming his innocence.

Prosecutorial misconduct

As noted earlier, the pressures on prosecutors may lead not only to legal shortcuts such as plea-bargaining but also to stratagems that constitute legal misconduct (and are usually recognized as such when detected). Some of these stratagems are, as we saw, used in the plea-bargaining process that seeks to avoid going to trial, but others are sometimes, and perhaps even frequently, used in the trial. In the latter case, an attempt is made to sub-vert or compromise the fundamental essence of a trial. A trial may be fairly described as the process in which the state is burdened to rationally estab-lish its claims against a defendant through the presentation of evidence, to respond to challenges to that evidence, and to seek through a fact-finder – which can be a judge or jury – to come to a determination of the truth of

---

[22] *Cook* v. *Texas*, 940 S.W. 2d 623 (1996). Similar agreements occurred in the cases of Joseph Spaziano (see *State* v. *Spaziano*, 692 So. 2d 174; [S. Ct. Fla. 1997], <www.upress.umn.edu/Mello/Spazianotimeline.html>) and Charles Zimmerman (see *Zimmerman* v. *State*, 750 S.W. 2d 194 (Tex. Crim. App. 1988) and "Death Row Inmate Accepts Plea Bargain," *Dallas Morning News*, October 18, 1989, 16A).

its claims. Prosecutors may attempt to subvert or compromise this process in a number of ways.

Jury skewing

As we will see later (Chapter 10), jurors are supposed to be selected for their capacity to view the facts that are presented at trial with an open (but not empty) mind. But in an adversarial system, there is a temptation for each side to select only jurors who are deemed sympathetic to its contentions. The desire to choose jurors who are sympathetic to one's case even before they have heard the case has generated a veritable industry of firms and individuals who profess to be able to judge which potential jurors are likely to have the appropriate sympathies and therefore should, on that account, be selected for placement on the jury. Although each side can challenge the other's selections, with judges also functioning as a possible "corrective" during the voir dire process, an astute prosecutor (or defense lawyer) will – as we will see later – sometimes strategically outmaneuver the other.[23]

Indeed, the process of jury selection can bring into relief a deep tension within the adversary system. For, although a trial pits prosecutors and defense lawyers against each other as adversaries, they should not be true adversaries. To be sure, their respective roles give them fundamentally different commitments, prosecutors embodying the state's commitment to justice, and defense lawyers being committed primarily to the rights of their clients. But the prosecutorial focus should not be seen simply as one of winning an adversarial contest but of ensuring that the argumentative process is one in which (actual) guilt is established and justice will therefore prevail. That of course is easier said than done, because prosecutors often find it difficult to differentiate the triumph of justice from the securing of a conviction. It is because of this that prosecutors may attempt to "stack" a jury by choosing jurors who are already positively disposed toward arguments that they plan to present.

Since the landmark case of *Batson* v. *Kentucky* in 1986, the US Supreme Court has sought to exclude various discriminatory factors, including those

---

[23] In the United States, jury selection is made after a "voir dire," in which jurors are questioned about matters that the opposing counsel deem of importance to their case. In some other democracies (e.g., Australia), jury appointment is made almost exclusively on the basis of random selection and (possibly) responses to a general questionnaire.

pertaining to race, ethnicity, and gender, from being used in jury selection.[24] The use of such discriminatory factors usually becomes apparent in the longstanding provision for peremptory challenges that allow both prosecution and defense to reject potential jurors "without cause," that is, without indication of the reason for the rejection. As a result of *Batson*, if it is suspected that a peremptory challenge has been used to eliminate a juror on grounds that involve illicit discriminatory factors, it is open to an opposing party to provide a plausible (though not necessarily conclusive) reason to support that suspicion. And if that reason proves persuasive to the court, the onus then falls on the person who made the peremptory strike to articulate a nondiscriminatory basis (which might fail if it turns out that others with similar characteristics were not struck from the jury). The court then determines whether purposeful (or perhaps subconscious) discrimination was or was not involved. Of course, though one may state what should not count as grounds for excluding a juror, it is impossible to guarantee that no juror will ever be excluded on those grounds. Racial or ethnic grounds for exclusion can be obscured by reference to other factors about a person (such as suspicious appearance or a prejudicing social experience) that may be allowable as grounds for exclusion. Indeed, many once nakedly discriminatory exclusions are now clothed in deceptive apparel, a situation which – despite the significant (though varying) restrictions that are now placed on the number of peremptory challenges available to the parties – has prompted some judges to argue for doing away with peremptory challenges altogether.[25] This is an issue to which we will return in Chapter 10.

Withholding of information that could affect the outcome of a criminal case

The temptation for prosecutors to compromise their contribution to a fair and unbiased trial is greatest when it comes to disclosure of information that may influence the trial's outcome in favor of the defendant. Because

---

[24] *Batson v. Kentucky*, 476 US 79 (1986), the beginning of a series of cases that expanded the number of factors that could not be used to exclude potential jurors.

[25] Peremptory challenges were abolished in England and Wales in 1988, though the English and Welsh jury selection process is markedly different from that in the United States.

the standard of proof in criminal trials is so high, prosecutors who wish to make their cases will be strongly tempted to engage in limited disclosure and a selective presentation of what they know. For example, a prosecutor may fail to mention that police had evidence that someone other than the defendant was reported to have been near the scene of the crime for which the defendant is on trial, or she may conceal her suspicion that police violated constitutional safeguards when they arrested the defendant. True, an astute defense lawyer will often be able to ask questions pertinent to disclosing such facts, but for many (and especially so for the poor) in the criminal justice system an astute lawyer may be hard to come by. In any case, prosecutors have an affirmative obligation to disclose to the defendant's attorney whatever may be relevant to the defendant's innocence or guilt. As Justice Souter put it, "The individual prosecutor has a duty to learn of any favorable evidence known to the others acting on the government's behalf in the case, including police," and to make it available to the defendant.[26]

A court will not reverse a conviction for reasons of withheld evidence unless the court believes that that evidence would have affected the outcome of the trial. But it is sometimes difficult to know what would or would not have affected a jury's deliberations. Even if the withheld information would not in and of itself have created the level of doubt deemed sufficient for acquittal, it might, when taken together with other factors presented at trial, have served to tip the balance in the minds of jurors regarding their certainty of guilt. But of course this is a determination that is extremely difficult to make.

A challenging case – one that clearly illustrates how law and ethics may part ways – occurred in 2003 when Ed Rosenthal, a deputized grower/supplier for the Oakland medical marijuana program, was convicted for violating the *federal* Controlled Substances Act. The Oakland program, sanctioned by Californian Proposition 215 (known as the Compassionate Use Act), distributed marijuana to qualified patients for medical use. The federal prosecutor sought and received permission to withhold from the jury the fact that the distribution was state-authorized and that Rosenthal was a state-deputized supplier. The prosecutor successfully argued that, because

---

[26] *Kyles* v. *Whitley*, 514 US 419 at 437 (1995). The Supreme Court has prohibited even the unintentional failure to produce potentially exculpatory evidence, *Brady* v. *Maryland*, 373 US 83, at 87 (1963).

federal law takes precedence over state law, it was irrelevant that jurors know that the purpose for which Rosenthal was growing the cannabis had state approval. The jury's knowledge was therefore restricted to the fact that Rosenthal had been caught growing marijuana in contravention of the Controlled Substances Act, which, according to an earlier Supreme Court decision, had no legitimate exceptions for appeals to medical/compassionate use.[27] Rosenthal was therefore to be viewed like any other drug-dealer. The only question left open at trial (a question whose answer was relevant to the severity of his sentence) was whether the hundreds of tiny plant structures found on his property were mere cuttings or had developed root systems and thus constituted independent plants.[28]

The Rosenthal case is clearly one in which nondisclosure by the prosecutor of information that, though irrelevant to the legal question of the violation of the federal law for which Rosenthal was being tried, would nevertheless have affected the jury's decision to convict him and, therefore, in some significant sense, the "justice" of the outcome of the trial. Indeed, when the jurors subsequently learned that the distribution of cannabis by Rosenthal had official (albeit not federal) sanction, seven of them signed a petition to overturn his conviction. There was no denying that the prosecutor had the law on his side, because federal law took precedence over the state law under which Rosenthal's actions were completely legitimate. But jurors responded to the ethical objectionableness of the prosecutor's withholding of information that was surely salient to their deliberations concerning Rosenthal's conviction.[29] In the end, the dilemma was acknowledged in the one-day sentence that Rosenthal received.

Use of questionable expertise

Though both prosecution and defense may seek to bolster their factual cases by means of dubious expertise, the prosecution is more likely to do so because of the resources it commands and the often problematic

[27] *United States* v. *Oakland Cannabis Buyers' Cooperative* et al., 532 US 483 (2001).

[28] *US* v. *Rosenthal* (2003). The twists and turns of this case are reviewed in the Ninth Circuit appeal *US* v. *Rosenthal* (2006), <http://caselaw.lp.findlaw.com/data2/circs/9th/0310307p.pdf>.

[29] This raises questions about the jury as "the conscience of the community" (*Witherspoon* v. *Illinois*, 391 US 510, 519 [1968]) to which we will return in Chapter 10.

relationship that forensic laboratories have to the government case.[30] The expertise in question may relate to *physical* evidence (such as bite marks or hair) or *psychological* judgments (say, about the dangerousness or mental condition of the defendant). And sometimes, of course, the problem is not simply excessive zeal but also an unjustifiable reverence for what poses as scientific.

The problems generated for defendants by the differential in resources available to the prosecution relative to those available to the defense is illustrated by the Krone case. Ray Krone, on trial for the murder of a female bartender, was convicted – despite his confirmed alibi that he was sleeping at home with a roommate at the time of the murder – on the basis of a forensic dentist's expert testimony that bite marks found on the victim's body matched an impression made by Krone on Styrofoam. It was only after Krone's case was taken up by the Innocence Project, and DNA tests showed that it was not Krone but another person (already known to the criminal justice system) who was the biter, that Krone was released in 2002, after spending ten years on death row. Most troubling about this case is the fact that bite mark analysis of the kind used was known to be problematic *before* its presentation at Krone's trial, a fact that bespeaks not merely poor judgment on the part of the prosecutor and/or incompetence on the part of the defense, but something more disturbing, namely, that the pressure to get a conviction may have overridden the caution that an alibi should have signaled, and that, even had the defense been doubtful of the "expert testimony" given at Krone's trial, it did not – so the public defender's office argued – have the resources to hire a "counter-expert." The frequency with which expert testimony is not tested (either for lack of resources or for other reasons) and because of which juries may be swayed toward conviction is, of course, a cause for serious concern.[31]

---

[30] See, for example, D. Michael Risinger, Michael J. Saks, William C. Thompson, and Robert Rosenthal, "The Daubert/Kumho Implications of Observer Effects in Forensic Science: Hidden Problems of Expectation and Suggestion," *California Law Review* 90 (2002): 1–56.

[31] Since the original decision against Krone, the Supreme Court has (in *Daubert* v. *Merrell Dow Pharmaceuticals*, 509 US 579 [1993]) "improved" the rules governing the admissibility of expert testimony, though it is doubtful whether this will prove sufficient to exclude what should be excluded and include what should be included. A bias in favor of the prosecution remains. See Craig M. Cooley, "Reforming the Forensic Science Community to Avoid the Ultimate Injustice," *Stanford Law and Policy Review* 15, no. 2 (2004): 381–446.

Coaching witnesses

In preparing their witnesses to testify, prosecutors are not permitted to foster consistency of testimony between or among them (so as to make their testimony more credible to the jury) by letting one witness know what another had said. The sentencing trial of Zacarias Moussaoui, who allegedly withheld information that might have prevented the terrorist attacks of September 11, was thrown into chaos when it was learned that one of the lawyers on the prosecution team had sent several witnesses transcripts of the earlier testimony of other witnesses and coached them on how they should respond to questions put to them on the stand. Although this was a particularly egregious case of witness preparation – indeed, on learning of the preparation, the judge refused to allow the coached witnesses to testify – it is likely that many cases of illegitimate coaching do not come to light because there is no contemporaneous record kept of the interactions and communications between members of the prosecution team and the witnesses they call upon to testify.

Prosecutors (and defense counsel) may – and indeed should – prepare their witnesses. In the United States, this can involve the mounting of mock examinations and cross examinations by "experts." But what such preparations may not involve is dictating how witnesses should respond or seeking to produce consistency in testimony by reporting to one witness what other witnesses have said. (Witnesses are in fact barred from the courtroom when other witnesses are testifying.) However, prosecutors (as well as defense lawyers) have been known to illicitly coach witnesses in ways that are subtler than outright telling them what they should say. They can alert witnesses to what may be perceived as inconsistencies in their testimony, leaving it to the witnesses themselves to revise what they would otherwise have said so that inconsistencies are removed; they may indicate that certain things may best be left unsaid or should not be said in a particular way; they may suggest that a witness craft her testimony so that matters that might affect her credibility or reveal that the prosecutor is withholding information are excluded. And a witness who shows that his memory is a bit fuzzy might have it "clarified" as a result of the prosecutor's suggestions. Such manipulative smoothing of testimony occurred in *Kyles* v. *Whitley*, cited earlier, in which the prosecutor coached the major witness to provide a detailed eyewitness account of the murder that, as it turned out, was totally at variance with his earlier statement to police – a statement that was then (of course) withheld from the defense.

One of the forms of witness "preparation" that has proven especially problematic is the use of hypnosis to "clarify" a witness's recall.[32] Although the use of hypnosis is not impermissible, its use must be made known to the defense, lest information be "introduced" into the memory of a hypnotized subject under conditions that make him especially vulnerable to suggestion. Because of this concern, some courts exclude the use of hypnosis to "refresh" testimony.[33] The worry is well illustrated in Joseph Spaziano's case (referred to in note 22). Spaziano was convicted of a number of murders largely on the basis of testimony provided by a witness whose hypnotically assisted "memories" eventually reverted to memories that were more clearly aligned to Spaziano's own account of events. This suggests, of course, that the account evinced under hypnosis was more invented than veridical.

Admittedly, the line between legitimate preparation and illegitimate coaching is a fine one, and some of what is allowable in the United States would probably cross the line in both Australia and the United Kingdom. When it comes to witness preparation, then, prosecutorial zeal, as with so many other matters in the criminal justice system, needs to be informed by thoughtful and discerning discretionary judgment.

Opening and closing misconstruals

As readers will probably remember from the widely publicized O. J. Simpson case, the opening and closing arguments (though particularly the latter) by prosecution and defense can be a time of high drama. It can also be a time of critical importance, as each side, true to the adversarial tradition, attempts to solidify its contentions, the prosecution arguing that what will emerge or has emerged in the course of the trial establishes the government's contentions beyond reasonable doubt and the defense arguing to the contrary.

---

[32] See the review in Nancy Mehrkens Steblay and Robert K. Bothwell, "Evidence for Hypnotically Refreshed Testimony: The View from the Laboratory," *Law and Human Behavior* 18 (December, 1994): 635–51.

[33] Even that can be problematic, however. In *Rock* v. *Arkansas*, 483 US 44 (1987), it was determined that the *per se* exclusion of hypnotically refreshed testimony violated the defendant's constitutional right to present a defense.

But such opportunities may also be corruptive.[34] The prosecutor may, in her opening statements, allude to what was revealed in sealed grand jury proceedings but will not receive examination during the trial, a maneuver that can sow an early bias among jurors who will not later have a chance to review these claims as they will not be aired again during the trial. In the prosecutor's opening statement there is also a temptation to overstate what will be shown, and, in her closing statement, what has been shown.

Oftentimes the opening and closing statements of prosecutors will contain insinuations that have little basis in the trial record. No doubt, not every exaggeration and baseless assertion on the part of the prosecutor will be seen for the overreaching that it is (at least not in the original trial), though sometimes opening and closing arguments by the prosecution have served as the basis for appeals of the convictions that they helped to influence. In a series of investigative articles written for the *Chicago Tribune* in 1999, Maurice Possley and Ken Armstrong indicated that, out of 207 reversals of judgment in Cook County, Illinois, 107 related to missteps in closing arguments.[35] We should not, however, assume that, because such overreaching on the part of the prosecution has sometimes subsequently provided grounds for reversal, it will always meet its comeuppance. Not every case that might and ought to be appealed on those grounds will be appealed, and the fact that overreaching is later caught out is, of course, no justification for engaging in it in the first place.

Resistance to post-conviction appeals

Sometimes evidence emerges after a conviction that appears to call into question the process by which a defendant was found to be guilty. It may

---

[34] Although we focus here on prosecutors, the defense is not exempt. I suggest, however, that, because of the special responsibility that prosecutors have to secure a fair trial and just result, it is a worse failing when prosecutors misuse the opportunity provided by opening and closing arguments.

[35] Maurice Possley and Ken Armstrong, "The Flip Side of a Fair Trial: Some Cook County Prosecutors Break the Rules to Win," *Chicago Tribune*, January 11, 1999. The temptation to overreaching is particularly egregious in capital trials; see Judy Platania and Gary Moran, "Due Process and the Death Penalty: The Role of Prosecutorial Misconduct in Closing Argument in Capital Trials," *Law and Human Behavior* 23 (August, 1999): 471–86.

be DNA evidence that puts someone else at the scene,[36] testimony that is revealed to be tainted (say, by the newly discovered fact that a witness had reason to lie), a confession obtained through coercion, or even, as in a 1997 case, a mistake that the prosecutor was willing to acknowledge, though not accommodate. In the latter case, prosecutors failed to get their sequence of dates right when Michael Haley was convicted of stealing a calculator from Wal-Mart. Because he had been convicted for theft on two previous occasions, he was eligible for up to two years in prison. Haley had other convictions as well, and this fact, together with the fact that prosecutors overlooked the dates on which one of those convictions became final, allowed Haley to be declared a habitual offender and be sentenced to sixteen and a half years' imprisonment. The mistake with respect to dates was noticed, however, only after Haley had exhausted his appeals, rendering him ineligible to lodge yet another state appeal as a result of the discovered mistake. Nonetheless, the Texas Attorney General refused to budge, even though it meant an extra fourteen years in prison. Finally, in 2004, the Supreme Court reversed.[37]

In many cases, as in the latter, prosecutors zealously resist any attempt to change a decision that reflects on their work. Sometimes this can be traced to prosecutors firmly believing that the person *is indeed* guilty of the offense for which he was convicted, even though the conviction or sentence would have been unlikely had what is now known been known beforehand. Or there is the belief that even if the trial was flawed, the defendant was guilty of *something*. Prosecutors must often regret the "ten guilty who go free in order that the one innocent not be convicted."[38] Nevertheless, it is of enormous importance that the one innocent not be convicted, and prosecutors must work within the rules that have been set and, plea-bargaining notwithstanding, the presumption of innocence that informs those rules.

---

[36] Though we should not forget that a number of US states still prevent general post-conviction access to DNA testing, seeing it as vexatious and expensive. Even where it is permitted, the cost may be placed on the prisoner.

[37] *Dretke* v. *Haley*, 541 US 386 (2004).

[38] A variant on William Blackstone, *Commentaries on the Laws of England*, Book 4, ch. 27 (1765–9; repr. Boston, MA: Beacon Press, 1962), 420.

Conclusion

The issues discussed above represent only some of the ways in which pros-ecutors may be tempted to subvert their role. What ultimately is required is an increased sense and culture of professionalism in which reputation is associated with integrity and a passion for justice rather than the more popular passion for winning. Mechanisms of accountability need to be estab-lished that will encourage rather than weaken the personal and cultural commitment to seeing justice as going both ways: ensuring that the guilty are punished but also that the innocent are not. This can be helped by having better mechanisms of accountability supported by legislatures that, on the one hand, adequately fund prosecutorial offices, and on the other, rethink the issue of overcriminalization. Perhaps most of all, it will require the support of a public that does not confuse being "tough on crime" with ensuring that justice prevails.

8 Defense lawyers: zealous advocacy?

It is the job of the defense attorney – especially when representing the guilty –
to prevent, by all lawful means, the "whole truth" from coming out.[1]

The view that every person who comes before the court as a defendant
should have access to legal representation was not always embedded in
our legal system. English common law made no such provision, and in the
United States it was only in 1963 that the right to counsel became generally
available to criminal defendants charged with serious crimes. This entitlement to legal counsel was as long overdue as it was crucial, for the court
is an arcane institution whose rules and procedures, quite apart from the
complexities of the law with which it engages, are likely to be bewilder-
ing to outsiders. Moreover, those who come before the court as defendants
come before an institution with enormous strategic, personnel, and financial resources and, unless there is provision for someone to be at their side –
indeed on their side – both to guide them through its intricacies and to some
extent to counterbalance its power, defendants will almost inevitably be at
a substantial disadvantage.

Of course, the inequality of power between accused and accuser (that is,
between the defendant and the prosecutor) may remain even if defendants
have legal representation, and this is so because many who come before the
court lack the wherewithal to obtain "strong" representation, and in some
cases, any representation at all. In the latter case, defendants must settle for
legal counsel assigned to them by the court, and sometimes this legal counsel is not only less than ideal but also well below even minimal standards of
competency. Stories of unprepared, underqualified, and inattentive defense
lawyers are legion, even if sometimes overplayed. Though it would be unfair

[1] Alan M. Dershowitz, *The Best Defense* (New York: Random House, 1982), xix.

to say that, generally speaking, ineffectiveness is characteristic of assigned counsel – the public defender programs and legal aid organizations of many large jurisdictions have members, who, though frequently overworked, are often unusually dedicated – it is nevertheless true that resources can and often do make a difference. (In an old joke, the defendant insists to her lawyer: "I want justice!" "Certainly madam," is the reply. "And how much justice can you afford?") The upshot is that although the inequality of power between the state and the defendant appears to have been addressed, the inequality between rich and poor is hardly erased (though in some jurisdictions administrative guidelines on trial conduct narrow the gap between "affordable" and "true" justice).

The continuing gap between the ideal embodied in representation for all defendants and the reality of inadequate representation for many poor defendants poses a significant and ongoing ethical and legal challenge for the adversarial system. It may appear that moral worries concerning differential representation for rich and poor are ameliorated by the fact that most criminal cases are resolved through plea-bargaining (or, in the United Kingdom and Australia, charge-bargaining). A lawyer's skill in creating reasonable doubt is not as likely to be on display. But even the outcome of a plea process can be heavily influenced by the "quality" of a defendant's representation. A highly paid lawyer is likely to be able to cut a better deal for his client.

In this chapter we focus on three general issues. First, we consider the ethical foundations of the right to counsel; second, we consider, as an ethical issue, what defendants may reasonably expect from defense counsel; and third, we look at what the defense may ethically do in and on a defendant's behalf.

The right to counsel

We have already noted that when the state prosecutes, it does so from a position of relative strength, given its substantial material and intellectual resources. The result is that what is intended to be the presentation and examination of evidence constrained by rules that work to ensure a fair fact-finding process tends – unless defendants are able to rely in court on the assistance of counsel – to be a process that is unfairly and unconscionably one-sided. As Justice Black put it in the US case that established the right to counsel for all poor defendants facing significant jail time, "[defense] lawyers in criminal courts are necessities, not luxuries."[2] In addition to lawyers for the defense being moral necessities, they are, if the Constitution's sixth and fourteenth amendment guarantees of a fair trial are to be satisfied, also legal necessities.[3] And even if fulfillment of the legal requirement of legal assistance for defendants does not always result in high-quality legal advocacy for the defendant, it at least bespeaks the recognition that legal advocacy for the defense is very important and not in any way a trivial matter.

Defendants are not *required* to have the assistance of counsel – counsel is a *right*, not an *obligation* – and a defendant may decide to refuse such assistance for a wide range of reasons, whether religious, ideological, or other. However, because it is sometimes difficult to determine whether a defendant's waiver of her right to counsel is truly "voluntary, intelligent, and unequivocal," as, according to the law, it must be, the US Supreme Court has disallowed waivers of the right to counsel when a person is appealing a conviction.[4] Too much is at stake.

The right to court-appointed counsel (if that is necessary) applies not merely to defendants who are unable to pay for their own legal representation but also to those who are accused of – and are strongly believed to have committed – horrific crimes (though the two categories will no doubt overlap). Those accused of terrible crimes are entitled to the same quality of representation and zealous defense as those entitled to court-appointed counsel on grounds of penury. Even though defense lawyers who specialize in cases involving those who are accused of shocking crimes often find that their reputations suffer because of an air of "unseemliness" that the nature of their clientele gives them, this should not blind us to the importance of representation for all.

The right to counsel has partial roots in the presumption of innocence (a principle that precedes the common law but which has been incorporated

---

[2] *Gideon* v. *Wainwright*, 372 US 335, at 344 (1963).

[3] Similar derivations from the right to a fair trial are found in English and Welsh and Australian law. However, the European Convention for the Protection of Human Rights and Fundamental Freedoms (1950) and the UN International Covenant on Civil and Political Rights (1966) both recognize a right to legal assistance for those lacking "sufficient means to pay" for it.

[4] *Martinez* v. *Court of Appeal of California*, 528 US 152 (2000).

into liberal democratic theory). For the presumption of innocence embodies a recognition that it is for states to establish their cases against the individual, not vice versa, and that they must do so "beyond reasonable doubt." It is because we presume innocence that judgments of guilt must meet this high standard of proof. Were the presumption otherwise, individuals would be subservient to the power of the state.

Nevertheless, the importance of defending even the apparently undefendable is not to be understood as an ethical license to use whatever tactics one chooses. When Marvyn Kornberg, the defense attorney for Justin Volpe, the police officer who was accused of shoving a wooden stick into the rectum of Abner Louima (a Haitian immigrant, who was assaulted in a Brooklyn, NY police station), opened his argument by saying that he intended to establish that Louima's injuries were consistent with his having engaged in consensual anal sex, he sought to tap into residual societal prejudices against gay sex. Given that there was not a shred of evidence for either the insinuation that Louima might have been gay or that the injuries were of a kind likely to have arisen from engagement in gay sex, the attorney for the accused officer crossed over an ethical, even if not a legal, line. (In some jurisdictions, particularly in rape cases, some legal limits have been placed on the tactics that may be used in court, and we will have something more to say about this later.)

Defense counsel–client relations

An individual attorney's decision to represent (or even not represent) a client may be made for reasons that are morally appropriate or inappropriate. In the case of a privately retained attorney, the desire to take on a case simply for the money or publicity may be ethically problematic. But the decision to represent a particular defendant can also be made for appropriate reasons – a commitment to the presumption of innocence, or a desire to assist the poor, or a belief that the client had a constitutional right to act as he did, or that even those who have the cards stacked against them possess a right to the assistance of counsel (notwithstanding that their guilt may appear obvious and the crimes of which they are accused heinous). There are good social reasons for this, exemplified in one of John Stuart Mill's key arguments against censorship. He writes that the "opportunity for contesting" an opinion "is the very condition which justifies us in assuming its truth for purposes of action; and on no other terms can a being with human faculties have any rational assurance of being right."[5] The same is true of criminal defense. If, in the face of a vigorous defense, the state is able to establish its claims beyond reasonable doubt, we can have warranted assurance that our beliefs were not misplaced.[6]

Once a lawyer accepts responsibility for a client, the lawyer becomes that client's agent. The nature of that agency has generated much debate and many questions, among which are: Is the lawyer required to do whatever the client asks? Are there any constraints that apply to what the lawyer may do to advance her client's interests? May the lawyer sometimes act paternalistically (that is, act for the benefit of the client even without the client's consent, and perhaps even without her knowledge)? Is the professional relationship between lawyer and client more like friendship than that between other professional service-providers and their clients? How is the lawyer's duty to the client balanced against other duties that the lawyer may have to the profession and court?

Clearly, the lawyer–client relationship is both complicated and paradoxical. The client comes to or needs the lawyer because of the lawyer's superior knowledge and skill, and yet the lawyer must act at the behest of the client. In the United States, it is the defendant's constitutional right to have the final say on whether to plead guilty or to go to trial; whether a jury or a judge should act as the fact-finder in the case; whether or not to testify on his or her own behalf; and whether or not to appeal a conviction. These prerogatives of the client, however, do not prevent a lawyer from advising or even pressuring her client to come to one decision rather than another on such matters. Nor do these prerogatives of the client address many strategic issues that may arise in preparation for and in the conduct of a trial, such as whom to call as witnesses, the form that questioning should take, and the best defense strategy.

If clients may sometimes find their freedom to instruct their lawyers as they see fit practically constrained, so too may defense lawyers – particularly privately retained ones – sometimes feel put upon to act inappropriately on behalf of their clients. Although lawyers are said to owe their clients an

---

[5] John Stuart Mill, *On Liberty*, ch. 2.

[6] This may need some qualification, given that the rules of evidence are only contingently structured to assist the search for truth, and do so with an eye to fairness as well.

"overriding duty of loyalty," they should not be viewed as – and should not become – simply sophisticated mouthpieces of their clients. Lawyers have professional and other responsibilities. It is often helpful to think of the relationship as fiduciary rather than merely contractual. The lawyer's primary concern is not merely to satisfy the terms of an agreement between herself and the defendant, but to advance the client's interests before the law. The lawyer is part counselor or advisor, part deputy or representative, part expert, and part friend. One expects that the client will be able to appreciate the lawyer's multifaceted role and will not see her as a legal hired gun, merely there to follow the client's orders and to be ruthless in their execution. The idea of the defense lawyer as a hired gun is a distinctly modern one. One would also hope that the client does not view the defense lawyer as a Houdini, able to extricate him from an impossible situation.

Defendants are said to be entitled to both loyalty and "zealous" or "vigorous" advocacy from their defense counsel. The loyalty and zealous advocacy to which defendants are said to be entitled are underlain by two critical requirements of advocacy – those of disinterestedness and confidentiality. Each is a precondition of the trust that should govern the lawyer–client relationship. The trust in question is that the lawyer will devotedly and competently pursue the defendant's best interests. We will now briefly consider the expectation of loyalty and then look in more detail into the ethical questions raised by zealous advocacy.

Loyalty

Loyalty is an associational virtue, a virtue of our connections with others. We think of the loyal person as one who, against odds and in the face of opposition, devotedly advances another's interests. But the person whose interests are advanced by the loyal person is not someone unrelated to him. Rather, loyalty expresses an *attachment* to the other and the other's well-being. Although loyalty may at times degenerate – and be perverted – into complaisance or servility, loyalty is not a variant of these. Indeed, being loyally devoted to others' well-being may at times require opposition to what they have done or propose to do, even though the opposition will not be of the kind that would undermine the interests of those others. A loyal defense lawyer may thus reasonably advise a client against acting on his wish to take the stand or against his wish to adopt a particular argumentative strategy, but though this advice may sometimes go against the client's desires, it will not knowingly go against the client's interests. The defense lawyer's duty of loyalty is often said to be "overriding" – that is, of first importance – but this is not quite the same as saying that it is absolute. Although it places a strong premium on the quality of loyalty that defense attorneys owe their clients, it does not exclude the possibility that clients may forfeit their claim to that loyalty. The hard question concerns the circumstances under which the otherwise steadfast loyalty expected of the defense counsel may be attenuated, trumped by other considerations, or forfeited by the client himself.

Disinterestedness

In order that a defense may be appropriately vigorous, lawyers are asked to suspend professional judgment concerning the guilt of those they defend. It is, after all, for the court to decide guilt, not for one of the opposed parties to the process. Of course, defense lawyers often suspect that those they defend are guilty, but this should not disqualify them from providing defense counsel unless their suspicions are such as to hobble their ability to vigorously advocate their clients' cases. This is what is known as the ability to provide a "disinterested" defense. However, the requirement of disinterestedness does not preclude defense lawyers from counseling defendants to plead guilty rather than to go to trial, should those they are charged with defending choose to confide their guilt. Given an admission of guilt (albeit a confidential admission), defense counsel may consider it in the best interests of the client to enter into a plea agreement or simply to plead guilty. (In the latter case the defendant's willingness to take responsibility for his actions and convey contrition may lead to a mitigation of sentence.)

Confidentiality

It is plausibly argued that if lawyers are to provide the best representation they can for their clients, they must have defendants' confidence, for only in that way is there a likelihood that matters that may be material to the defense – even if secret or private – will be disclosed to them. Moreover, since the state has access to impressive investigative resources, defense lawyers who have not been spoken to frankly by their clients run a heightened risk of showing up in court and having matters of which their clients could have apprised them beforehand now revealed in a way that will publicly undermine whatever defense strategy they and their clients had decided upon.

A breach of confidentiality by the attorney will normally constitute a breach of the loyalty owed to the client. And this breach is taken so seriously that only rarely will other, competing obligations be taken to justify it. Indeed, it is only in two cases that the law recognizes the loyalty owed to a client by her attorney as justifiably compromised: when the defendant confides to the attorney that he intends to place someone at grave risk (in which case the attorney's duty of loyalty is overridden by her duty to protect others[7]) and when the defendant involves the defense lawyer in some criminal enterprise (in which case the client forfeits the loyalty owed to him). In all other cases, the duty of loyalty remains paramount. Should a defendant confide that he was responsible for some past unsolved crime – even murder – it is the lawyer's obligation to respect that confidence and not to reveal the disclosed information. Sometimes, the duty of the defense attorney to respect confidences shared by defendants may have extremely painful consequences for others, but even so, the confidences may not be breached. Such a situation occurred, for example, in what is commonly referred to as the Lake Pleasant Bodies case, when a client told his lawyers the whereabouts of bodies for which police had been fruitlessly searching, and, having verified what had been told them, the defense lawyers kept the information to themselves.[8] It was later argued that the obligation to respect client confidentiality not only entitled but legally bound the lawyers not to disclose the information their client gave them. Moves were made to discipline the lawyers for concealing the information (partially on the grounds that concealment led to further work for the police and continued

---

[7] In the USA, this was first established in *Tarasoff* v. *Regents of the University of California*, 551 P.2d 334 (Cal. 1976). But see the recent reviews in *University of Cincinnati Law Review* 75 (2006).

[8] The defendant was being tried for another murder. One of the lawyers involved, Frank Armani, subsequently coauthored a book on the issue. See Tom Alibrandi and Frank H. Armani, *Privileged Information* (New York: HarperCollins, 1984). A later Canadian case, involving a lawyer associated with the Scarborough Rapes case, is even more problematic, for there it involved the (temporary?) concealment of material evidence to whose existence and location the defense lawyer had been directed by the defendant. See *R.* v. *Murray* (1999), 136 C.C.C. (3d) 197, <www.criminallawyers.ca/murrayjudgment.htm>.

suffering for the families of the victims), but the position of the defense lawyers was eventually upheld: loyalty to clients and the duty to provide zealous advocacy for them was taken to override the moral requirement that we should not cause either needless trouble or avertable human suffering. It is not that the important moral duty to forestall needless trouble (in this case on the part of the police) and avert the suffering of others (in this case the families of the victims) was set aside; it is rather that it was overridden by what is regarded – in the context of the relationship between a defendant and his lawyer – as of paramount importance if defendants are to be adequately represented before the court.

Obviously, the critical question about when a defense lawyer should breach a confidence placed in her by her client concerns where we are to draw the line between what, generally, is and what is not permissible within that relationship. We should also want to know whether the legal and moral lines between the permissible and impermissible are the same. At least part of what we must take into account in answering the question whether a breach of confidentiality should be permissible is whether breaches are likely to have a negative impact on the trust that clients can reasonably expect to have in their attorneys. What is important to consider, however, is not the consequences of such a breach in a particular case but the impact on the general practice of respect for client confidentiality if particular reasons are taken to justify it in some cases. Nevertheless, though the system of respecting confidentiality is of crucial importance, one must be mindful of the possible negative impact that concealment may have on the administration of justice. This is well illustrated by what took place in the Scarborough Rapes case (see note 8). In that case, the defendant, having made video-recordings (with his wife) of his raping and torturing several young girls, directed his lawyer to go to his home to retrieve and secure these highly incriminating tapes that he had secreted but which police had not been able to find. The lawyer did as his client bade him (perhaps intending to use some of the tapes to undermine the credibility of a prosecution witness or even to broker a plea agreement). When a second defense attorney was appointed and the concealment of the tapes became known, the question arose as to whether this concealment had constituted tampering with the evidence. Was the offense of the defendant (and the video-recorded material of that offense) so egregious that – morally, at least – concealment of the tapes on the part of the defendant's attorney went too far?

Zealous advocacy

Discussions of zealous advocacy almost invariably take as their starting (and sometimes finishing) point Lord Brougham's famous statement in behalf of Queen Caroline:

> An advocate, in the discharge of his duty, knows but one person in all the world, and that person is his client. To save that client by all means and expedients, and at all hazards and costs to other persons, and, amongst them, to himself, is his first and only duty; and in performing this duty he must not regard the alarm, the torments, the destruction which he may bring upon others. Separating the duty of a patriot from that of an advocate, he must go on reckless of consequences, though it should be his unhappy fate to involve his country in confusion.[9]

Reminiscent of – but even more radical than – the invocation to do justice though the heavens fall, Brougham's remarks were probably not hyperbolic. For George IV, newly acceded to the throne, had sought to divorce Caroline for adultery, and Brougham's statement ominously hinted that, were steps taken to proceed with the charges against Caroline, it would be revealed that before his marriage to Caroline the king had secretly "married" a Catholic – a revelation that would surely have thrown the country into "confusion." The charge against Caroline was eventually withdrawn.

Brougham's remarks bring into relief a basic question about the adversarial system: To what extent, if at all, should zealous advocacy by the defense, so critical to the adversarial system, be constrained in the interests of other concerns?

In response, we might fruitfully distinguish different accounts of the interchange among its parties. One somewhat cynical account views the adversarial system in *gladiatorial* terms as a form of (mostly) nonviolent combat in which the opposing parties "have their day in court" or "strut their stuff," seeking by whatever wiles and stratagems they can to gain the upper hand and get the referee's nod. The situation is not quite a free-for-all, for even gladiatorial contests have rules.

Nonetheless, even if some courtroom encounters appear this way, the gladiatorial model leaves too much of importance out of account. The

---

[9] Joseph Nightingale (ed.), *The Trial of Queen Caroline* (London: J. Robins & Co., 1820–1), vol. II, 8.

rules of court engagement require that participants testify under oath, and abstain from both perjury and the presentation of false documents. They also outlaw the coercion of witnesses and tampering with juries. Indeed, to the extent that the process is (or perhaps even appears to be) an argumentative free-for-all, the process, which should be constrained by certain normative rules, may be viewed as having been corrupted.

Another account, often thought to have Brougham as its champion, is *civil libertarian* in nature. On this account, since the central purpose of the courtroom engagement – grounded as it is on the presumption of innocence – is protection of a defendant's rights against the resources and awesome power of the state, defense counsel should be given great latitude in how they operate, even, if necessary, to the point of embarrassing and humiliating witnesses, attacking their credibility, and indulging in dramatic flourishes. In Alan Dershowitz's view (expressed in the epigraph to this chapter), a defense lawyer owes it to her client "to prevent, by all lawful means, the 'whole truth' from coming out." For Brougham, as we saw, a client's interests are an advocate's "first and only duty," and in pursuit of those interests the advocate may cause alarm and bring torments and destruction upon others, even if it plunges the entire country into "confusion." No doubt Brougham makes his point too strongly, for his point is not that it would be justifiable to lie, or to threaten jurors, or to kill witnesses, should that aid a client's case. Zealous advocacy, as it used to be put in the ABA Model Code of Professional Responsibility, must operate "within the bounds of law." (Brougham's making good on his threat to make public King George IV's clandestine relationship with a Catholic woman, were the issue of Caroline's infidelity to be pursued, would not have violated those rules, even if George IV's secret was not at all germane to the question of Caroline's fidelity.)

Although the civil libertarian model has a significant following, its invitation to "work the margins" or "push the limits" of what is permissible behavior in court also runs the risk of being self-defeating. Lawyers who act in accordance with that model tend to become known not primarily as protectors of civil liberties but as "hired guns." And though we may reasonably accept that defense lawyers owe their "first duty" to their clients, it is surely more problematic to see that duty as their "only duty." Lawyers operate within an institution that is committed – ultimately – to justice, not only for defendants but also for victims, and though the defense and prosecuting attorney's roles are differentiated from each other, that differentiation is, nevertheless, bounded by a common, overriding objective. If the impression is given that lawyers are "hired guns," the larger purposes of the criminal justice institution will have been lost sight of. What we hope for from a robust adversarial system is that the state's massive power will be matched by an equally skilled advocacy for the defendant, that the truth will, in the end, prevail, and justice be done. If it appears that one of the parties to the court proceedings can, with impunity, act so as to undermine the institution's larger justifying purposes, the institution as a whole will be brought into disrepute. There are of course occasions when each of the parties to court proceedings – prosecutors (and victims), defense lawyers (and defendants), judges, and juries – will be tempted to conduct itself inappropriately, but the importance and expectation of zealous advocacy for defendants provides an especial lure to excess on the part of defense lawyers.

The traditional or *classical* account of the adversarial system sees the goal of court processes as the provision of a fair trial and (relatedly) of decision-making that is just. The likelihood that this will take place is optimized if the court processes are directed to truth-finding via a formal procedure in which opposed parties present their case and challenge opposing contentions before an impartial fact-finder (which can be a judge or a jury). In other words, legal decisions are to be made as the result of a *rational* process of challenge and counter-challenge. Given that the prosecution is backed by the resources of the state in making a case against the defendant, only a zealous advocate for the defense can present the defendant's claims with the argumentative forcefulness that is required if the argument presented in court is not to be one-sided. Such, at least, is the theory. In practice, it is not clear that the adversarial approach yields better decisions than alternatives, such as the inquisitorial approach used in Europe, in which the court's investigation is directed and conducted exclusively by the judge. (Well-trained inquisitorial judges can be quite relentless in the pursuit of the truth in cases over which they preside, and they are not encumbered, as are prosecuting and defense attorneys, by the need to argue for a specific "side.") In any case, there is no doubt that, however worthy particular theories of legal decision-making may be, all will run into problems of one sort or another at the level of implementation.

Each of the foregoing models of the adversarial system – the gladiatorial account, the civil libertarian model, and the classical view – has a place for zealous advocacy of the defendant, and each has a rationale for such advocacy that puts specific limitations on the zeal that the defense may show. In what follows we will review the kinds of limitations that might be justified under the classical model.

The limits of advocacy

However much defense lawyers are committed to the zealous advocacy of their clients' causes, they also have a duty to the court, to their profession, and, of course, to the wider community that is served by the institutions of criminal justice. The duties owed to these different entities are distinct, but they are not necessarily incompatible with one another. Indeed, sometimes a defense lawyer's multiple duties – professional, legal, and civil – are inseparable. This is so because defense lawyers' obligations to the court are to a large extent intertwined with their role as professionals and so with duties owed to the profession itself. Furthermore, since it is because of its service to the wider community in which it functions that the legal profession has the particular legal obligations and responsibilities that it has, and is endowed with its specific but extensive legal prerogatives, its professional activities must be conducted in ways that are deemed acceptable to the community. As we shall see, a lawyer's duty to be a zealous advocate for his or her client is linked with (though is not collapsible into) the duties that the lawyer owes to the profession, to the court, and to the community. What are the wider duties to the court, to the legal profession, and to others, that lawyers have, and what should be done if any of these duties come into conflict with the advocate's duty to the client? Does duty to the client always take priority? To unravel some of these complexities here, consider the following.

The problem of perjury

Because the court functions as, among other things, a fact-finder for the cases that are brought before it, it requires of defense lawyers that they not perjure themselves or induce, encourage, or condone perjury on the part of their clients. Rather, the court requires testifying witnesses to tell "the truth, the whole truth, and nothing but the truth," a requirement that is, of course, critical to the fact-finding process. If participants fail to testify truthfully, the fact-finding process will be threatened and perhaps undermined.[10] But the duty to tell the truth is not always an unproblematic one, where zealous advocacy is concerned. Because a significant number of defendants who plead "not guilty" are in fact guilty more or less as charged, efforts will be made by these defendants to mislead the court – a fact that, of course, defendants will try to conceal, even from their lawyers. When defense lawyers become aware that their clients have lied to the court or intend to do so, it is the lawyers' duty to the court not to disregard the perjury, actual or intended, but to address and oppose it. But how, exactly, is the defense lawyer to discharge this duty consistent with her duty to the client? The answer to this question is a matter of ongoing dispute. Some argue that in such a situation the defense lawyer must confront the client and have him withdraw his false or deceptive remarks. Others claim that the defense should simply refuse to use what is said in arguing the client's case. And still others maintain that in such a situation the defense counsel should withdraw her services. There are also those who claim that the defense attorney should report the matter to the court. Different circumstances may dictate different responses, but almost all agree that, however it is to be discharged, the defense lawyer's duty to the court is significant and to be taken seriously. This could hardly be otherwise given that the processes of the court are intended to serve the cause of justice. Although zealous advocacy is absolutely critical if the adversarial process is to work effectively as a fact-finding mechanism, the point of the adversarial process is not merely to establish the facts, but to do so for the purpose of, and in a way that reflects our concern with, what is fair and just.

The following case (and its progress through the courts) illustrates some of the professional ethical and legal quandaries that may arise because of a conflict between a defense attorney's duty to his client and his duty to the court.[11] Emanuel Charles Whiteside was charged with the murder of Calvin Love. According to the court record, Whiteside and two others went to Love's apartment to obtain marijuana. They found Love in bed with his girlfriend. At some point during their visit an argument started and Love asked his girlfriend to get his "piece," after which he himself got up and then returned to bed. A little later, Love reached under the pillow and moved

---

[10] Constraints include the right against self-incrimination and (more problematically) public safety or national security considerations.

[11] *Nix* v. *Whiteside*, 475 US 157 (1986).

in Whiteside's direction, at which point Whiteside fatally stabbed Love in the chest. Whiteside initially told his court-appointed lawyer, Gary L. Robinson, that he stabbed Love as the latter "was pulling a pistol from under the pillow on the bed." The police found no gun and no one apart from Whiteside claimed to have seen one. Robinson probed Whiteside, asking whether he actually saw a gun. Whiteside admitted to Robinson that he had not actually seen a gun but was nonetheless convinced that Love had one. Robinson informed Whiteside that to claim he killed Love in self-defense it was not essential that Love actually had a gun. All that was necessary was that Whiteside reasonably believed there to be a gun. At some point while preparing for trial, Whiteside changed his story and claimed that he had actually seen "something metallic" in Love's hand. He stated that this addition to his story was necessary for winning the case. Robinson assured Whiteside that this "addition" was not only not necessary for his defense, but would constitute perjury. He warned Whiteside that he would have a duty to advise the court of this fact, and that he would seek to withdraw as his defense attorney should Whiteside insist on going ahead with his testimony that he had seen something metallic. In the end, Robinson testified that he "knew" Love had a gun, even though he had not actually seen it. Robinson argued that Whiteside's belief that Love had a gun was not unreasonable, as demonstrated by evidence that Robinson presented that on other occasions Love had been seen with a sawn-off shotgun. Furthermore, on the night he was killed Love may very well have had a gun that the police did not turn up, since their search may have been careless. And finally, the police report that there was no gun was difficult to verify because the victim's family had cleared out the apartment soon after the police inspected it.

But Robinson's argument did not convince the jury and Whiteside was convicted of second-degree murder. Whiteside appealed the verdict, claiming that his defense attorney's refusal to allow him to testify that he saw something metallic deprived him of a fair trial. Robinson countered that his duty as defense counsel did not extend to permitting the defendant to perjure himself. Though Whiteside's conviction was upheld by the Supreme Court of Iowa (and a federal District Court denied relief), it was reversed by the Federal Court of Appeals for the Eighth Circuit on the grounds that, although the defendant certainly had no right to commit perjury, Robinson's threat to Whiteside could reasonably be seen as a threat to violate his duty of confidentiality to his client, thereby undermining Robinson's right to effective representation. Ultimately, this decision was reviewed by the US Supreme Court, which reversed it yet again, this time in Robinson's favor. The grounds for this last reversal were that Robinson's conduct in the trial did not constitute a lapse of such a kind as to "undermine confidence in the outcome." The Court did not deny that Robinson might have dealt with the situation in some way other than the way he did, but it determined that the way in which he did in fact deal with it fell within the range of reasonable professional options.

Despite continuing controversy, I believe the final decision in the *Whiteside* case was a morally appropriate one. Some critics of the final exoneration of Robinson have argued that Robinson was wrong to view his client's intention to add to his original testimony as an intention to perjure himself, for it might have been that the added information had been blocked out by his client in the stress of the moment and had come back to him only later. Robinson could not have known with any certainty that this was not the case. This is correct, but in determining what we should do and in assessing what others have done, we need to know more than what was possibly true about an event. Since no evidence was offered to support any view other than the view that Robinson himself had, there is no reason to call into question Robinson's assessment of what was going on. Of course, had circumstances been different, we might have come to a different conclusion as to the rightness of Robinson's judgment of his client's intentions and so of his actions in response to that judgment.

No doubt Robinson could have tried to dissuade Whiteside in a less heavy-handed fashion. He might simply have pointed out to him that to claim falsely that he saw something metallic would be unlawful, and then if that did not deter Whiteside from going ahead with his false testimony, he might have indicated that he would not support such conduct in court. Should Whiteside have persisted in his intention to perjure himself, Robinson could have made it clear to him that he would have to take some action, for otherwise he himself would be in violation of the law for "suborning perjury." Perhaps Whiteside would have gone ahead anyway, taking the chance that Robinson would let his false testimony pass. Indeed, had Robinson been privately retained by Whiteside, perhaps he would have let it pass. But though the reality is such that a privately retained lawyer may be less likely than a court-appointed one to take action in the face of a client's intention to perjure himself, that says little about the rights of lawyers, privately retained or not. One cannot validly argue that Robinson should have done what privately retained lawyers are sometimes willing and able to get away with. I think it is fair to say that at trial Robinson could hardly have done more than he did: he presented a plausible (even if not ultimately convincing) reason for viewing Whiteside's action as one that was reasonably taken in self-defense, and he provided his client with this defense without at the same time violating his professional obligations.

No doubt, some will respond to my affirmative assessment of Robinson's actions with the claim that Robinson's loyalty to Whiteside committed him to keeping whatever Whiteside told him in strictest confidence, for otherwise Robinson could not have expected Whiteside to fully confide in him and thereby provide him with the wherewithal for the strongest possible defense. In short, lawyers who cannot assure their clients that they will keep to themselves whatever they are told in confidence will not gain the full trust of their clients. But the answer to this is, first, that the law does indeed recognize some exceptions to lawyer–client confidentiality (though these exceptions do not bear on Whiteside), and second, that it is not clear that the defense attorney's refusal to permit his client to perjure himself impinges on the duty of confidentiality to the client in such a way as to undermine the causes of fairness, truth, and justice. Not even the staunchest civil libertarian (for whom the client's rights are paramount) would have objected to Robinson's saying to Whiteside at the outset: "We cannot go forward with any perjured testimony." But it is not clear what such lawyers would have seen as their professional obligation had Whiteside, despite his lawyer's admonition against it, gone on to perjure himself anyway.

Finally, although some might argue that Robinson's action intruded unreasonably on Whiteside's right to testify on his own behalf, thereby denying him the freedom and dignity to pursue his defense according to his own judgment, this argument overlooks the way in which Whiteside's perjurious testimony would have implicated Robinson. Upon Robinson's refusal to countenance Whiteside's intended perjury, Whiteside had the option of either defending himself or dismissing Robinson in favor of another defense attorney. But, given that he chose to continue as Robinson's client, he could not ethically involve Robinson in his own perjurious design. And Robinson, aware of what his client intended to do, could not simply turn a blind eye to his client's actions without sharing in that act.

Client misconduct

Zealous advocacy has constraints in addition to those discussed above, constraints that also relate to the court's justifying purposes. For example, should the defense lawyer discover that the defendant had been tampering with witnesses or jurors by means of threats or offers, he would not be prevented from disclosing this to the court. Indeed, he may have a duty to disclose it. The overarching concern is with fairness, truth, and justice. Though the upholding of these values may not be the defense lawyer's direct and primary professional concern, he cannot ethically stand by when these values are, to his knowledge, being corrupted.

Courtroom tactics

Yet another way in which the lawyer's various duties to the court, the profession, and the community may come into tension with the duty to be a zealous advocate for one's client is suggested by the disparaging description of defense lawyers as "hired guns." Such a characterization hints – not too subtly – that the lawyer is an unprincipled bully whose motivations are money (and power) rather than respect for the principles of justice and fairness. This assessment is held to be supported by tactics sometimes used by defense lawyers – discovery tactics that delay and courtroom tactics that intimidate, harass, embarrass, or humiliate. In the course of cross-examining prosecution witnesses, it is of course not only appropriate but also obligatory for the defense lawyer to challenge their credibility and to try to expose their testimony as inconsistent or false. But sometimes defense lawyers go too far and deliberately and maliciously confuse witnesses they are cross-examining. Such lawyers "play" to juries in ways that are not designed to get at the truth, or even, except accidentally, the truth as the defendant sees it. Their tactics reflect a passion to win, and win at almost any cost (though sometimes such tactics backfire and alienate the jury they are intended to convince). In theory, the adversarial structure has correctives within it that allow such overreaching on the part of defense lawyers to be counteracted, but in practice it is not so easy. In some areas (such as trials for sexual assault) rules have been put in place that limit the kinds of evidence that can be used. But for a large range of cases there are no clear rules to tell us when a defense lawyer has overstepped the line. The issue is not one of regulation but of professional ethics, of refusing to act in ways that bring the profession, and with it the system, into disrepute.

There is no simple solution to the defense lawyers' dilemmas. On the one hand, they are there to champion their clients' interests. On the other hand, they cannot exempt themselves from responsibility for the tactics they employ on and in behalf of their clients. This does not mean that they can therefore sacrifice their clients' interests on the altar of their personal moral opinions. They have professional obligations, and the professional ethic that shapes those obligations embeds them in a system that ought – ultimately – to be structured around the demands of justice, demands that are most likely to be realized when the system's processes are fair and therefore conducive to the discovery of truth.

9   The impartial judge?

Four things belong to a judge: to hear courteously, to answer wisely,
to consider soberly, and to decide impartially.[1]

Within the adversarial system, judges and juries function as fact-finders –
that is, as those who, having heard the arguments both for and against
a particular construction of the facts of a case, are called upon to decide
whether the construction of the facts presented by the prosecution (in a
criminal trial) reaches an appropriate level of certainty: beyond reasonable
doubt. Fact-finders are concerned with the truth of the matter at issue –
whether, for example, given the evidence and arguments, it is the case that
Smith embezzled the funds of Alpha Inc. or assaulted Bill Bloggs. However,
because the determination of truth is the basis for the just disposition of a
case, fact-finders may be said to be concerned with justice as well as truth.

But judges do not always function as fact-finders. In jury trials they do
not. In the US criminal justice system, in serious cases defendants have a
right to a jury trial, and in those cases, the judge who presides over a case
will function as a "master of ceremonies" and interpreter of the law. Presiding judges also have a critical role in determining that the trial is fair
and (with varying degrees of discretion) making sentencing decisions should
the defendant be found guilty.[2] They must also research the law, approve

---

[1] Attributed to Socrates in *Etzel* v. *Rosenbloom*, 83 Cal. 2d 758, 765 (Cal Dist. Ct. App. 1948);
People v. *Hefner*, 127 Cal. 3d. 88, 92 (Cal. Dist. Ct. App. 1981), though I am unable to find
any textual support for this attribution.

[2] The issue of judicial sentencing discretion has recently been thrown into some confusion in the United States. As a curb on judicial discretion (and inconsistent sentencing
decisions), the federal government and many states introduced mandatory sentencing
guidelines that severely limited judicial sentencing discretion. But a recent series of
cases has determined, on the one hand, that judges may not vary upwardly the sentence that a jury verdict would have warranted (without agreement by the jury), and on

special requests from police and others, write opinions, and approve plea agreements, all of which are important aspects of their role. Of course, because the judiciary is a complex and hierarchical institution with its own internal checks and balances, judges operating at different levels of the system have different responsibilities and prerogatives, and perform different activities. The responsibilities of, say, trial judges differ from those of appellate judges, and yet again from Supreme Court judges. Moreover, the judicial responsibilities and prerogatives of judges vary with jurisdictional differences. Nevertheless, some expectations are invariant for almost all judges, even if the activities through which these expectations may be fulfilled vary with the level of judicial operation and the jurisdiction of operation.

In this chapter, we review the importance of the judiciary, focusing particularly on the role of judges in criminal trials. We consider the ethical qualities that judges should display if they are to fulfill their judicial role. And we shall reflect on strategies for creating and sustaining a healthy judicial culture.

The critical importance of the judiciary

Recall the Lockean observation that humans in a state of nature will do a poor job of judging in situations in which competing interests have to be adjudicated. Either they will be prejudiced in their own cases or they will not be sufficiently interested in others' cases to give them the attention that those cases deserve. What is needed, Locke says, is an institution dedicated to the impartial interpretation and application of the law. In short, what is needed is an impartial judiciary. Unfortunately, however, though it has sometimes done well, the judiciary has never managed to transcend the flawed humanity of its occupants. (Historically, God, the divine judge, has been presented as the aspirational model for human judges, but even in the Old Testament, where the divine exemplar was most vividly represented, human judges, as described there, tended to be woefully corrupt and so to fall clearly short of the model of judgeship.)

---

the other, that the guidelines should not be seen as mandatory, but only as advisory. See, in particular, *Blakely* v. *Washington*, 124 S. Ct. 2531 (2004) and *US* v. *Booker*, 125 S. Ct. 738 (2005). Since then, about 60 percent of decisions have conformed to the guidelines.

It is difficult both to design institutions and then to nurture their cultures so that they are immunized against all the failings of the state of nature, especially given that the state of nature was as precarious as it was because of the same tendencies and flaws that characterize those who establish and enter into our institutions of civil society. To be sure, some environments are less corruptive than others, but all fall well short of perfection. In his classic work on political economy, A. O. Hirschman builds on the view that all institutions, like their individual members, have an endemic tendency to decline (sometimes referred to as institutional entropy).[3] He considers it a major social challenge to devise ways of conserving what is good in institutions and reviving what has declined. Although the judiciaries of liberal democratic societies have gradually developed cultural traditions that are relatively resistant to corruption, or at least possess active mechanisms for tracking and dealing with corruption, they still fall short unacceptably often,[4] whereas the judiciaries of societies that have not (yet) developed strong liberal democratic traditions often remain deeply corrupt, both systemically and individually.[5]

Corruption in *any* social institution is a serious problem because it involves the betrayal of a public commitment – it diverts institutional energies from their larger social purposes into more limited or self-interested pursuits. But judicial corruption is almost always more troubling than other forms of corruption because, at least for liberal democratic societies, an honest and impartial judiciary is necessary to ensure the rule of law that sustains those societies. The judiciary is the final arbiter of the general framework for the conduct of public life.[6] As the final arbiter that brings social closure, the judiciary bears a heavy burden of responsibility. Moreover, even if a judiciary's basic structures remain sound, judicial misconduct and

---

[3] A. O. Hirschman, *Exit, Voice, and Loyalty* (Cambridge, MA: Harvard University Press, 1970). On "institutional entropy" generally, see David A. Whetten, "Organizational Growth and Decline Processes," *Annual Review of Sociology* 13 (1987): 335–58.

[4] For a good overview, see Geoffrey P. Miller, "Bad Judges," *Texas Law Review* 83 (2004): 431–87.

[5] See Edgardo Buscaglia, *Judicial Corruption in Developing Countries: Its Causes and Economic Consequences* (Vienna: UNODCCP, 2001), <www.unodc.org/pdf/crime/gpacpublications/cicp14.pdf>, and the work of Transparency International, <www.transparency.org>.

[6] Not every judge of course is a final arbiter, because decisions taken in one court can be appealed to another, but the system as a whole functions in this way. Nevertheless, corruption at lower levels may function to diminish trust in the process at higher levels.

corruption are deeply problematic because they undermine the authoritativeness of judicial judgments and also the social trust that must be placed in them for them to be effective guarantors of the justice of the law and the fairness of its application. For these reasons, a judiciary characterized by independence, impartiality, and integrity is critical to the preservation and health of other social institutions.

Norms of judicial conduct

Judges make their determinations not in isolation but as part of an institution – the court system – which is embedded within larger institutional frameworks such as the criminal justice system, the market system, the administrative system, and so on. Judges cannot be impervious to these larger frameworks, even though the demands of their immediate institutional framework will bear most directly upon them. Despite claims to the contrary,[7] there are many instances in which judges have taken account not only of the social impact of their decisions but also of (what they have referred to as) the "evolving standards of decency that mark the progress of a maturing society."[8] Indeed, even at the highest level – the US Supreme Court – judges have often waited for "suitable" cases to come along before granting review (certiorari) so as to minimize the possibility that their decision will result in large-scale social disorder.

Some judicial norms are more closely associated with the judiciary or court system as a whole than with its individual members, but each of the norms that we consider here can be attributed either to the whole or to its individual members. For example, the impartiality of individual judges is often said to depend on the independence of the courts or judiciary, but along with the impartiality of the institution the independence of individual judges will also be considered.

---

[7] Former US Chief Justice Warren Burger argued that "judges . . . rule on the basis of law, not public opinion, and they should be totally indifferent to pressures of the times." *Christian Science Monitor*, 11 February 1987. The first part may be correct, but the second part surely overreaches.

[8] *Trop v. Dulles*, 356 US 86, 101 (1958). It should be acknowledged, though, that some judges – most notably Justice Scalia on the current US Supreme Court – are strongly resistant to the notion of a "living Constitution."

It is not easy to provide an authoritative enumeration of the norms of judicial conduct. For among these norms there is often overlap, differentiation, expansion, and contraction. (Thus, what is seen as a single norm in one context may be viewed as an umbrella term for a number of variously individuated and differentiated norms in another. For instance, the judicial norm of integrity may be viewed in some but not other contexts as a broad-spectrum norm that encompasses the more specific ideals of honesty, fairness, and even-handedness.) The influential United Nations-sponsored (*Bangalore*) *Principles of Judicial Conduct* (2002)[9] enunciates six values – independence, impartiality, integrity, propriety, equality, and competence/diligence. Here, though, we will focus on the first three of these, and the ways in which they implicate both one another and the remaining others.

Independence

As noted, "judicial independence" may refer either to the independence of individual judges or to the institutional independence of the judiciary/court system, though independence in the one is often connected with independence in the other. In the case both of individual judges and the judiciary/court as an institution, "independence" is often taken to refer to an independence from improper influence by others – including, in the case of individual judges, the improper influence of fellow judges, and in the case of the institution, the improper influence of the legislature, other government officials, corporate interests, or powerful individuals.[10] To claim that individual judges must be independent is not to deny that judicial 'bullying' ever takes place or that compromises are not sometimes struck so that court decisions do not become too fragmented.[11] Nor is the understanding of "independence" of the court always uncontroversial. A recent example of

---

[9] *Principles of Judicial Conduct*, <www.unodc.org/pdf/crime/corruption/judicial_group/ Bangalore_principles.pdf>.

[10] Consider the phenomenon, more common in nondemocratic countries, of "telephone justice," when powerful parties indicate how they wish for cases to be decided. See Justice Stephen Breyer, "Fair and Independent Courts" (speech delivered at Georgetown University Law Center, Hart Auditorium, Washington, DC, September 28, 2006), <www.law.georgetown.edu/news/documents/CoJ092806-breyer_edited.pdf>, 4ff.

[11] It is usually considered that a Supreme Court decision with too many sub-opinions is problematic.

the way in which the "independence" of the judiciary as an institution was viewed by individual judges is reflected in the response of some of them to the "threat" made by some members of the US Congress that judges be monitored for "downward departures" in what was felt to be the too lenient sentencing of certain kinds of offenders such as child-molesters.[12] Monitoring by members of Congress was viewed by many judges as a threat to their independence.

In higher courts, judicial independence is frequently fostered by giving judges lifetime tenure or by instituting a mandatory retirement age. In lower courts, as we shall see when discussing impartiality, independence can be much more problematic. Tenure – the guarantee of one's position against dismissal for political reasons – helps to assure independence of judicial judgment from political influence, for it helps to insulate members of the judiciary from reprisals in cases in which they do not support initiatives or actions taken by the incumbent legislature or executive. By the same token, it assures judicial continuity through changes of political leadership. Mere continuity of tenure, however, is not sufficient to guarantee judicial independence. There must be assurance that the courts, like other social institutions, are equipped with the infrastructure and resources necessary to maintain them: without an ample and secure budget judges may be so poorly remunerated and resourced that they may find themselves under pressure to toe a political line to ensure that needed resources are not withheld. At the higher judicial levels, such resources can be of critical importance, since the judiciary may be called upon to pass judgment on governmental initiatives, including those relating to criminalization.

Judicial independence is an important part of what is needed to correct the deficiencies that Locke identified with living in a state of nature. According to Locke, it is only through the drawing up of distinct and independent institutions to interpret public policy (including criminal law) that we will have a winning chance of not regressing to a political state that has the markings of the very authoritarian (monarchical) institution against which Locke's treatises were directed. Although Locke was not especially pessimistic about human beings' capacity for virtuous behavior, he also believed

[12] See Tom Feeney, "Reaffirming the Rule of Law in Federal Sentencing," *Criminal Justice Ethics* 22, no. 2 (Summer/Fall 2003), 2, 67–73. It attracted a strong riposte from the late Chief Justice Rehnquist, <www.supremecourtus.gov/publicinfo/speeches/sp_05-05-03.html>.

that if the human tendency toward self-centeredness is not checked, then, even in established civil society, social decision-making will be susceptible to tyranny. What we need, therefore, are institutions that are separated in their powers rather than closely intertwined, so that "checks" of one are provided by the others and none is disproportionately powerful relative to the others (hence the idea of "checks and balances"). In addition, it is also no accident that in liberal democracies the highest courts comprise a plurality of judges. This keeps judicial power out of the hands of a single individual. And insofar as the judges are plural not only in number but also in outlook, there is the likelihood that there will be independence not only from any outside authority but, as well, from one another – a further check against those who might attempt to exert tyrannical influence.

Judicial independence, then, is both a mechanism that structures judicial institutions within democratic societies and also a value of democratic culture. Both as a structural mechanism and a cultural value, independence works against partiality in judicial judgment, a partiality that would violate a central principle of liberal democratic thought, namely, that each person has an equal claim to the consideration of his or her interests.

Impartiality

When Locke speaks of the need for an "indifferent" judge, he has in mind not one who is "uninterested" or "unconcerned" but one who has no stake in a particular judicial outcome beyond the fact that it has been brought about as a result of adherence to legal procedures. This is what it means for a judge to be impartial.[13] Impartiality is the central judicial value, but even though it is partly secured through independence, it is (as we shall see) also sustained by integrity.

The idea that judges are answerable only to the law is not, admittedly, a completely transparent idea, because – at least at higher judicial levels – judges do not merely "discover," "report," and "apply" the law but to some extent also determine it. As we have already seen in other contexts, it may be unclear (to varying degrees) what the "law" is. This is so because our

---

[13] The demand is not for some unattainable absolute impartiality, but rather for freedom from certain partialities – for example, with regard to the guilt or otherwise of a defendant prior to trial.

concepts frequently have fuzzy edges and the concrete realities of the world may change in ways that make it unclear whether a case under review falls within the boundaries of a particular prohibition. For example, although it is illegal to buy votes or engage in bribery, it may not be clear whether, in today's world, contributions to US politicians or political campaigns from lobbyists, large institutions, and corporations should be seen as attempted (or even actual) bribery. If we respond in the negative, the question we should ask is: What *would* need to be the case for a contribution to cross the line and be considered attempted bribery? (US politicians have a considerable stake in the answer to this question, and perhaps it is for this reason that they have not shown themselves capable of providing a satisfactory answer to it.) Clearly, what we need here is the assistance of an impartial body, untainted by interest, that can draw the lines between the permissible and the impermissible and articulate the principle that distinguishes them. (In some liberal democratic societies, traditions of primarily state-financed elec- tioneering have already been established to attempt to circumvent what has become a quagmire.)

Attributions of impartiality and partiality (like attributions of indepen- dence and dependence) may be made with respect to the courts and to those who preside over them, and in both cases expectations of impartiality are fraught with difficulties. This is amply illustrated by recent debates con- cerning membership of the US Supreme Court, debates that make clear that legal interpretation does not take place in a social and theoretical vacuum, neither does it occur in a vacuum of personal, political, and professional commitments. Laws passed at one time may need to be interpreted at a later time, or decisions that were reached at one time may have to be revis- ited at another. And some jurists profess to place primary weight on the intentions of the original drafters of constitutional provisions or legislation (presuming that there is something to be identified as such), or to be "strict" constructionists (placing primary weight on the meaning that the constitu- tional text originally had), whereas others give considerable weight to the changing social environment within which the Constitution or legislation must be interpreted. If the collective that comprises the Court is too heavily populated with judges who identify with one rather than another tradi- tion of interpretation, then, in a strongly diversified community, the Court risks losing its reputation for impartiality. Because particular traditions of interpretation tend to express themselves in substantive social positions, an apparently "stacked" Court will be seen as continuous with the political process, even though, given tenure, it is less vulnerable to rapid change. In recent public debates over Supreme Court appointments, much attention has been given to the need for "swing votes" – in other words, judges whose interpretive traditions and substantive social views are not too closely identified with a particular political position – for otherwise the Court will come to mirror (and perpetuate) the values of the political power prevailing at the time of their appointment. One expects politicians to vote their partisanship. In the case of judges, though, one expects a greater openness to argument, so that their judgments will reflect a broader sense of what is rationally defensible.

Of course, it is not the mere fact that judges come to the bench with different traditions of statutory interpretation that in and of itself impugns the impartiality of the Court. (Indeed, different ways of interpreting the laws and the Constitution are what we might expect given the liberal democratic milieu from which judges are drawn.) The perceived threat to impartiality comes rather from the fact that different interpretive traditions are often believed to have different and predictable implications for a variety of pressing social issues – such as abortion and capital punishment – that, in our society, have been found to be divisive. A court that is too heavily freighted with people belonging to a particular tradition of interpretation is likely to be characterized in a particular way – say, as conservative or liberal – and a court so characterized will find its impartiality impugned, especially if the process of selection is seen as highly politicized.

Issues of partisanship (and the partiality that goes with it) that are both prevalent and visible at the level of the US Supreme Court have been even more prevalent, even if less publicly visible, in lower courts. Like prosecutorships, in many state courts judgeships are elected offices and, though seemingly open to general scrutiny, are effectively products of a party machine or of the kind of privately financed campaigning that is associated with political office. It is in these lower courts that most corruption, misconduct, and incompetence are found.[14] Lower court judges who are not elected are often appointed, a process that also tends to impugn independence and

---

[14] See, for example, Max Boot, *Out of Order: Arrogance, Corruption, and Incompetence on the Bench* (New York: Basic Books, 1998), an informative though somewhat polemical cataloguing of problems.

impartiality, not to say integrity. Admittedly, the fact that judges (usually) have to go through a process of reelection or reappointment may tend to ameliorate the situation. But if the local area is strongly committed in a particular ideological direction over a number of judicial terms (as has been the case, for example, in Brooklyn, New York), this check may not amount to much: judicial nominations and support have often been tied to political contributions and other partisan activities.

The challenges to judicial impartiality that are the most widespread as well as the most subtle arise from what are technically called "conflicts of interest." Conflicts of interest occur when those who are expected to make judgments concerning others have interests that tend to interfere with their ability to make those judgments properly. What is crucial here is not merely the inability to exercise proper judgment: a judge whose preoccupation with her currently sick daughter makes it difficult for her to concentrate on the arguments and therefore to come to a fair decision has an interest that conflicts with her ability to exercise her judgment properly but is not to be seen as having a prejudicial "conflict" of interest. Rather, a judge is said to have a conflict of interest when the factor that interferes with the ability to exercise proper judgment results from the judge having an interest that is essentially connected to the substance of the case. Thus, were a judge asked to make a decision or even preside in a case involving a relative (or other intimate) charged with reckless driving he would have a conflict of interest.

It must be said that having a conflict of interest does not, of itself, prevent a judge from judging fairly, for even with a conflict of interest, the judge may resist the effects of bias or prejudice. To have a conflict of interest is to have an interest that *disposes* one toward biased conduct, a tendency that the judge might be able to set to one side so that she still adjudicates the case before her with commendable impartiality. Nonetheless, because it may be very difficult when a conflict of interest arises – difficult both for others and for the judge herself – to know whether there has been undue influence in conducting affairs or rendering a decision about the case, it is best for judges who have conflicts of interest with respect to a given case to recuse (disqualify) themselves from presiding over or deciding matters with respect to that case. Were the judge to agree to be involved in the case and the relative found guilty, it might be reasonable to assume that the judge was able, in court proceedings, to discount the familial connection. But were the relative found *not* guilty, we might not be clear whether that verdict came about because there was insufficient evidence in support of the charge or because the judge's relationship with the accused got in the way of a fair assessment of the charge. For this reason, in cases in which judges are aware of a conflict of interest, disqualification from the case seems the best policy.

Because of the damage that might be done to the just disposition of court cases as a result of judges' conflicts of interest (and the subsequent undermining of the confidence that we have in the impartiality of judicial decisions), we are often concerned not merely with *actual* conflicts of interest but also with *potential* conflicts of interest and even with *apparent* conflicts of interest. A potential conflict of interest is one in which a person is not currently in the position in which she has to make a judgment concerning a matter on which she would have conflicting interests, but would come to be in this position were she to take the case on. Thus, in a criminal case concerning corporate malfeasance, a judge may ask to be excluded from the roster if she holds shares in the corporation that is under indictment. The judge wishes to avoid a situation in which she would be asked to judge on the merits of a case whose outcome could affect her financially. In the case of what is only an "apparent" conflict of interest, circumstances are such that they create an appearance of a conflict of interest where there is in fact no actual (or even potential) conflict. However, it is incumbent on the judge in such cases to show why the apparent conflict of interest is only that, and to dispel any notion that, with respect to a given case, there is any actual (or even potential) conflict of interest. Cases in which there are apparent conflicts of interest thus place judges under the burden of demonstrating that no true conflict of interest exists. It is not enough that a judge may know that what appears to be a conflict of interest is not one in fact. Because the appearance of a conflict of interest may be sufficient to undermine public confidence in the impartiality of a judicial decision-maker, that in itself constitutes a very important reason for the decision-maker to show that the appearance of a conflict of interest is only that, and that no true conflict of interest exists. Justice, as the saying goes, must not only be done but be seen to be done.

In January, 2004, US Supreme Court Justice Antonin Scalia went duck-hunting and dining with Vice-President Dick Cheney. The outing occurred three weeks after the Supreme Court agreed to hear a case involving the Vice-President's unwillingness to accept the decision of a lower court that he hand over the internal files of an energy task force he headed. It was claimed that the outing created an appearance of favoritism toward the Vice-President – that is, it constituted an apparent conflict of interest. There were calls that Justice Scalia recuse himself. Scalia refused, and in the public debate that followed he produced a twenty-one-page memorandum in which he sought to defend his remaining on the panel for the case.[15] He argued that the outing had been planned long before the Supreme Court had agreed to take the case (that is, before it granted *certiorari*); that he and the Vice-President were old friends; that the duck-hunting trip did not provide an intimate setting or one in which the case could have been reasonably discussed (had that been desired); that by recusing himself he would create the possibility of a tied (4:4) vote; and that the issue at stake was one of the Vice-President's official actions and not some matter involving friendship or financial benefit. Scalia noted that the circles in which he moves are ones in which he and many of the Justices have historically had close personal relationships with people whose official actions might come before the Court and that it would disable the Court were mere friendship a ground for recusal. One might reasonably agree that Justice Scalia met the onus placed on him. The case does, however, indicate some of the complexities involved in determining whether there is a conflict of interest. We will shortly have more to say on this.

Clearly, conflicts of interest occur in many contexts other than those of judicial decision-making, but they are never so deeply problematic as they are in judicial contexts. For this reason, judges often (rightly) take precautions – likely regarded as excessive in other contexts – to avoid the appearance of such conflict.

Integrity

Independence and impartiality are important to the quality of judicial decision-making; they must be in evidence if judges are to show themselves to be beyond reproach. And beyond reproach they must be if their authority and that of the court/judiciary is not to be called into question. In a liberal democracy, maintenance of judicial authority is critical, for the power of the

---

[15] 541 US 913 (2004), <http://fl1.findlaw.com/news.findlaw.com/hdocs/docs/scotus/chny31804jsmem.pdf>.

judiciary *resides* in its authority. We refer to the probity expected of judges as their "integrity."

Although integrity is often understood narrowly to mean "honesty," it also carries the sense of *wholeness*. Indeed, in many contexts "integrity" has come to stand in for a cluster of concepts which cover a range of character traits or virtues. In the judicial context, it refers to the uprightness and decency that constitute a judge as someone to be respected and trusted, someone whose private and public behavior will sustain "public confidence in the administration of justice." Clearly, this is not a simple matter of popularity but rather of personal and professional behavior that is not only compatible with, but positively conducive to, respect for the court, its officers, and ultimately, the rule of law.

The qualities of character and forms of conduct that are constitutive of judicial integrity include (but are not confined to) those qualities and behaviors that are strictly necessary to the exercise of judicial judgment. What links these qualities and behaviors is the bearing that each has on the authority that the judge is likely to summon and, more generally, on the ability of each to promote respect for the judiciary as an institution. Authority, as we have previously observed, is a social relation in which someone or some institution is not only trusted as an appropriate provider of some good but also acknowledged as such. As a social relation, authority will be sustained only if personal and professional behavior is conducive to trust.

What kinds of behavior might be encompassed by judicial integrity? A wide variety. One obvious expectation is that judges not be corrupt or be seen as corrupt or even corruptible. Although concern with judicial corruption has often focused on the issue of judicial bribery, it can refer more generally to actions that place a question mark against a judge's impartiality or that smell of self-servingness of other kinds. It is indeed the self-servingness of public officials – particularly actions by public officials influenced by considerations of private gain – that is the usual way of construing "corruption of public office." But one can corrupt an institution other than through self-seeking behavior; there is a classical sense of corruption in which it refers to any form of degeneration or decay – the failure of a person or an institution to live up to the standards by which it is appropriately judged.

Corruptive influences may be of various sorts. Some may be directly related to the way in which judges conduct themselves in court. If, for example, a judge appears to act in a friendlier and more supportive way to witnesses for the prosecution than to witnesses for the defense (or vice versa), or overrules defense objections but not similar objections by the prosecution, that suggests corruption in the form of bias, whether the reasons for the bias be political, social or economic, religious, racial, gender-related, or any other.

Conduct related to court proceedings, but not specifically to the impartiality of the court and its officers, may also reflect on the integrity of the judiciary and so on its dignity and authority. If a judge comes unshaven and dishevelled to court, reads the paper or opens his mail during proceedings, nods off after lunch, speaks rudely and sarcastically to the parties, or "goes along with" overly aggressive or otherwise bad behavior by the various parties involved (whether police, prosecution, defense, or jury), he corrupts the court by flouting its traditional and expected rules of decorum, efficiency, and gamesmanship. The same goes for behavior that leads one to think that the court winks at or sanctions harassment via delays or other egregious but not necessarily illegal behavior; here too, the dignity of the court will be impaired and respect for the rule of law will be diminished.

There are other forms of behavior that reflect on the integrity of judges, though some of these are more closely associated with questions of competence. Competence is not itself an *ethical* requirement, though issues related to competence often have an ethical dimension. For example, judges who are notorious for dillydallying over decisions or written opinions, or who become careless, or who fail to acknowledge their growing forgetfulness, may no longer be sufficiently competent to continue to serve in their capacity as judicial decision-makers. Their persistence in their behavior or, if they no longer have control over it, their refusal to leave the bench, is a mark not merely of loss of competence but, as well, of a failure of integrity.

So far we have focused on actions that are court-related. But out-of-court actions may be no less suggestive of bias or at least of improper influence, and therefore be undermining of authority. Consider the following.

Public pronouncements. Judges who make strong public pronouncements or who publish heavily slanted articles may generate questions about their capacity to be impartial in certain kinds of cases. Although judges should not be muzzled in public, they should exercise considerable care in how they present themselves lest they or the court be seen as biased. Sometimes, even past public pronouncements should be grounds for their seeking recusal from impending cases.[16]

Financial disclosure. Although US judges are required to satisfy financial disclosure regulations, it can be very difficult (supposedly for security reasons) for interested parties to obtain such information, and therefore difficult to determine whether conflicts of interest lurk beneath the surface of a judge's decision-making. (Sometimes the secrecy that surrounds financial disclosure statements appears to outstrip security needs.)

Perks of office. "Educational" seminars – "junkets for judges" – that are sponsored by ideological organizations and law firms, but which may be little more than occasions for wining and dining at fancy resorts, can raise eyebrows if not questions about "influence." Like pharmaceutical dinners for physicians, they easily leave the impression that professional judgments will be affected in an inappropriate manner.

Social connections. If judges are known to fraternize with business people whose companies are frequently involved in litigation or with those known to have significant criminal records or associations, suspicions about integrity and impartiality may be created. To be sure, it is sometimes difficult to walk the line between immersing oneself in the larger world of which one needs to be aware and to which, ultimately, one must answer, and engaging in social activities that will lead to apparent (or actual) conflicts of interest. We do not want judicial recluses, but neither do we want a judiciary fraught with conflict-of-interest problems.

Private conduct. Where private conduct calls into question the wisdom or competence of the actor's public judgment, authority may be eroded. After the breakdown of an intimate relationship, the (then) Chief Judge of New York State began harassing his former lover and threatened to kidnap her daughter.[17] Quite apart from being criminal, such behavior called into question the judgment of a person who, till then, had been considered a brilliant judge. Even though *he* may have been able to compartmentalize his personal problems so that his judicial role was performed without their

---

[16] This is one reason why appointments to the US Supreme Court have become so fraught in recent years. A candidate's previous pronouncements are relentlessly scrutinized for evidence of certain kinds of ideological or other bias that might provide some ground for disqualification.

[17] See Linda Wolfe, *Double Life: The Shattering Affair Between Chief Judge Sol Wachtler and Socialite Joy Silverman* (New York: Pocket Books, 1994).

corrosive interference, his judicial stature was nonetheless greatly diminished by the events. And when an Australian politician (falsely) suggested that a High Court judge trawled the streets for young male prostitutes using his official car, the integrity of the judge, and thus his authority and with it the authority of the office, was called into question.[18] Or, to take a case that is more likely to occur, what if a judge is pulled over and charged with reckless driving or driving under the influence of alcohol? Not only is the judge's integrity called into question, but the judge's lapse – particularly if replicated – may be thought to reflect poorly on the court in general (as unable to police its own members).

These latter examples are not meant to suggest that out-of-court behavior must be illegal in order for it to demean the judicial office. Even small things like the inappropriate use of the official letterhead, or the use of office facilities or perks such as an official car for personal purposes, may detract from the respect that judicial officeholders seek to preserve as they uphold the "majesty of law."

As should be clear by now, judicial integrity may be compromised in many ways, large and small, and by different actions in different contexts. In addition to the ways that we have already discussed and alluded to, questions of judicial integrity may be raised by what appears to some to be insensitivity to the very people who are most affected by the decisions that judges make, an insensitivity exacerbated by the fact of a class difference between many (perhaps most) judges and a large majority of those who come before them as defendants. Such insensitivity as there is may be additionally fostered by the very different social circles which judges inhabit relative, generally speaking, to those charged with criminal activity. The quandary, of course, is that while, on the one hand, we expect judges to exercise care about their social contacts, on the other hand, if they limit their contacts too narrowly, a large comprehension gap may develop between them and the world of those they are expected to judge. If the gap is great enough, confidence in the judiciary as an agency of unqualified justice may be eroded, for what appears to be just from the perspective of someone deeply immersed in legal arcana may look very different from the perspective of an "outsider." (Juries,

---

[18] *Hansard*, March 12, 2002 <www.aph.gov.au/hansard/senate/dailys/ds120302.pdf>. A record of some of the repercussions can be found at <www.cpa.org.au/garchve5/1084kirb.html>.

on the other hand, may be both more aware of and also more sensitive to the thinking and feeling of "the general public.") We see some evidence of social distance between members of the judiciary and "the common man" in the US Supreme Court case, *Herrera v. Collins*.[19] Leonel Herrera had been convicted of killing a police officer (two, in fact) ten years previously and was now seeking to present affidavits to the effect that it was his (deceased) brother who had done the killings. Justice Scalia took the view that a person who had "received, though to no avail, all the [judicial] process that our society has traditionally deemed adequate," had *ipso facto* been treated justly, and that there was therefore no reason to set aside a decision on the basis of a claim of factual innocence. He noted that provision for executive clemency was available in such cases. The courts, he considered, should be required to do no more: "If the system that has been in place for 200 years (and remains widely approved) 'shocks' the dissenters' consciences . . . perhaps they should doubt the calibration of their consciences, or, better still, the usefulness of 'conscience shocking' as a legal test." Herrera's contention was probably bogus. But there is something disconcerting (indeed, out of touch) about the view that, as long as the processes have been properly followed, evidence of factual innocence is irrelevant. In the mind of many, what, indeed, *is* justice if it is not the acquittal of the innocent? Apart from our increasing familiarity with cases in which the processes have been properly followed but in which, say, DNA evidence has subsequently established innocence, the insensitivity displayed by Scalia's view might be taken to reflect a willful and disdainful insularity, and to that extent a reflection of diminished integrity.

Even more troubling challenges to integrity than most of those already mentioned (and also to independence and impartiality) come from the mechanisms of judicial appointment and reappointment. In the United States, this process has sometimes become so highly politicized that judicial decision-making often appears to be more about "having the numbers" than the quality of argument. Wrangles over Supreme Court appointments have been distasteful and destructive, weakening the authority of the Court. But the problems extend to lower courts as well. As we have already noted, many state and local judges are elected, and that requires campaigning, financial contributions, and even a parading of "values" in order to secure the support of particular constituencies. Not that appointing judges offers an

---

[19] *Herrera v. Collins*, 506 US 390, at 428–9 (1993).

adequate alternative, for that can also reflect strong ideological preferences. Bipartisan review may go some of the way toward the avoidance of "extremist" appointments, but even that can be circumvented – as it was when two federal appeals court judges were appointed during a congressional recess in early 2004.[20]

What we see, then, is an intertwining of independence, impartiality, and integrity. In classical images, judicial authority is represented by the Roman goddess, Justitia. In one hand she holds aloft the scales of justice whose empty pans, in equipoise to show the absence of bias, are ready to weigh the competing claims of those who come before her. In the other hand, she carries a sword to represent the power of the state that enforces her judgments. In many representations she is also blindfolded, to show that she is "no respecter" of the persons who come before her – whether rich or poor, high- or low-born. Her impartiality is fostered by her independence and her authority is sustained by her integrity.

Judicial accountability

Juvenal famously asked: "But who is to watch the watchers?"[21] The courts are the watchers, but who watches over them? To whom are they accountable?

Let us first take a look at the idea of accountability. We are inclined to think of it as a type of social audit in which officeholders are expected to answer for their actions, showing how they were justified. That is indeed a dimension of accountability, but within a professional context – such as that of the judiciary – it is a secondary one. Professional accountability is most directly an individual and communal activity, whereby the members of a profession personally and collectively hold *themselves* to account for how they perform their role. Their holding themselves to account is shown in their individual and collective commitment to the standards that are implicit in their role. In the professions generally and the judiciary in particular,

---

[20] William Pryor and Charles Pickering, both of whom had been strongly opposed for their alleged partisanship. Although recess appointments are authorized by Article II, Section 2, of the US Constitution, they were originally intended to avoid unnecessary delays in filling vacancies (at a time at which the Senate met less frequently). But they have now become "back doors" for the appointment of those whose confirmations face significant opposition. They thus serve to erode the separation of powers.

[21] "Sed quis custodet ipsos custodes?" *Satires*, VI, line 292.

we expect there to be a culture of accountability in which those who are initiated into judicial office are at the same time inducted into a community or professional environment marked by a vital concern for the values that underlie and justify it.

Of course, personal accountability for one's professional actions is not, nor should it be, the only accountability that is relevant, or expected. Because the role of the judiciary is one of public service (even though judges are not strictly public servants), those in a judicial role are concerned with meeting a public need, and this means that they will *see themselves* as answerable not only to each other directly but also indirectly – via the rule of law – to the broader public that authorizes the institutions of civil society.

To the extent that a judicial culture is one of professionalism, recourse to indirect mechanisms for accountability will be minimal. Various self-policing strategies will tend to operate. Either judges will voluntarily recuse themselves when they perceive a conflict of interest (or when appropriately challenged) or, if they refuse to do so, a petition for mandamus (mandatory recusal or disqualification) may be successful. So in the end the judiciary is counted upon, for the most part, to ensure its own professionalism. Some judiciaries have disciplinary boards or other internal mechanisms for reviewing the conduct of judges.

To a considerable extent, this is probably how it should be, though where judges are elected there will obviously be a regular public opportunity to hold judges accountable. The real problem is to develop effective mechanisms of accountability that do not compromise legitimate judicial independence. That is most likely to occur when the workings of the judiciary are transparent. If, for example, there is a complaint mechanism, it may work best if, after complaints are reviewed and dealt with internally, their dispositions are recorded in suitably detailed annual reports. Open courts and written opinions also constitute transparent means whereby independence can be sustained and accountability served, though there is probably an argument for a more extensive use of written and other records of judicial proceedings.

Obviously judges cannot be shielded from the criminal law should their behavior warrant its attention, and there probably should be some provision for the rare impeachment of judges and their removal by a legislature. However, impeachment can be politically motivated. What is more important is that the various forms of incivility, incompetence, disproportionality, procrastination, and bias that sometimes infest the lower courts and bring the judiciary into disrepute should be taken seriously enough by the courts themselves to be dealt with effectively so that confidence is restored. It should be sufficiently in the interests of the courts to ensure their independence that they effectively address their own problems and remove pressures for external oversight.

Prophylactic solutions that require educational programs, selection of judges according to merit, review of judicial performance with quality ratings, and so on, may go some way toward preventing some problems and lowering the number of others. But they are by no means foolproof. Geoffrey Miller has suggested a strategy that would identify and respond to bad judges without the problems generated by external review. In brief, he proposes that a court administrator randomly select a panel of three or five judges (depending on the number of judges required by a particular court), from which the attorneys on each side will be allowed to privately eliminate one.[22] Over time such a system would result in the development of a profile of professional satisfaction with judges that would then form the basis for internal judicial review. Naturally, the actual procedure would have to be more complex than this; its main benefit, though, would be its responsiveness to the demand for judicial accountability without the sacrifice of judicial independence.

In transitional societies, however, stronger and more intrusive measures for judicial assessment and oversight may be required. In those societies, the judiciary may need the presence of external oversight mechanisms until it is able to create and perpetuate its own culture of impartially administering the law. What will be critical to such mechanisms is that they are governed by a sunset clause requiring their periodic review and reaffirmation (or lapse) and that they are crafted to foster and sustain professional accountability, not stifle it.

[22] Miller, "Bad Judges," Section III, 482–7.

10 Juries: the lamp of liberty?

No tyrant could afford to leave a subject's freedom in the hands of twelve of his countrymen. So that trial by jury is more than an instrument of justice . . . it is the lamp that shows that freedom lives.[1]

The jury is an ancient institution. It was, after all, a jury that in 399 BCE (by a vote of 281 out of 501) sentenced Socrates to death for corrupting the youth of Athens. But even the "modern" jury pre-dates the emergence of the liberal democratic societies with which we now associate it. After the Norman invasion of England in 1066 CE, a system of grand and petit juries that Charlemagne had developed in eighth-century France was introduced to Britain. In 1215, the English Magna Carta – a formative document for democratic polities – provided for jury trials by peers, and it was about that time that the determination of guilt became the jury's primary role. In early juries, jurors were usually familiar with defendants; it was not till relatively recent times that such familiarity would serve to disqualify a person from participation. By the time of the American Revolution, the jury had arrived at pretty much its present form – though, as the revolutionaries complained, jury trials were frequently corrupted or circumvented by those in power. After the New World colonists broke from the distant and centralized power of England, the "American experiment" accorded to jury trial a much greater symbolic and practical role than was found in its countries of origin. Today, even though the jury trial has been overwhelmingly displaced by plea agreements, its iconic status remains and the ever-present prospect of a trial still influences the process of plea-bargaining.

When the Bill of Rights was appended to the US Constitution (and ratified in 1791), it included a guarantee that, "in all criminal prosecutions, the accused shall enjoy a right to a . . . trial, by an impartial jury of the State

---

[1] Lord Devlin, *Trial by Jury* (London: Methuen, 1956), 164.

and district wherein the crime shall have been committed, which district shall have been previously ascertained by law."[2] This federal provision was formally extended to all state criminal trials in 1968.[3]

The precise wording of the sixth amendment was vigorously debated at the beginning, and its elements have remained the subject of ongoing discussion. A key concern has been the apparent tension between the requirement, on the one hand, that the jury be impartial and, on the other, that it be drawn from the district in which the crime was committed. One might well imagine that, depending on the circumstances of the case, jurors drawn from the vicinity of the crime would be partial to either the perpetrator or the victim. In our contemporary world, characterized as it is by aggressive and often emotional media coverage, it has sometimes seemed impossible to put together an impartial local jury, and trials have needed to be moved to more remote venues. This was the case when Timothy McVeigh was tried for the 1995 bombing of the federal building in Oklahoma City. But the original purpose of the local jury requirement was not to create problems for impartiality. It was, rather, to register the importance of local knowledge for competent decision-making, to reflect a shared understanding of the law, and to protect defendants against prosecutorial tyranny. There was, in other words, a deeply democratic intent to the geographical provision of the sixth amendment.

Although there is wide support for the requirement that those who go to trial for their alleged crimes have the right to have their fate determined by an impartial jury, a great deal of controversy has surrounded its application. Here the presumption that competent local knowledge will operate becomes problematic. What if the perpetrator or victim is not local? More seriously, how do we ensure that, by the time a trial is called, jurors will not have been exposed to opinions about the crime that taint their objectivity? Should we expect jurors to be completely ignorant of the case? Should we presume that any and all knowledge that they have will be tainted? Or, if they have been exposed to reports, are we justified in thinking that they will not be able to set aside whatever opinions about the case they may have encountered or even formed? If we expect jurors to have minimal knowledge of the case, might we not then be forced to favor as jurors those who take only a minimal interest in what goes on around them? These questions are not just

---

[2] US Constitution, sixth amendment.   [3] *Duncan v. Louisiana*, 391 US 145 (1968).

rhetorical; they identify a range of concerns that arise even as jury pools are being increasingly widened and deepened. What we hope for, of course, are people who are concerned with truth and justice and who will come with open (but not empty) minds, and who will be willing to allow their judgment to be determined by the facts presented at trial.

So, then, how do we account for the persistence and shape of jury trials within a broadly liberal democratic framework? What powers and responsibilities do jurors have? And who should serve on them? These are the broad questions that will occupy us for the remainder of this chapter.

Jury foundations

Despite his influence on the justificatory framework for liberal democratic polities, juries do not figure in Locke's account of the institutions necessary for the adequate functioning of society. It is the judiciary to which he gives the task of interpreting and applying the law, and it is not unreasonable to think that judges are better trained to make the kinds of decisions that jurors are expected to make. So, does the jury represent anything more than a historical hangover, a residue of anticolonial feeling, or a symbolic reminder of past tyranny?

But even though juries do not figure in Locke's discussion, it is possible to interpret their carryover into liberal democratic polities in a way that reflects liberal democratic concerns.[4] As we have already claimed, underlying the Lockean "social contract" is the idea that each person has a right to determine the conditions under which his or her life is to be lived, subject, of course, to others being able to make similar determinations with respect to their own lives. Civil society is viewed as a strategic (and morally sensitive) attempt to implement this foundational understanding. Now, it is at least arguable that this consensual strategy anticipates that each person will have some input into an understanding of the various conditions necessary for an orderly social life – that is, into the formation, application, and enforcement of social rules. Such an expectation, however, if taken literally, would be much too strenuous and difficult for every individual to manage. And so, instead of having a fully participatory political and legal

[4] Though juries, where used, tend to operate differently and in different ways in European courts.

order, we would settle for a representative one in which we choose those who will act on our behalf. But because the resulting system is imperfect – even those whom we choose to represent us will fail – we utilize various instruments that we hope will minimize or counteract its imperfections. Jury trials can be construed as one of those instruments. Instead of having a single detached judge (often socially remote from those who are being judged) determine how a particular law is to be interpreted and applied in a particular place and set of circumstances, the process of decision-making employed is one that places important determinations back into the hands of the people who – in social contract theory – are the ultimate agents of the conditions of their social life. The point of having a plurality of jurors is that through their deliberative engagement with one another they will be enabled to come to a decision that better expresses the understanding and will of those whose system it ultimately is than would be the case were such determinations left entirely in the hands of judges. Having experienced the rulings of "monarchical" judges, the fathers of the American tradition were not so sanguine about judges as to think that they would naturally be "oracles of the law" rather than proponents of particular ideologies and policies, and often associated too closely with the political powers of the time. And so an ancient institution was taken over and reclothed in liberal democratic garb, often to be spoken of as the "palladium of liberty."[5]

But there was another dimension to jury decision-making in the emerging republic that also contributed to the symbolic significance that jury decision-making has come to have. The jury came to be viewed as a site for training in and the exercise of civic virtue. In his classic nineteenth-century report on American society, Alexis de Tocqueville put it thus:

> The jury invests each citizen with a kind of magistracy; it makes them all feel the duties which they are bound to discharge towards society and the part which they take in its government. By obliging men to turn their attention to other affairs than their own, it rubs off that private selfishness which is the rust of society.[6]

[5] The phrase, though not in exactly that form, goes back at least to William Blackstone's *Commentaries on the Laws of England* (1765–9; repr. Boston: Beacon Press, 1962), Book 4, ch. 27.

[6] Alexis de Tocqueville, *Democracy in America* (1833), trans. Phillips Bradley (New York: Vintage, 1945), vol. I, 295.

But Tocqueville's characterization of the "magistracy" with which the jury invests "each citizen" is misleading if read through twenty-first-century eyes. For early juries in the United States consisted exclusively of white male owners of property. African Americans began to be included from about 1860 in some states, although – until the 1960s – African Americans were routinely excluded from Southern jury pools by administrative fiat. Women were sometimes included from about 1898. But even less than fifty years ago discrimination was often perpetuated through the use of blue-ribbon juries and jury lists that disqualified daily-wage-earners or were skewed to favor white males. Until recently, eligibility lists were also restricted in other ways – for example, they included only registered voters, thus disproportionately omitting the young, Hispanics, Native Americans, and those of low socioeconomic status. Lately, though, this has changed. Most US jury lists are created from several sources – for example, from holders of drivers' licenses, utilities' customers, telephone directories, tax rolls, public assistance rosters. Moreover, in many places "routine" exemptions (of lawyers, doctors, teachers, undertakers, and so forth) have been eliminated. There are still some exclusions – those deemed mentally ill or of poor character by virtue of a criminal conviction are still disqualified (though rules regarding some of these disqualifications vary greatly from state to state, and in some countries those convicted of crimes are only temporarily excluded).

Jury powers and responsibilities

On the surface, the jury's task is relatively simple: it is to determine whether or not the person is "guilty." However, that characterization of the jury's task conceals a major shift that has occurred over the past two centuries – in both the United States and elsewhere – in the jury's formal role. Juries were originally empowered to interpret the law as well as to act as fact-finders. But at least since 1895 in the United States they have been expected to confine their determinations to *factual* matters and to yield their understanding of the *law* to judges.[7] In most contemporary courts, this limited role of the jury is made quite unequivocally and jurors are expected to commit themselves explicitly to an acceptance of the judge's interpretive role.

---

[7] See *Sparf and Hansen* v. *US*, 156 US 51 (1895).

One reason for making an issue of this lies in the fact that although the judge has formal responsibility for interpreting the law, the jury retains an indefeasible *practical power* to nullify it – that is, not to follow the law as officially interpreted. Later judicial decisions have made it clear that juries that take matters of *law* into their hands have neither a (legal) *right* nor a *privilege* but only a *power* to do so. A potential juror who exhibits an awareness of this power is likely to be considered a loose cannon, and will probably be excused.[8]

Jury nullification entered the criminal courts in 1670 in London, when the Quaker William Penn, along with an associate, William Mead, held a peaceful worship service in a London street. He was charged with disturbing the peace (though it was really because his religious position did not have official sanction), but the jury – recognizing what was going on – refused to convict. In retaliation, the jurors were fined for their refusal to obey the direction of the court to convict. The charges that were brought against Penn and Mead reflected governmental tyranny and judicial collusion, and provided stark evidence of the value of jury trials as well as a vivid example of the kind of occasion for which jury nullification might be deemed ethically appropriate. The bench's attempt to confine the jury to matters of fact also showed how interrelated matters of fact and law could be. Fining the jurors for making their own judgment magnified that wrong by "depriving" them of their voice regarding the justice of a law, its application, or its consequences in a particular case.

The classic American case involved Peter Zenger, publisher of *The New York Journal*, who – in 1735 – was charged with committing seditious libel because he had printed articles critical of the British colonial government. Because the judge had ruled as a matter of law that the articles were libellous, the jurors' only task, it would have appeared, was to determine whether Zenger had in fact printed them. But the colonists' antipathy toward the British politicization of the law prompted the jury to acquit Zenger. Although American history books celebrate this as a triumph of press freedom, it also involved a jury "taking the law into its own hands." In doing so, however, the Zenger jury did not abandon the rule of law. Rather, it rejected an understanding of the rule of law as being simply a mechanical application

---

[8] The problem for the courts is exacerbated by the fact that there are some activist groups that foster an awareness of this power and probably encourage its more frequent use.

of statutes or unquestioning acceptance of a judicial interpretive directive, and saw itself as an agent of justice.

But jury nullification is a double-edged sword, despite the potential that it has for countering government oppression. As an uncheckable power, it can also be made into a vehicle of injustice. Such has been notoriously the case in the long struggle that the United States has had with racial prejudice: Southern juries often refused to convict whites charged with killing blacks despite overwhelming evidence to the contrary. Moreover, in the interests of upholding tough law enforcement, especially with regard to those seen as the "criminal classes," nullification has also been used to exonerate police officers patently guilty of using excessive force.

There are in addition theoretical problems with jury nullification. My foregoing comments on the Zenger jury notwithstanding, the "rule of law, not men," a pillar of liberal democratic order, arguably requires that social life be regulated by means of previously determined and transparent procedures, and, further, that procedures for determining and applying the law be stated in advance. The rule of law is intended to exclude the arbitrary judgments of a single individual (or group). Jury nullification appears to fly in the face of the view that, if we do not like the way things are done, change ought to be brought about through established (that is, legislative) procedures. The unappealable "right" of a jury (or juror) to make legal (as against factual) determinations seems to leave it unclear (though not usually punitively so) how a person might order his life to conform to the law; it would, moreover, also litter the judicial landscape with decisions that lack precedential value.

And yet, like civil disobedience, with which it is frequently compared, jury nullification may also appear to be a morally necessary option in a less than perfect world. Even in democratic societies, legislative power can be used to enforce the morally suspect interests of a particular group of people, or particular laws may be too coarse to exclude from their purview certain actions that should be permissible, or the sanctions attached to certain breaches may be unconscionable. The problem is to keep the jury's nullification power from getting out of hand. In the case of civil disobedience, it is usually accepted as the price of conscientious disobedience that those who disobey will or should be willing to suffer the consequences of their disobedience. That will give pause to those contemplating it, as they weigh the cause against the costs. But there are no sanctions against jurors who nullify. True, jury nullification (in practice) imposes no legal sanction and that no doubt diminishes its social and institutional costs. Nevertheless, when the nullification option has been used in prejudicial ways (as in the acquittals of Ku Klux Klansmen), its effects have been grossly demeaning and unfair to the immediate victims, to their loved ones, and to the groups from which they were drawn.

In point of fact it is now rare for juries consciously to disregard judges' instructions and to acquit those who are unmistakably guilty. For the most part, the power to nullify is a power that is conscientiously exercised. This has led to the suggestion that in some cases – such as those in which horribly brutalized women have killed their abusive husbands but cannot claim self-defense or provocation – jurors be given nullification instructions that explicitly permit them to acquit in order to avert injustice. But others have condemned such license, arguing that it opens the door to jury arbitrariness and caprice. In the words of one appeals court, when it rejected the request of a defendant in a Vietnam War protest case that jurors be told explicitly that they had no obligation to follow the law: "What makes for health as an occasional medicine would be disastrous as a daily diet . . . An explicit instruction to the jury [of their right to set laws aside] conveys an implied approval [of such a practice] that runs the risk of degrading the legal structure."[9] It is likely that the status quo that permits jurors to nullify without telling them that they can do so will continue indefinitely.

The nullification option is further complicated by the fact that even if, as Locke claimed, we accept that the (moral) law of nature is clearly "discernible to the eye of reason," the criminal law in complex industrial and postindustrial societies is often not transparent to the lay person. In addition, fact patterns may be exceedingly complex, demanding a great deal of those who must make sense of them. These considerations may be taken to strengthen the argument for a division of labor that allocates to judges the responsibility for determining applicable law and interpreting it and that burdens the jury with no more than responsibility for judging the unique factual situation of the case before it. It is not simply that the criminal law in industrial and postindustrial societies has become increasingly complex,

---

[9] *US* v. *Dougherty*, 473 F. 2d 1113 (D.C. Cir., 1972). The argument is somewhat specious, because it was not claimed that juries should be told of their power to nullify "as a daily diet."

but also that the Lockean "eye of reason" no longer possesses its original argumentative appeal. In a homogeneous community one might presume that reasonable people would have a shared perception of right and wrong. In diverse modern societies it is questionable whether moral perceptions are shared. What we find is that the contours of criminal law result from social compromise as much as from any "natural law." Although criminal law has not completely abandoned its moorings in moral judgment, the high seas of diversity have left its determinations increasingly in the hands of experts. We may not like that, but it is something with which we have had to come to terms.

That said, the division of labor between judge and jury is not altogether helpful to the practice or significance of the jury trial. Just because criminal jurors are called to pronounce on questions of *guilt*, it is important that they see themselves as engaging with the substance of the law and not simply with neutral determinations of fact. Even though they are triers of fact, their task is ultimately a normative one, and any suggestion that they are merely passive appliers of law puts them in a morally impossible situation. They are judges not of neutral facts but of criminality. Now, we can probably pursue a practical middle path. If the division of labor is seen as strategic – that is, one that for reasons of practicality rather than principle gives primary responsibility for matters of law to the judge and for matters of fact to the jury – jurors will not be prevented from appreciating the normative and moral dimensions of their task and even, in rare instances, from legitimately exercising a nullifying or, as it might better be seen, a "merciful" power.

Indeed, empirical studies have demonstrated rather convincingly that jurors' reliance on their own values is far more subtle than the purposeful abandonment of the law involved in radical jury nullification.[10] Although most jurors make sincere attempts to follow the law and base their verdicts on evidence, sometimes legal ambiguity and factual uncertainty give them sufficient opportunity to incorporate personal sentiment into their exercising of conscientious judgment. The adversary process itself, with its presentation of opposing arguments and evidence, permits the jury such leeway. There is almost always some fragment of evidence, some line of argument or legal definition, that will enable jurors to justify the outcome

[10] Norman J. Finkel, *Commonsense Justice: Jurors' Notions of the Law* (Cambridge, MA: Harvard University Press), 1995.

they consider to be preferable. People can see the same facts differently and draw different inferences from the same information. Thus jurors who desire acquittal can take a "merciful view of the facts,"[11] and those wanting conviction can look at much the same facts vindictively.

The O. J. Simpson case was a striking example of this phenomenon. Although a majority of Americans who followed the televised trial thought that the sportscaster and former football star was guilty of murdering his wife and her friend, the jury that acquitted him thought otherwise. Many critics of the verdict claimed that the predominantly black jury showed favoritism toward a black hero. As *New York Times* columnist Maureen Dowd put it: "Mr. Simpson's jury in the criminal trial had plenty of evidence, but made a decision based on race."[12] But the jurors themselves disavowed such a contention, claiming that the police investigation was muddled, that the evidence was inconclusive, and that the forensic experts were divided. As one of them emphatically defended the verdict: "I was brought up to love everyone. I'm not for anyone, yellow, black, blue, green. I'm just for justice . . . We were fair. It wasn't a matter of sympathy. It wasn't a matter of favoritism. It was a matter of evidence."[13]

Composition and deliberation

Although the criminal jury is a political institution, its *modus operandi* is deliberative rather than political. Its function is to determine the facts of a criminal matter before the court. Jurors are to come with their understanding of the facts presented at trial and, through a process of reflective interchange, seek to arrive at some agreement about whether or not the defendant is guilty as charged (or sometimes, guilty of some lesser offense available to them).

Although the role of the jury is to determine the facts, it can be subverted in a number of ways – some of which relate to the jury's composition, and others of which relate to the deliberative process.

---

[11] Patrick Devlin, "Morals and the Criminal Law," in *The Enforcement of Morals* (London: Oxford University Press, 1965), 21.

[12] Maureen Dowd, "The Sound and the Fury," *New York Times*, November 21, 1996, A29.

[13] Whether or not we agree, we should accept that this, at least, was how they understood it. Lorraine Adams, "Simpson Jurors Cite Weak Case, Not Race," *The Washington Post*, October 5, 1995, A1, A26.

We have already noted how, in times past, jury pools were often skewed in race, class, and gender terms. But even if the jury pool is broadened to reflect the local community, it can still be distorted in other ways. The jury selection process is a case in point. In Chapter 7, we discussed the longstanding practice known as peremptory challenge, whereby potential jurors can be ruled out for no articulated reason. This has often been used to exclude jurors who are thought to be unfriendly to a particular outcome. Peremptory challenges have an honorable intention: it is thought that those with interests at stake (particularly defendants) ought to have some say in determining those who make the judgment, and that leaving such decisions in the hands of a single, fallible judge would not be sufficient to secure those interests with any reliability. But it is just as likely, however, that they will be used to "stack the deck" with a jury that is questionably partial to the prosecution or the defense. Although use of the peremptory challenge has been curbed in recent years,[14] mainly to inhibit the exclusion of people on account of their race or gender, it remains a problematic entitlement. Some judges have called for its abandonment altogether – they have argued that race and gender can be brought in by the back door when rejecting potential jurors.

In addition to peremptory challenges and the questioning process that usually occurs prior to selection (voir dire), there has been an increasing use of jury consultants to "craft" juries that will underplay or overemphasize certain social factors considered to be relevant to the ways in which jurors will deliberate. A particularly dramatic example occurred in the 1991 trial of El Sayyid Nosair for the murder of Rabbi Meir Kahane. Kahane, a militant Zionist, had just completed a speech in a midtown Manhattan hotel when Nosair walked up, shot him, and ran off. After a running gun battle, Nosair was captured and charged. Jury consultants advised the defense lawyer to include as jurors people who would not only lack sympathy for Israel but also be open to claims about Nosair's marginalized social status. Anomalously, Nosair was acquitted of murder, though not of the lesser charge of illegal gun possession. Because the adversary system encourages both the defense and prosecuting lawyers to do what they can for those they represent, zealous advocacy can be exploited to subvert fairness in the name of

---

[14] In the United States, see *Batson* v. *Kentucky*, 476 US 79 (1986) and a line of subsequent cases – e.g. *Powers* v. *Ohio*, 499 US 400 (1991); *Georgia* v. *McCollum*, 505 US 42 (1992).

victims' or defendants' rights. Not that jury consultants need be used to gain an unfair advantage. Prosecutors and defense lawyers owe it to those whom they represent to form a jury that will not be unfairly disposed to their clients. It is not clear, however, whether defense (or prosecution) attempts to make "scientific" selections succeed in sufficient numbers to make them worthwhile.[15]

Besides attempts to diminish the discriminatory use of peremptory challenges, other efforts to make the jury better fitted for its purpose have also been undertaken. Some of these can be criticized for losing sight of the theory that underlies a jury trial. Juror diversity ought not to be understood as a response to identity politics (or even as proportional representation) but rather as an expression of John Stuart Mill's contention that truth and our assurance of it are most likely (albeit not guaranteed) to be achieved when the available data are exposed to those with varying opinions and perspectives.[16] The purpose of jury decision-making is not democratic majoritarianism, but consensus or at least concurrence achieved after a situation has been scrutinized from a suitably diverse set of perspectives. The end is truth, not cross-sectional representation. Were it the latter, we would then have to worry about the representativeness of the representatives. We would have to worry whether, for example, a particular black or female juror would adequately represent the interests of the group from which he or she was drawn. It is, moreover, not easy to decide in advance what groups should be included: Should gay-bashing cases include homosexual jury members? Should jury selection in cases of violence against abortion clinics include both pro-choice and right-to-life supporters? And so forth. Only at its best will some form of cross-sectional representation increase the likelihood that in the search for truth salient dimensions of a situation will not be left out of account or excluded.

Nevertheless, behind the problematic idea of a demographically structured jury there lies a valid recognition that even if those who become jurors can be presumed to be free from certain kinds of disqualifying prejudice, they cannot be expected to shed all past beliefs, preconceptions, values, and ways of thinking. Moreover, they may suffer from certain kinds

---

[15] For one assessment, see Neil Kressel and Dorit F. Kressel, *Stack and Sway: The New Science of Jury Consulting* (New York: Perseus Books Group / Westview Press, 2002).

[16] John Stuart Mill, *On Liberty*, ch. 2.

of prejudicial ignorance. Prejudice varies greatly in its subtlety, and even those who have the best of intentions may be subtly but significantly influenced by, say, sexist or racist perspectives. Moreover, even though jurors may not be interest-group representatives, they are not blank sheets either. The deliberative ideal of juror engagement is that each will enrich and correct the others' perceptions in ways that will lead to a common or at least integrated understanding that might not have been available to them individually. Via their deliberative engagement, the truth of a matter is more likely to emerge than would have been the case had the decision been left to a single individual or determined through an interest-based poll.

As a matter of policy, however, that may not be the last word on this issue. If, despite attempts to ensure jury openness, actual practice suggests a persisting bias, quotas may appear to offer a pragmatic solution. When prosecution and defense both have an interest in a partisan jury, prejudice may veil itself in ways that are manifest only in aggregate outcomes. That, certainly, is the continuing danger posed by peremptory challenges, and is one of the factors that has led to calls for their abandonment.

The deliberative ideal that we have spelled out is just that – an ideal. Although jury research is forbidden in the United Kingdom, the secrecy that cloaks jury deliberations has been lifted to some degree in the United States.[17] Talk of "deliberation" conceals what is often a passionate and angry debate among jurors. It may involve name-calling, ganging up, gamesmanship, and compromise decisions. There are difficult questions about what constitutes going too far – presumably, what subverts the ideal of trial before an impartial jury. Jurors who vote a certain way because of threats made to them or whose decisions are determined by sources outside them (say, their pastors) subvert that ideal. But in many cases it may be difficult to distinguish robust debate from coercive tactics.[18]

---

[17] See Penny Darbyshire, Andy Maughan, and Angus Stewart, "What Can the English Legal System Learn from Jury Research Published up to 2001?" <www.kingston.ac.uk/~ku00596/elsres01.pdf>. See also Valerie P. Hans, "Jury Research Ethics and the Integrity of Jury Deliberations," in John Kleinig and James P. Levine (eds.), *Jury Ethics: Juror Conduct and Jury Dynamics* (Boulder, CO: Paradigm Publishers, 2006), 247–64.

[18] See Jeffrey Abramson, "Jury Deliberation: Fair and Foul," in Kleinig and Levine, *Jury Ethics*, 181–207.

At its best, trial by a local jury might be seen as an attempt to secure the consensual account of governmental power that underlies the liberal democratic tradition. Although those who pass the laws are elected representatives of the people, there is no guarantee that their legislative decisions will always reflect the nuanced understanding of those who elected them; furthermore, although judges are supposed to be impartial interpreters of law, there is no guarantee that they will always be sensitive to the ways in which local knowledge impacts on its interpretation and application. Determinations by a local jury have the potential for ensuring that the judgments of civil society are products of consensus rather than the pronouncements of an elite. As Alexander Hamilton put it, it is the task of jurors "to see with their own eyes, to hear with their own ears, and to make use of their own consciences and understandings in judging of the lives, liberties or estates of their fellow subjects."[19]

A jury also serves the more pragmatic purpose of diminishing the temptations for engaging in judicial misconduct. In many parts of the world, as we saw in Chapter 9, the potential for bribery and other perversions of justice remains strong despite the high ideals of judicial office, and judicial power is legitimately balanced by a jury of twelve rotating individuals. Of course, the benefits of this pragmatic corrective are at best only relative, as is made clear by the history of racial prejudice displayed by juries and occasional scandals of jury-tampering.

Size and unanimity

The desire to maximize the probability of reaching a correct assessment of the fact pattern has implications for two other questions, one concerning the size of a jury and the other concerning the kind of conclusion that it reaches (for example, whether or not it should be unanimous). There are probably no timelessly correct answers to these questions, though the development of jury practice has to some extent reflected the exigencies of the times.

We are accustomed to think of juries of twelve (fifteen in Scotland), though some US states have recently opted for juries of six, at least for

---

[19] James Alexander, *A Brief Narrative of the Case and Trial of John Peter Zenger*, ed. Stanley Nider Katz, 2nd edn. (Cambridge, MA: Harvard University Press, 1972), 93.

less serious criminal trials and for civil cases. Trials that might result in a death penalty have continued to require juries of twelve. Is there any magic to the number "twelve"? The legal cases that address the issue suggest that it was simply happenstance that arrived at the number twelve.[20] One might suspect, given the environment in which the modern jury developed, that it tapped into a certain Judaeo-Christian fondness for the number twelve.

There is probably no more magic to twelve than there is to the age of majority. It is a workable convenience that bears some reasonable relation to the purposes for which it is designed. Having been fixed upon, it then exercises its own influence on public consciousness. Just as recognition of eighteen as the age of majority has subsequently influenced the nurturing and educational process by providing a socially determinate "cut-off" point, so the need to have twelve persons agreeing on an outcome has provided a certain operational framing of our deliberative processes. Getting three people to agree is not the same as getting thirty people to agree. Getting twelve to agree has acquired a certain conventional weight or *gravitas*.

Fixing on a number to comprise a jury also influences the kind of rationale that might be presented. In a fairly diverse community, we might consider that twelve is a sufficiently large number to reflect that diversity in a relatively fair manner. (It would not, of course, be a sufficient number were we to insist on cross-sectional representation. But that political ideal of the jury should not be supported.) It is also large enough to enable us to draw reasonably firm conclusions about the existence of systematic bias when it occurs. If the number on the jury is twelve rather than six and we begin to observe a pattern whereby members of certain groups (and, along with that, an appropriate diversity of perspective) are being regularly excluded from jury service, it is easier to argue that this is due to bias rather than to bad luck.

Other factors may also be relevant to the likelihood that a jury's decision will represent a genuinely deliberative outcome. Having too many on a jury will make it difficult for all jurors to have a proper say. Having too few might deny a jury the insights that come from a plurality or diversity of initial perspectives. Although some who argue for smaller juries suggest that twelve makes it too easy to be a free-rider and increases the likelihood

---

[20] See the discussion in *Williams* v. *Florida*, 399 US 78 (1970); *Colgrove* v. *Battin*, 413 US 149 (1973).

of there being a holdout, it may be countered, on the one hand, that relative silence during deliberations cannot be equated with a lack of participation and, on the other, that the proportion of single holdouts is very small.

None of the arguments has "twelve" as its necessary conclusion, though together they make a reasonable case for the number being as it is. As has been the case with the age of majority, we might think that for certain cases a different cut-off would be acceptable. As we may allow consent to medical procedures at an earlier age, we may also think that a smaller jury is adequate for certain kinds of cases. In any event, the US Supreme Court has determined that six is the lower limit of jury size.[21]

What about unanimity? Once again, certain religious considerations may have originally influenced such a requirement. The "one mind" that was said to characterize the early church was seen in part as assurance that its mind was the mind of God, and those acting as his earthly agents might have sought similar assurance.

Although unanimity has been the dominant tradition, since the 1970s a number of US states (Louisiana and Oregon, for example) have qualified it. A similar easing took place at about the same time in England and Wales. And some Australian states have followed suit. Scotland allows a simple majority. For many cases some jurisdictions require only majority or super-majority decisions. A unanimity requirement has seemed costly and ineffi-cient. Drawn-out jury deliberations, hung juries, and, no doubt, unconvicted offenders have disposed some jurisdictions to loosen the requirement that a verdict be unanimous.[22] And even where the unanimity requirement has been formally observed, it has sometimes reflected a jury-room compromise in which, in order to secure a conviction, an offender has been dealt with more lightly than might otherwise have appeared to be warranted.

But even if one might want to make some concessions to less than unani-mous decision-making, there are strong reasons why we should pursue una-nimity as an ideal. If the point of a jury is to seek, through a deliberative process, an outcome that is sensitive to the diversity of considerations that might be brought to bear on the case – an outcome that might be said to have taken adequate cognizance of the various perspectives and understandings

---

[21] *Ballew v. Georgia*, 435 US 223 (1978).

[22] Broadening the jury pool might be thought to have increased the likelihood of unpro-ductive dissension.

of its members – then unanimity might reasonably be seen as the goal of, and expectation in, such deliberations. If the unanimity requirement is compromised there is a significant danger that jury decision-making will take on the character of political decision-making, with its members seeking to persuade one another to their side rather than focusing on the deliberative challenge posed by a diversity of understandings. A jury must attempt to give such diverse views their due weight in the process of arriving at a factual conclusion that is not predetermined by or merely reflective of interests. It is the fact of a jury trial that reflects liberal democratic values – an opportunity for those who are under law to participate in its determinations. But the jury process is directed to the establishment of certain factual conclusions – concerning guilt or innocence – and not merely to the representation of preexisting interests in a political process.

There is another factor of moment. The outcome of a decision to convict, particularly in a criminal trial, is the imposition of some penalty on a human being, and governmental authority for that needs strong justification. If a strong justification is not provided, the very purpose of a civil order – the preservation of a person's life, liberty, and projects – is subverted. Thus a high level of concurrence should be expected before the power to penalize is exercised. Although this may not require unanimity, it pushes in that direction.

In upholding less than unanimous decisions, it was Justice Lewis Powell's contention that the unanimity requirement forced juries into compromises that were unsatisfactory to all.[23] And no doubt that is one possibility. But not every compromise creates dissatisfaction (for reasonable people can agreeably disagree), and there is no more reason to seek a compromise that is unsatisfactory than to acquiesce in a hung jury. Compromises do not necessarily depart from an ideal of truth. For human behavior is sometimes too complex to fit neatly into the categories provided for it by law, and a compromise position may better reflect the awkwardness of fit than a majority decision would have. Although retrials may be costly and inconvenient, they can provide a socially acceptable option where matters of social importance are at stake.

No doubt the deliberative ideal of jury decision-making is sometimes breached – an outcome likely to be of greater media interest than its

---

[23] *Johnson* v. *Louisiana*, 406 US 356, at 377 (1972).

opposite – but this is not a sufficient reason for abandoning it. The expectation that twelve people, contributing their varied understandings and perspectives to a conversation in which they are expected to reach a consensus or at least a concurrence, affirms the seriousness of the responsibility they have as well as the fundamental commitments of a liberal democratic polity. Their goal is truth, not numbers. And each has standing as a rational being equal with others, respected and respecting.

As we noted early in this chapter, except in capital cases, trial by jury is a right rather than a requirement. It cannot be said to be essential to just decision-making, though its continued presence is an enduring symbol of self-government.

Part IV

Corrections

At this point we assume conviction and consider appropriate institutional responses. Although punishment is usually taken for granted as the appropriate institutional response and has generated a vast and sophisticated literature in its own right, we endeavor not only to introduce some of the central elements of that discussion, including the capital punishment debate, but also to raise for consideration some of the restorative justice challenges that have recently been made to the punishment paradigm. Again, the discussion is intended to be suggestive rather than definitive. Beyond that, we consider the form that punishment should take – focusing particularly on the recent heavy reliance on imprisonment. Although we question that reliance, we look at the ethical obligations of prison officers and society's larger obligations to ensure that those who go into prison not only have the opportunity to come out better but are also enabled to reestablish their place in society.

11   Punishment and its alternatives

> My object all sublime
> I shall achieve in time –
> To let the punishment fit the crime.[1]

A person who pleads guilty to or is convicted of a crime normally faces punishment. Should this be the case and, if so, why? Responding to these and some related questions will be our central concerns in this chapter. Of all the ethical issues in the criminal justice system, punishment – at least as a general response to wrongdoing – is the topic that is most thoroughly explored. But it is also riven by deep and persisting disagreements, disagreements that go to the heart of ethical theory. Although we will address some of them, many will have to be put to one side. There is an extensive and rich literature that can be consulted.[2] Our first stop will be to review the nature of punishment – what makes what one person imposes on another a punishment rather than, say, an assault, and how punishment differs from other, similar impositions. We will then briefly review some of the classical debates concerning its justification. And finally we will ask: Are there legitimate alternatives to punishment for crime?

What is punishment?

Although the primary context in which we will be discussing punishment is that of the criminal justice system, it is important to remember that punishment is not limited to and in fact preexists the criminal justice system. In fact, the various less formal contexts in which punishment is administered

---

[1] W. S. Gilbert and Arthur Sullivan, *The Mikado* (1885), Act II: "A More Humane Mikado."
[2] Some of this literature is indicated in the "Selected Further Reading" at the end of this volume.

(such as families and voluntary associations) provide a valuable framework for understanding its imposition in the context of criminal justice.

Punishment is first and foremost an imposition – a burden or hardship. Usually it is experienced as unpleasant, often as painful – though we are nowadays more likely to conceive of it as a deprivation (of certain rights) than as the infliction of pain. It is, moreover, deliberately imposed. Unlike quarantine, which interferes with us only contingently, the interference constituted by punishment is *intended* as a hardship. However, not every deliberately imposed burden is a punishment. Those who violate the rules of a game are (normally) penalized rather punished; and those who are taken into protective custody are not thereby punished. Although some would say that penalties are for actions whereas punishment is of persons, this is a difficult distinction to maintain with any consistency.

Unlike penalization, which is simply an imposition for a rule violation, punishment is *expressive* – it communicates censure or condemnation. It denounces what was done and to some degree stigmatizes the doer. That for which people are said to be appropriately punished reflects on their moral character, either on a persisting flaw that has issued in the condemned conduct or on a lapse that is expressive of weakness of will. We punish people for wrongdoing, where the wrongdoing involves some form of moral defect or discredit. Although this is the implication of punishment, the implication may sometimes be wrongly drawn. Nevertheless, those who punish rather than merely oppress must believe that what they are imposing is imposed *because of* wrongdoing.

It is the character of punishment as an imposition for wrongdoing that helps to explain why, in Chapter 2, we saw in *crime* a reference to some moral failure, and not merely a violation of rules. We are penalized for overparking or driving with an expired vehicle registration; such administrative penalties are not usually seen as punishment for crime because they are not thought of as involving moral dereliction. The crimes of theft and assault, on the other hand, are believed to involve moral wrongdoing.

Let us grant that punishment is imposed for moral wrongdoing (including crimes). The critical questions that now arise are: Does moral wrongdoing justify *punishment*? And, if so, why? These are the central and most contentious (though not the only) ethical questions confronting punishment. We will need to go on from there to consider the *authority* to punish, *legal* punishment, and also questions of *severity* and *form*. But because punishment involves an imposition on someone who normally has a right not to be imposed upon, the onus of justification in the central questions lies on those who would advocate its infliction.

Justifying punishment

In the vast literature on punishment it has been common to "take sides" in a debate between "consequentialists" and "retributivists" – that is, between those who seek to justify punishment by reference to certain benefits it is said to convey and those who seek to justify it by reference to the wrong-doing that occasions it. Or, as it is sometimes put, it concerns the relative importance of forward-looking and backward-looking considerations. Punishment, indeed, has often been used as the arena in which proponents of two approaches to ethical theory have sought to assert their claims to superiority. We shall largely sidestep those battles. Grand theory – and the choice that is often posed between consequentialism and deontology – is unlikely to be resolved (even if it may be illuminated) by such struggles. Moreover, it is probably unhelpful to cast the debate in these terms. On the one hand, a simple either/or approach conceals the complexity of the underlying issues. On the other hand, the seemingly simple dichotomy is not so simple. Let us expand briefly on each of these points.

Multiple questions

Some influential contributors to the debate on punishment have sought to distinguish two central justificatory questions, one relating to the general practice of punishment and the other to its imposition in particular cases. They have suggested that some form of consequentialist answer might be given to the former question (by suggesting, say, that the general practice might be justified in terms of social protection) whereas the latter should be answered in retributive terms (through its imposition only on wrong-doers).[3] When such writers refer to "the general practice," what they usually have in mind is legal punishment (and therefore the kinds of considerations that justify legal constraints). In line with this, others have argued that

---

[3] For a good example, see H. L. A. Hart, *Punishment and Responsibility* (London: Oxford University Press, 1968), ch. 1.

appropriate consequentialist ends (such as rehabilitation) are justifiably pursued only if punishment is retributively imposed, and that one should therefore not seek to play them off against each other. On this view, retributive considerations act as side constraints or limits on consequentialist ends in punishing. Yet others have suggested that whereas a retributive response might satisfactorily answer the central moral question, consequentialist considerations might well enter into determinations of the authority to punish. We may wish to restrict the authority to punish to those who can provide socially significant ends or purposes for imposing it.

Multiple options

Each of the so-called sides in the punishment debate comprises a variety of sometimes competing alternatives. For example, the consequences that are appealed to include general and/or specific deterrence (that is, the attempt to deter others from engaging in the punished conduct and/or the attempt to deter the punished person from repeating that conduct), reform, rehabilitation, or moral education, and incapacitation. These aims – though often put forward in the literature on punishment – need not be (and often are not) compatible. Deterrence, for example, may clash with rehabilitation. On the retributive side, it is sometimes said that punishment is a form of emphatic denunciation, a vindication of the law, or an expression of just deserts. Casting the debate, then, as one between consequentialism and retributivism (or, more generally, deontology) tends to obscure this complexity.

In seeking to address the central ethical issues of punishment, we do better by offering specific responses to specific questions. Let us begin, though, with the deepest and most difficult question: What justifies us in punitively imposing on people? Or, to characterize it slightly differently, but maybe more helpfully, if A wrongly imposes on B, what – if anything – then makes it morally permissible to impose on A? Isn't one wrong just being added to another?

Nearly all would agree that punishment is not justified *unless* some wrong (or, in the context of this study, crime) has been committed. That is, if punishment is justified, wrongdoing will be a necessary condition for it. The question is whether the wrongdoing can also be sufficient to justify punishment. I believe that a strong case can be made for thinking that the wrongdoing that is necessary if punishment is to be justified is also defeasibly sufficient to justify it. First, what is meant here by "defeasibly"? The idea is that wrongdoing is a *sufficient though not necessarily overriding reason* for imposing punishment. In claiming that wrongdoing is defeasibly sufficient, there is an acknowledgment that there may be countervailing reasons – such as the status of the punisher or considerations of mercy – that would make punishment inappropriate in a particular case.

That of course puts my response into what is commonly considered to be the retributivist camp, though what is more salient at this point of the argument is the particular account one gives of the "sufficiency" of the wrongdoing to justify punishment. A more specific account might be as follows: Wrongdoing (or crime) *deserves* punishment, or, even more precisely, those who do wrong deserve to be punished for their wrongdoing. Insofar as justice consists in people receiving what they deserve, then punishment will be seen as an expression of justice. Such just deserts are constituted by past conduct, not future outcomes. Punishment is deserved not because it will rehabilitate or deter, but because wrong has been done and it is argued to constitute an appropriate and (in general) proportionate response.[4] Those who are not believed to have done wrong cannot be punished (though they may be persecuted); the innocent can be punished only by mistake. What this means is that we have already embedded in our concept of punishment a reference to the kinds of considerations that not merely differentiate it from other impositions but also serve to justify it.[5]

Let us press the issue further. By virtue of what do wrongdoers deserve punishment? The answer that I wish to defend here is that punishment is deserved by wrongdoers because their wrongdoing involves a *moral* transgression. To see how this might be sufficient, it is helpful to remind ourselves again of the role that morality is accorded in human life. Put generally, what we construe as our moral obligations are those basic deliberative behaviors that inform our interactions with each other – whether we conceive of those interactions individually, collectively, or through the structures of our communal life. Morality is concerned with those interactions not simply in terms

---

[4] However, the issue of proportionality also goes to the matter of severity, and we will tackle that later as a discrete issue.

[5] That, of course, does not prevent someone from asking whether we are justified in conceptualizing punishment in this way, any more than, given certain beliefs that we may have about the existence of God, we are prevented from asking whether blasphemy, although conceptually characterized as an offense, is really wrong.

of the consequences they have for others but also and especially because of *what we are* in those interactions. That is, morality is also concerned with the reasons, motivations, and attitudes that we express in those interactions. It is concerned with the quality of our relationships and not simply with their externalities. This is one of the things that distinguishes morality from law. Legal rectitude is concerned primarily with externalities – more with the fact that what we do does not interfere with others' autonomy than with why we do not interfere with it.

It is through the structures of morality that we are able to flourish as human beings. The moral domain provides the relational context within which our lives come to express themselves in their multiple dimensions and through which we are recognized as objects of dignity, warranting the respect of others. One critical reason why this is so is that the development and sustenance of our human capacities are not "natural" in the sense that the development and sustenance of a tree are natural. We do not come into the world fully formed or with our persons narrowly fixed by our genetic endowments. Our formation as the persons we become and desire to be requires more than the presence of chemical nutrients (oxygen and food). Human growth is a *social* achievement, the outcome of a process of learning and nurture rather than the endpoint of some impersonal maturational or biological process. Not any kind of social or communal environment will do for this. Although humans are remarkably resilient, some social environments will be much more conducive to our flourishing than others. The substance of morality is constituted by those conditions (that is, those understandings and forms of interaction) that conduce to – and to some extent are constitutive of – our human flourishing. Some of these we consider important enough to secure through the criminalization of their breaches. Others we may leave to less formal or localized enforcement.

An understanding of morality such as this helps us to appreciate why moral dereliction is so significant – why, that is, wrongdoing deserves a response as serious as punishment. Punishment is conditionally called for as an index of the seriousness that we attach to moral breaches and, in the case of crimes, to the social importance we attach to certain of these breaches. Because much moral dereliction explicitly or implicitly challenges the moral equality of standing that we have with others and threatens to undermine the conditions for our individual and collective human flourishing, failure to act in a negative or critical manner when moral norms are breached displays a failure of regard for ourselves or others.

Having said that, it might be argued that more is still called for. For why, it might be asked, is it that the hard treatment of *punishment* is called for as an index of the seriousness with which we take morality? Why is it not sufficient to blame, reprove, or censure those who violate moral norms? A partial answer may be that the contingency of an offender's awareness of others' blame, reproof, or censure of his or her actions renders it questionable whether any of these would be adequate unless made known to him or her. But if they are made known to the offender, why should more be required? Why should we not simply confront a person with the seriousness of what he or she has done? The answer to this must also take into consideration the contingencies of our human condition. Sometimes, to be sure, it may be enough to denounce and censure: a person may be shamed, humbled, penitent, and desirous of making amends. But generally our human sensitivities are too dull, and our propensity for hypocrisy is too great, to appreciate the full measure of what we have done to others. What Locke saw as the deficiencies of the state of nature also affect our response to our own wrongdoing. Punishment – hard treatment – expresses and communicates the measure of what we have done (provided, of course, that it is proportionate to the offense).[6]

Those who accept the seriousness of what they have done will generally see punishment as a fitting response to it, whether or not it is actually inflicted. But for those who fail to see what they were accused of doing as unjustified (or who do not care that it was), there remains the possibility that the punishment may powerfully confront them with the evil of what they have done and thus bring them to remorse and repentance. Not that this is necessary to the punishment or even part of its justification. For punishment is not primarily appropriate for the corrigible and inappropriate for the incorrigible. With regard to the latter, punishment may still be justified as an emphatic statement of the seriousness with which we view what was done.

To argue in this fashion is not, of course, to approve of our current punishment practices. As we will see later in this chapter and in the next, there is still much to question in that regard. Nevertheless, the argument I

---

[6] In *The Philosophy of Right* (§ 220), Hegel mounts a similar argument in relation to legal punishment: if we do not punish those who violate the law we send a message that the law in question is of no great moment. If this failure occurs too frequently, the authority of law as a whole will be undermined.

have offered attempts to account for the widespread intuition that punishment represents a fitting response to wrongdoing.

The authority to punish

So far our discussion has focused on punishment primarily as a response to wrongdoing and has had only a passing concern with legal punishment – punishment for *crime*. Although our earlier discussion in Chapter 2 indicated why we might choose to label some kinds of wrongdoing as criminal and leave others to be dealt with in other ways, more needs to be said. In older debates, it was sometimes claimed that were punishment to be imposed simply for moral wrongdoing, only God would be in a position to mete it out, since only God would be capable of looking into the human heart. Now that may underestimate our ability to divine the intentions and motives of those who do wrong, even though it may often be difficult for us to do. But the claim that only God can punish wrongdoing does draw attention to a distinct question that is often left unaddressed in the literature: Who has the authority to punish? Might punishment be justified in certain cases but no one be in a position to impose it? Or, might punishment be justified but it not be for the state to impose it?

We can see the salience of such questions if we consider a situation in which, say, my child hits another person's child and a bystander who sees this happen then takes it upon himself to punish her. The punishment may have been deserved, but it may also be appropriate for me to say: "It was not for *you* to punish her, but for me." There are, as it were, jurisdictional issues involved as a result of my being her father and the other person having no special authority with regard to her. What, then, gives the state the right to punish rather than, say, the victim or the victim's friends?

One response that is implicit in our earlier discussion of liberal democratic theory starts from Locke's claim that the right of retaliation (that is, the right to punish) is not safely left in the hands of individuals, including victims. Particularly in the case of the latter, as we know from vengeance and vendettas, feelings may run too high for a measured response. Through its criminal justice processes, the state thus assumes responsibility for ensuring that, with respect to wrongdoing that possesses public significance (crime), it will act appropriately and proportionately. The state's institutions are supposed to be crafted in such a way that they secure basic rights, that just (deserved) responses are made to violations of those rights, and that, within that framework, they will also minimize future violations through processes of deterrence, rehabilitation and, if necessary, incapacitation. Social institutions are justified partly in terms of advantages accruing to those affected by them, and it is here, at the level of institutionalized punishment, rather than at the level of its basic justification, that various consequentialist considerations come into play.

The state's authority to punish, then, rests on the twin considerations of the public character of criminal wrongdoing and the ability of its punitive practices to serve appropriate state functions. At least, that is the theory.

Quantifying punishment

We are taken some of the way through the thicket of moral issues posed by punishment once we have provided an account of its basic justification and have supported its institutionalized expressions. But we are still left with the immensely difficult question of "How much?" How do we determine the severity of deserved punishment?

Some writers who have endeavored to answer the basic justificatory question by reference to deserts have then gone on to suggest that we can appeal to consequentialist considerations for determining quantity – punishment calibrated to considerations of deterrence or rehabilitation or incapacitation. But this hybridization – or at least this way of creating it – is almost certainly inappropriate, for it ignores the proportionality implicit in the central claim: It is not simply that punishment must be justly deserved; so also must its severity. If a person's punishment is justly deserved, but its quantum is then determined by reference to its deterrent or rehabilitative value, its moral acceptability will be at best coincidental. What is just as likely is that what is required by considerations of, say, deterrence will be excessive in terms of deserts, and a deserved punishment will no longer be so. Desert should figure not only in determinations of eligibility but also in determinations of quantity.

But how should such deserts be determined? Here we confront some of the most difficult questions in punishment theory. There are (at least) two issues here, commonly spoken of as ordinal and cardinal. The ordinal one concerns the ranking of offenses; the cardinal one concerns their relative seriousness. And in each case there must be some correspondence (proportionality) between the offense committed and the punishment imposed. Both cardinal and ordinal issues have problems associated with them. We may not have much difficulty in judging rape to be worse than petty theft, but is assault after provocation worse than tax fraud? Just ranking offenses in terms of their seriousness is difficult to do. The problems are exacerbated when we add questions of cardinality. How much worse than petty theft is rape or tax fraud? Is one three times as bad as the other? Is the difference between a minor assault and armed robbery greater or less than the difference between burglary and embezzlement? The judgments become even more difficult when we move from generalities to particular cases. For then we need to factor in issues of intentionality (Was the offense committed purposely, knowingly, recklessly, negligently?), motive (Was it done out of greed, for revenge, from a sense of duty . . .?), and justification or excuse (Was it done from necessity, under duress, mistake of fact, provocation, intoxication . . .?). Not only is it difficult to give such factors an appropriate weight, it is even more difficult to trade them off when they come into conflict. The motive for stealing may have been to feed a family, but the penury may have been caused by gambling. How should one consideration moderate another? These are challenging matters of judgment, and not amenable to easy formulaic resolution. But neither can we avoid making some such judgments.

Historically, determinations of the seriousness of an offense (and hence the severity of the penalty to be imposed) have been left mostly to judicial discretion (the presumption being that judges are professionally skilled at making such determinations) or to juries, and though this may have worked tolerably well when liberal democratic societies were more homogeneous, it has increasingly led to bizarre sentencing disparities. To counter this, the federal US government and many US states developed sentencing guidelines that provide (relatively) uniform criteria for sentencing. Until such guidelines recently became advisory rather than mandatory, discretion was often quite limited, even though a range of penalties was indicated. Sentence maxima are specified, and various factors, such as the degree of culpability, the seriousness of the harm, recidivism, and other aggravating or mitigating circumstances (say, racial motivation or remorse) are weighted in an almost algorithmic way. But although the vagaries of individual judicial discretion may have been lessened, the results have not always inspired confidence in the justness of outcomes. For example, in the US federal sentencing guidelines, the differential weighting of powder and crack cocaine (treating possession of the latter as much worse than the former) has played out badly for African Americans, for whom it has been the most accessible and/or preferred form.

Even without the anomalies, sentencing guidelines have not cured the most critical moral difficulties involved in determining what sentences should be. Part of the problem is that more than one range of penalties could express the same ordinal/cardinal values. Suppose A, B, C, and D represent the ordinal rankings of four offenses, and that 1A, 3B, 4C, and 8D represent their cardinal relations. Each of the following sentences would reflect this relation: fines of $1, $3, $4, and $8, and imprisonment for one year, three years, four years and eight years, respectively, assuming that there is no diminishing value with the penalty increase. Clearly, though, there is no parity between a $1 fine and one year in prison and an $8 fine and eight years in prison. This matching problem is the most difficult one that confronts desert-based approaches.[7]

The classic solution to the matching problem has been to argue for some kind of "equivalence" of offense and penalty. Traditionally known as the *lex talionis*, it is exemplified (more or less) in the biblical injunction to "give life for life, eye for eye, tooth for tooth, hand for hand, foot for foot, burning for burning, wound for wound, stripe for stripe."[8] If taken to refer to a literal equivalence, the principle quickly reduces to absurdity. Does one rape a rapist or remove the remaining eye of the one-eyed person who blinds one of another's two eyes? Of course not. But how, then, is the equivalence to be determined? However – except for its frequent invocation in favor of capital punishment – the *talionis* principle is not generally intended so literally. What is argued for is some parity or equality of value between the offense and what is exacted by way of punishment.

But though ideas of proportionality, commensurability, parity, or equality of value avoid the problems of literalism, they come with their own. How, for example, does one compare fines with imprisonments? Is a $500 fine equivalent to a day in jail, and, if we are inclined to think so, does this hold for rich and poor alike? Does a day in jail constitute the same for the

---

[7] In only partial defense, it should be stated that *every* theory of punishment has a matching problem, even if not the proportionality one of retributive theories.

[8] Exod. 21:23–5. In fact the biblical injunction was not intended literally, and the context was more compensatory than punitive.

homeless pauper and the wealthy executive? What should be our calibrating principle – some "objective" set of determinations (such as years in prison), or some subjective measure (that takes into account how different penalties will impact on different people)? Or some combination of them? I raise these questions not to ridicule notions of proportionality but to indicate the difficulty of making comparative judgments, difficulties that have increased as liberal democratic societies have lost whatever sense of common judgment they once may have had. Perhaps the best that can be said is that we now recognize that even though offenses can range from the relatively trivial to the almost unimaginably heinous, our punitive responses must be checked against the moral boundaries that make punitive responses appropriate in the first place. Insofar as we hold to the legitimacy of punitive responses to wrongdoing, our judgments of proportionality must be constrained by limits determined by our sense of what it would be wrong to impose on another. We should, for example, be morally inhibited from torturing torturers or dismembering thieves; proportionate responses can be determined only within the constraints of a society that justifies punishment rather than, say, revenge.

Capital punishment

The range of permissible punishments is and must be a matter of ongoing reflection. For much of human history, the death penalty has been officially sanctioned. But from the eighteenth century on – especially after Cesare Beccaria's influential *On Crimes and Punishments*[9] (1764) – a growing movement to eschew its use has developed in many liberal democratic countries. Countries entering the European Union must now forgo its employment. The most notable exception to this liberal democratic trend is the United States, which continues to impose and carry out the death penalty for certain classes of offenses (mainly aggravated murder). Apart from a short period during the 1970s when the constitutionality of its application was successfully challenged, the death penalty has retained judicial and public support.

At one point in its deliberations about "cruel and unusual punishment," the US Supreme Court spoke of a need to be responsive to "the evolving

[9] Cesare Beccaria, *On Crimes and Punishments*, trans. David Young (Indianapolis, IN: Hackett, 1986), ch. 28.

standards of decency that mark the progress of a maturing society."[10] However, the Court has not yet judged such evolving standards to rule out the use of capital punishment, for, quite apart from different traditions of constitutional interpretation, there is still considerable – though waning – support in the United States for the use of the death penalty.[11]

At the level of basic moral theory it is not easy to argue for one position against the other. Although our sense of the value of human life has arguably grown over the past few centuries, we do not regard adult human life as inviolable – most of us, for example, would accept that killing in self-defense can be justified. Why the taking of life as punishment should become unjustified as punishment is unclear. It would be understandably unjustified were it taken as punishment for burglary. But what if it is limited to cases of aggravated murder? Is there something less dignified about putting someone to death than – the usual alternative – incarcerating him for the rest of his natural life (life imprisonment without parole)? Perhaps there is, though it is not an obviously more humane alternative, and in any case life imprisonment without parole also needs to be rethought. Does the problem lie with the process? Some methods of execution are clearly dehumanizing or degrading, and it may be possible to argue that even more clinical methods, such as lethal injection, are unseemly,[12] though Kant's demand that the death of the murderer "must be kept free from all maltreatment that would make the humanity suffering in his person loathsome or abominable"[13] is not obviously incoherent. On the surface, at least, there is a reasonable proportionality between capital punishment and aggravated murder. Does such a judgment represent simply the subterranean influence of a particular religious tradition? It may, though even secular supporters of capital punishment have seen a certain moral symmetry in the permanence of loss that both murder and execution involve.

Very often, of course, those who have supported capital punishment have done so for consequentialist reasons (such as deterrence), although it is not clear that, apart from its incapacitative and specific deterrent powers, capital punishment has any wider societal value. Although the data are hotly

---

[10] *Trop v. Dulles*, 356 US 86, 101 (1958).

[11] The results of polls can be found at <www.pollingreport.com/crime.htm>.

[12] See, for example, Deborah W. Denno, "Death Bed," *TriQuarterly Journal*, 124 (2006): 141–68.

[13] Immanuel Kant, *The Metaphysics of Morals*, trans. and ed. Mary Gregor (Cambridge: Cambridge University Press, 1996), 106.

contested, there is little clear evidence to suggest that states or countries employing capital punishment have lower murder rates than those that do not. But in any case, consequentialist reasons must take a back seat to considerations of the justness or deservedness of such a penalty.

Much more troubling are the issues of its irrevocability and the tendency for its discriminatory imposition. Initiatives such as the Innocence Project in the United States[14] have shown how, even in capital cases, where one would assume that great care would be taken to establish guilt, miscarriages of justice have occurred with unnerving frequency. Given that these represent only cases for which DNA evidence is available, we have some reason to believe that they do not tell us the whole story about such miscarriages. Furthermore, at least in the United States, capital sentencing tends to reflect and exacerbate the history of racial division. It is significantly more likely that a black person convicted of killing a white person will be sentenced to death (and executed) than that a white person convicted of killing a black person will be so sentenced. It is of course arguable that both issues indicate no more than that there are flaws in the administration of the criminal justice system and that they do not amount to a decisive argument against the death penalty. That is true. But we should not ignore how difficult it has been to remove flaws in the administration of justice, given the rules of evidence, given unequal access to representation, and given the continuing legacy of racial discrimination. In any case, it is not as though we lack harsh alternative but somewhat more revocable penalties.

Restorative alternatives

There are some real difficulties with the penal status quo. Imprisonment has become a convenient but unsatisfactory social response to many crimes. It does not seem to "fit" the crime in many cases, and frequently leaves victims feeling dissatisfied. For victims as well as offenders, the processes of criminal justice have become alienating. Apart from a temporary warehousing of those who have offended against our public standards, relatively little social good appears to have come from our current practices. As we will note in the next chapter, it is not plausible to argue that imprisonment has had a significant effect on crime rates. Although the jury is still out on the

---

[14] The Innocence Project: <www.innocenceproject.org>.

causes of decline in crime, factors other than imprisonment are likely to have played a more significant role.

Overreliance on imprisonment – especially in the United States – has been recognized for a long time (though to relatively little effect). In some cases (particularly involving juvenile and drug offenses), diversionary programs and probation are resorted to, or community service. But in addition to these (and other) internal adjustments to the correctional system, there has also begun to emerge an alternative to current penal practices that goes under the name of "restorative justice." To speak of it as an "alternative" is not completely accurate. Restorative practices are sometimes used to supplement traditional penal responses, often as an adjunct to imprisonment. For some theorists of restorative justice, however, restorative practices are consciously crafted in opposition to punitive responses.

Interestingly, the logic of desert may include theoretical space for the introduction and promulgation of restorative options. We sometimes make a distinction between what is "naturally" deserved and what, given certain institutions (such as prize-giving), is deserved. We may think that someone such as Mother Teresa deserved to be rewarded for her charitable work: that is, that she was naturally deserving of some reward for her good deeds. However, in the absence of a set of institutions to provide rewards to the deserving it is not clear what form her reward should take. Once we have a set of rewarding institutions in place, however, it becomes much easier to nominate one of them (say, the Nobel Peace Prize) as an appropriate reward for the good she did. For the most part our desert claims presume some preestablished social institution, such as a reward or penalty structure. Thus, given that we have institutions of punishment, it is easier to argue that it is appropriately imposed as their deserts on wrongdoers. At least it is easier to argue that than it would be in an institutional vacuum. Thus, though it may be the case that doing ill "naturally" has negative deserts, the specific character of those deserts may not be determinable independently of a social institution of punitive impositions. But this relative indeterminacy of natural deserts also provides some moral space for restorative responses to wrongdoing. Certainly wrongdoing deserves some form of negative response, but why should that response always take the form of punishment (narrowly understood as fines or imprisonment) when it might more productively take the form of confrontation, blame, shame, reparation, apology, penitence, and so forth?

Restorative justice takes wrongdoing seriously, just as do the traditional institutions of punishment, but it tends to focus more on ruptures of interpersonal relations such as assault and theft than on "impersonal" wrongs such as tax fraud and insider trading (though of course it can be extended to these as well). But even when offenses involve individual victims, the focus tends to be on the fractured relations that have come about as part of the wrongdoing rather than on the formal violation of rights or rules. Though diverse in its expressions, much of the thrust of restorative justice can be characterized as an attempt to foster reconciliation among the parties to a criminal offense – offenders, victims, and the wider community whose terms of public engagement have been breached.

Instead of evocations of guilt, "reintegrative shame" has often been advocated, leading to the acknowledgment of responsibility, the offering of apology, and some act of restitution.[15] Rather than remaining on the sidelines or involved merely as witnesses, victims are given the opportunity to express the subjective significance of what has been done to them and to be actively involved in setting the terms of reconciliation. The aim has been to create conditions for forgiveness, or the forswearing of resentment.

Critics of restorative justice have sometimes complained that – whatever the failures of the criminal justice system – there should be no deep opposition between restorative and retributive justice. Indeed, it is sometimes claimed that a morally acceptable restoration requires that offenders accept their guilt and be prepared to suffer punitively for what they have done.[16] Further, it is claimed that even though victims ought to receive redress for what was done, the offense itself was no mere "private" wrong against the victim but also a "public" offense against standards recognized and established by the community or state. It should therefore not be left to the victim and offender to work out what the terms should be for the violation of what was also a communal standard. Admittedly, many theorists of

---

[15] There is a tendency in some of this literature to draw a sharp dichotomy between guilt and shame. Certainly there is a difference – crudely, guilt involves a consciousness of violated norms whereas in shame one has been exposed for what one is – but if, as we have previously suggested, morality is most deeply concerned with the terms under which we relate to one another, we might well expect them to occur together.

[16] See Antony Duff, "Restoration and Retribution," in *Restorative Justice and Criminal Justice: Competing or Reconcilable Paradigms?*, ed. Andrew von Hirsch, A. E. Bottoms, K. Roach, J. Roberts, and M. Schiff (Oxford: Hart, 2003), 43–59.

restorative justice give a significant place to the need for reconciliation with the broader community whose public expectations have been violated, but in practice there is often a tension between the two.

Practically speaking, the processes of restorative justice tend to be less formal and less bureaucratic than those of a trial (or even its more common plea-bargained agreements). Frequently they take the form of a "conference" or gathering of the relevant parties, facilitated by a restorative justice counselor. Although many early restorative meetings focused on adolescent offenses, they are now often advocated or employed when quite serious adult offenses are involved.

Critics of restorative justice, especially in its more radical incarnations, have argued that the due process guarantees of traditional criminal justice minimize disparities of outcome, whereas the less formal processes of restorative justice lay themselves open to widely divergent outcomes and discriminatory practices. Furthermore, such guarantees provide a formal environment in which neither victims nor offenders will be disrespected. In addition, it is claimed that, given the diversity of responses likely to be found among victims and offenders to what, respectively, they have suffered and perpetrated, it may be difficult to secure appropriate conditions for a respectful and productive exchange. Courts, on the other hand, have established ways of proceeding that, even if cumbersome, are well suited to bringing about a socially acceptable outcome. Finally, for the more radical defenders of restorative justice, there is an important question about what to do with recidivists. Should a re-offending person be given further opportunities to participate in a restorative process, or is there now a community interest in opting for a more traditional incapacitative response?

None of these objections to restorative approaches is decisive. Many of its defenders have not adopted a simple either/or approach that adversarially juxtaposes retributive and restorative understandings. What are more appropriately opposed are many of the actual institutions of justice in which retributive values are exemplified in ways that are inimical to restorative values. Thus, even if restorative justice may not offer a clearly workable alternative to the existing institutions of punishment, it calls attention to values that have been obscured. We will see this more clearly in the next chapter.

12 Imprisonment and its alternatives

> The degree of civilization in a society is revealed by entering
> its prisons.[1]

The prison is such a familiar institution that it is easy to forget how recently it has been socially normalized as – after fines – our most frequently used form of punishment. There has, of course, always been a need to detain those who are believed to pose an ongoing social threat or risk of flight pending legal judgment concerning their alleged offenses, and the imprisonment of debtors has also had a long history. But it was not until the late eighteenth century that imprisonment *as* punishment came into its own. Recent (2005) figures put the United States jail and prison population at over 2 million, an incarceration rate of 737 per 100,000 people, and the highest in the world (ahead of Russia, with 611). The rate for Canada was 107, for England and Wales it was 144, and for Australia it was 126. Within the United States, another 5 million are under some form of court supervision.[2]

In the wake of exposés of prison brutality and neglect, it is also easy to forget that imprisonment (along with transportation) was originally advocated as a more humane Enlightenment alternative to corporal and public punishments. As attitudes toward the body changed, confinement – albeit often with incapacitating forced labor – became the favored penalty. Subsequently, mostly under the reformist influence of religious dissenters, the penitentiary was introduced as a vehicle for remorse and rehabilitation. The transition was not rapid or smooth – provisions for whipping and flogging in

---

[1] Fyodor Dostoyevsky, *The House of the Dead*, trans. Constance Garnett (1860; New York: Grove Press, 1957), 76.

[2] Up-to-date correctional statistics for the United States can be accessed via the Sentencing Project, <www.sentencingproject.org/pdfs/1044.pdf>, or the Bureau of Justice Statistics, <www.ojp.usdoj.gov/bjs/correct.htm>.

England and the United States lasted until the middle of the twentieth century. Moreover, despite successive attempts at reform, prisons in English-speaking countries have only rarely lived up to the rehabilitative goals envisioned for them, often becoming little more than cheap labor pools or convenient warehouses for societies that have been unable or unwilling to address the problem – and causes – of crime in a more constructive manner.

Assuming that punishment for crime is sometimes justifiable, what rationale, if any, can be offered for employing imprisonment as a punishment? And, given that a rationale for imprisonment can be provided, who should be imprisoned? Further, what ethical constraints ought to be placed on the conditions of confinement? And finally, given the persistent failure of prisons to meet moral expectations, can imprisonment continue to be justified? These are the questions we will address in this chapter.

Justifying imprisonment

As we noted, the increasing use of imprisonment reflected a growing sense that corporal punishments constituted an unacceptable imposition on persons whose embodiment was seen as essential and central to their being and not simply as a temporary residence for the soul. But that still leaves unanswered the question: Why should an emerging concern about punishing the body have translated itself into imprisonment rather than, say, community service, restitution, banishment, and so forth?

For a time in England, deportation was viewed as a viable alternative. First North America and then Australia were popular convict destinations from the seventeenth century on, and transportation to Australia ended only in the mid nineteenth century. But deportation became increasingly impracticable, quite apart from other problems associated with it, and imprisonment became the preferred alternative to fines and floggings. The simple practical justification of imprisonment was that it ensured control of those facing trial or deemed appropriately punished. We cannot assume that those contemplating or in receipt of a conviction will readily accept its burden. Confinement resolves the issue: it ensures that those who face trial will be present and, in the case of those who have been convicted, it ensures that punishment will be carried out. Imprisonment *is* the punishment. In addition, it sometimes had social utility. In the USA at least, as slavery declined, prisons became a valuable source of cheap labor.

As with punishment generally, so too with imprisonment, the arguments have tended to be divided between consequentialist and nonconsequentialist options.

Consequentialist arguments

Even if – as we claimed in the last chapter – we locate the justification for punishment primarily in the wrongdoing for which it is deemed an appropriate response, it might still be possible to justify the *form* to be taken by punishment (and thus imprisonment) in consequentialist terms. Deserved punishments do not automatically translate into prison terms, even if prison terms can satisfy the proportionality requirement of desert. Assuming that imprisonment can satisfy that desert requirement, the question will then be whether it adequately fulfills legitimate consequentialist purposes – that is, consequentialist purposes that cohere with or advance legitimate state purposes. To the extent that it might – at least in theory – we will then need to consider whether it satisfies the means–end tests we proposed in Chapter 3.

We cannot isolate the consequentialist reasons that we might adduce in favor of imprisonment from the sociopolitical environment in which imprisonment occurs. Imprisonment and the broad conditions of confinement are, after all, state mandated. (Despite the increasing privatization of prisons, such institutions are overseen by the state, albeit not always effectively.) In that context, imprisonment in particular, and not only punishment in general, is often said to be justified because it serves legitimate state purposes such as rehabilitation or deterrence. As the name suggests, the *penitentiary* was originally intended to provide a solitary environment – away from the corrupting influence of others – that would lead offenders to reflect on the nature of their misdeeds, bring them to repentance, and thus prepare them to act in a socially responsible manner on release. Within such institutions, hard labor and strict discipline were often thought to increase prospects for law-abidingness and social responsibility. Later named *reformatories* were oriented to similar, though less religiously tinged, purposes. That name is now generally reserved for juvenile detention facilities. In the United States, jails and prisons[3] are still commonly referred to as *correctional facilities* – the

---

[3] Although we shall generally use the terms interchangeably, in the United States the term "prison" is often reserved for those institutions in which longer-term inmates are incarcerated.

intended implication being that they will rehabilitate or "straighten out" those who are admitted to them. In each case, the state seeks to legitimate the penal institution by reference to certain outcomes.

We have some reason to be skeptical of the efficacy of most actual imprisonment – at least so far as its rehabilitative purposes are concerned. The labeling of prisons as correctional institutions may have been aspirational, but for the most part confinement to a correctional institution appears to function as little more than a political expedient for warehousing. Boredom is the most common complaint of those who are imprisoned. The point is not that prisons can do no better. Despite Robert Martinson's notorious and long-lived claim that "nothing works,"[4] there *is* a significant literature to suggest that some prison programs can and do work. The problem, however, is that these programs have always struggled for survival. Because security is the dominant concern of politicians and often of those who run prisons, and taxpayer-supported prison budgets are not popular with the electorate, rehabilitative programs tend to be compromised or cut. In tight budgetary circumstances – a common occurrence – rehabilitatively oriented programs are among the first to go. This is not good for prison morale. Moreover, those who administer programs may not be well qualified and, even if they are, may have their professional judgment undercut by security concerns.

The failure of this somewhat disingenuous appeal to the rehabilitative value of prisons is not usually sufficient to disabuse their supporters of belief in the legitimacy of punishment by imprisonment. For when one justificatory outcome fails to be realized, another can be introduced to take its place. If prisons are not rehabilitative, then surely they will deter! Deterrence is a much more slippery notion than rehabilitation. There is of course the shuffle back and forth between specific and general deterrence, that is, between deterrence from future offending of those who have been imprisoned and deterrence of others who might otherwise have offended. Specific deterrence does not have too much going for it, if US recidivism statistics are any indication. Some two-thirds of those who are released from US prisons are rearrested within three years of their release, a figure that is increasing rather than decreasing. And any appeal to general deterrence is likely to

---

[4] Robert Martinson, "What Works? Questions and Answers about Prison Reform," *Public Interest* 35 (Spring 1974): 22–54. Martinson pulled back from this assessment in a later article: "New Findings, New Views: A Note of Caution Regarding Sentencing Reform," *Hofstra Law Review*, 7 (1979): 243–58.

be highly speculative. For we are not being asked to compare general deterrence as a result of the threat of imprisonment with what would be the case were there no punishment at all (where a general deterrence claim for imprisonment may have some intuitive plausibility), but we are being asked to compare general deterrence effected by imprisonment with the deterrent effects of threatening some other form of punishment. More salient, even if the threat of imprisonment has intuitive appeal as a general deterrent, it will be effective only if (potential) law-breakers believe that there is a high probability that they will be caught. At present, that is not a widespread or particularly well-founded belief.

The consequentialist defender of imprisonment will not be deterred! For even if the claims of specific and general deterrence are weak, there is still incapacitation. This, indeed, is what it often comes down do – "putting people away" or "getting criminals off the streets." That, surely, nobody can gainsay. But it is not so simple. Incapacitation has its own problems. For one thing, it makes the assumption – in many cases unjustified – that those convicted of offenses would have continued to offend (during the period of their incapacitation) had they not been prevented from doing so. Further, it presumes that incarceration is not itself criminogenic: if nothing else, the rate of recidivism should lead us to consider whether – because of associations formed, the treatment received, or the social setback that imprisonment constitutes – the experience of prison might often exacerbate social failure. Given that 95 percent of those who go to prison will eventually be released,[5] it is important to ensure that the prison experience does not itself worsen a person. But there is also a mythological dimension to incapacitation. Although imprisonment keeps prisoners away from the population at large (at least for a time), prisoners usually have considerable contact among themselves and with prison officers, and it is a sad fact of prison life that a significant amount of what goes on in prison would – if it happened on the outside – be classified as criminal. Why should we not factor in such activity? Might it be that we think prisoners deserve no better?

The bad effects of much imprisonment are not limited to those who are incarcerated. Frequently there are dependants left without adequate support, and – particularly in the United States – urban communities that have been decimated by high levels of imprisonment. We need to look at

---

[5] Currently, that translates into over 600,000 releasees per year.

the effects of imprisonment not only on those who are confined but also on those who are left behind. Ultimately, we need to look at the long-term effects of high imprisonment rates – effects on neighborhoods, on families, and on race relations.[6]

If we are really interested in rehabilitative punishment, then, for a significant proportion of those who are currently imprisoned, there are almost certainly more effective ways of achieving rehabilitative goals. In recent years, there has been some acknowledgment of this in the greater use of community-based sanctions, drug courts, restorative justice practices, and other diversionary programs. Nevertheless, imprisonment remains the punishment of choice and, given how deeply it has embedded itself in the politics and economics of our society, the so-called prison-industrial complex[7] is likely to remain with us for a long time. To avoid economic and social disruption, any diminution in the use of imprisonment is likely to be gradual at best.

The foregoing criticisms of consequentialist arguments for imprisonment do not amount to an argument for its abolition. But they constitute reasons for diminishing reliance on imprisonment as a medium for punishment. The apparent value of imprisonment is that it gives the state control over what it seeks to accomplish through punishment (apart from being a vehicle for dispensing just deserts). But the degree of control and conditions of control that (most) imprisonment involves are counterproductive for many of those who are imprisoned. More to the point, in many cases ample control can be exercised using alternative means of punishment. For many offenders, house arrest, the attachment of electronic monitoring devices, intensive probation, mandatory attendance at treatment programs, and supervised community service might provide as much control *as is required* as well as the opportunity for more productive intervention. It is easy to forget that a large number of the incarcerated are confined for minor offenses such as drug possession and use.[8]

---

[6] See, for example, Todd R. Clear and Dina R. Rose, "Individual Sentencing Practices and Aggregate Social Problems," in *Crime Control and Criminal Justice: The Delicate Balance*, ed. Darnell F. Hawkins, Samuel L. Myers, and Randolph N. Stone (Westport, CT: Greenwood Press, 2003), 27–52.

[7] Eric Schlosser, "The Prison-Industrial Complex," *Atlantic Monthly* 282, no. 6 (December, 1998): 51–77.

[8] If the likelihood of their re-offending can be attributed to their social or psychological circumstances, that may provide a better reason to address those circumstances than to incapacitate.

Fear of crime, however, is a potent motivator, and the risk of re-offending is easily magnified. Many hold that only the imprisonment of offenders offers adequate security. It might, however, be more realistic to confront the possibility that imprisonment may do relatively little to deter crime and more to foment it. Were crime clearance rates higher than they are and prisons better resourced and managed, there might be more reason to put one's faith in the long-term deterrent and incapacitative power of imprisonment.

Nonconsequentialist considerations

One might also try to justify imprisonment on nonconsequentialist grounds by appealing to underlying liberal democratic values that imprisonment could be argued to exemplify. Although such arguments are not common, it might be claimed that those who violate the laws of a liberal democratic polity lose some entitlement to its preeminent good – liberty. The laws that govern our public life are intended to secure our various rights, but the centerpiece of our liberal democratic tradition is liberty: freedom to pursue our lives in ways of our own choosing. Those who violate the rights of others act in ways that are subversive of that liberty. And so, however else we might want to punish rights violators, constraints on their liberty might be thought to appropriately express and communicate our condemnation of what they have done.

Still, this may not be enough to allay the worry that there is something intrinsically unacceptable about imprisonment as a particular constraint on liberty. Freedom of movement, access to certain qualities of human intimacy, privacy, and control over one's everyday affairs are so central to human dignity that their incarcerative contraction might be seen as inherently dehumanizing. It is not, after all, simply that one's liberty of movement is constrained. Along with the constraint on movement that imprisonment involves, many other restrictions are imposed.

Clearly there is an issue here. However, it is arguable that the constraint constituted by imprisonment is a matter of degree. At one extreme, were imprisonment to involve confinement to a straitjacket-like existence, this would surely dehumanize. At the other end of the spectrum, some low-security prisons allow for significant social interaction, reasonable privacy, and engagement in aspects of the life one had on the outside. At what point along this continuum do the conditions of confinement become morally troubling? One particularly troubling, but increasingly popular, form of confinement has been the development of supermax prisons, which maximize isolation, boredom, and disorientation, and eliminate privacy. The fact that some have managed to survive them relatively unscathed should be seen as a triumph of the human spirit and not as evidence of their basic humaneness. Supermax imprisonment is inherently problematic.[9] Still, as we will soon observe, there are many features of "ordinary" imprisonment that also make it troubling, even if contingently so, thus raising the question whether forms of imprisonment that are not inherently dehumanizing may nevertheless be so prone to conditions and practices that derogate from dignity that we should place a general question mark against imprisonment. Or, if that appears too radical, it should at least obligate us to make prisons more transparent and accountable than they currently are.

Privatization

Although legal punishment (and the imprisonment that it often involves) is a state function, its implementation has sometimes been placed in the hands of private – and profit-oriented – corporations. There are nineteenth-century precedents for what has reemerged with the rapid rise in incarceration over the past three decades.[10] In order to meet the pressing demand for prison spaces, or to respond to court orders concerning overcrowding, and/or to accommodate tight budgets, many states have contracted some of the building and running of new prisons to private and even international corporations. In some cases (as with Wackenhut), the organizations were already involved in the security business prior to their involvement with prisons, but in other cases (as with Corrections Corporation of America) companies have been set up to take advantage of a business opportunity. Apart from the need for an urgent response – for which governmental bureaucracies are not

---

[9] Leena Kurki and Norval Morris, "The Purposes, Practices, and Problems of Supermax Prisons," *Crime and Justice: A Review of Research*, ed. Michael Tonry (Chicago: University of Chicago Press, 2001), vol. 28, 385–424; Richard L. Lippke, "Against Supermax," *Journal of Applied Philosophy* 21, no. 2 (2004): 109–24.

[10] See <www.ojp.usdoj.gov/bjs/glance.htm#Corrections>. Even in countries that have not seen the same increase as the United States, privatization has been considered an attractive option. See <http://www.psiru.org/ppri.asp>.

usually well organized – it has been argued that the privatization of prisons constitutes a "cost-effective and efficient" way of dealing with imprisonment and thus represents a good stewardship of public resources.[11] In addition, it has been claimed that today's private contracts provide safeguards against the egregious abuses that had led to their cessation toward the end of the nineteenth century.

Opponents of privatization tend to disagree about the comparability or advantages of private prisons. On the one hand, they argue that there is something ethically unseemly about profiteering from the business of punishing others; on the other hand, they claim that the profit motive is likely to encourage various cost-cutting measures that will detract from the "quality" of the imprisonment experience. The two objections tend to coalesce. If, as part of a liberal democratic polity, we believe that legal punishment should involve both the humane treatment of offenders and the desire to maximize possibilities for human fulfillment, placing those expectations in the hands of profit-making organizations puts such organizations under a good deal of pressure. Although we need not think that those who run such organizations care only for profit (that, in any case, would probably be self-defeating), the fact that profit (and adequate shareholder returns) is a *sine qua non* of doing business will inevitably place pressure on liberal democratic expectations for imprisonment. The private prisons are likely to employ fewer, cheaper, and less well-trained prison personnel, and they will probably have an interest in security at the expense of rehabilitative programs. Moreover, rather than being focused on the larger public good of law-abidingness, such organizations are likely to be (and usually are) supportive of social measures designed to increase rather than diminish the prison population.[12]

Defenders usually respond that private prisons have records that are comparable with those of public prisons (and hence that the profit motive is not corruptive). But this is arguably a poor benchmark. "Doing as well as" is in fact "doing as badly as," and privatization might be seen merely as an extension of existing problems with even less public accountability. Maybe we should be grateful that private organizations were able to step up when

---

[11] This does not seem to be borne out by the evidence. See Douglas McDonald, *et al., Private Prisons in the United States* (Cambridge, MA: Abt Associates, 1998).

[12] For a helpful development of these themes, see Sharon Dolovich, "State Punishment and Private Prisons," *Duke Law Journal* 55, no. 3 (2005): 439–548.

the numbers of prisoners began to escalate in the 1970s; but it might have been better had the crisis generated a more radical rethinking of our criminalization practices and our social response to crime. A quick fix is not necessarily a fix at all.

I am not arguing that imprisonment should be abandoned or even that privatization is always wrong. But there are more fundamental issues that should be addressed at the level of public policy, and we tend to avoid them. What it is important to see is that the arguments in favor of imprisonment are quite modest. They do not come close to giving imprisonment the role that it has come to have. And they leave us with at least two major questions: (1) Whose punishment should take the form of imprisonment? and (2) What should be the conditions of their confinement?

Who should be imprisoned?

If nothing else, the United States' propensity for using imprisonment as punishment should prompt the question: Why? Why is its incarceration rate so much higher than that of other liberal democracies? Why does it incarcerate rather than punish in some other way? And why does it so much more readily incarcerate those who belong to particular socioeconomic and ethnic groups?[13] Although these questions are being asked, they have so far had little effect on the overall numbers of those incarcerated.

For our present purposes, we can set to one side those who are detained simply to ensure their presence during the criminal justice process. Although there are significant ethical questions concerning the justifiability and conditions of such confinement (especially given the presumption of innocence), our present concern is with those who have been fairly convicted and for whom the question is now: How shall we punish them?

Let us grant that in some cases fines and/or confiscation of property would be impracticable as forms of punishment (whatever else might be said about their appropriateness). What other options do we have? Corporal punishments are generally considered unacceptable, though there may

---

[13] For a strongly opinioned but useful overview of some of these questions, see Jeffrey Reiman, *The Rich Get Richer and the Poor Get Prison: Ideology, Class, and Criminal Justice*, 8th edn. (Boston, MA: Allyn & Bacon, 2007).

be room for some limited rethinking of this.[14] A better option might be an increasing use of a range of community service or restitutive penalties, along with a range of monitoring strategies. Given the failure of regard for others that crime generally displays, such service requirements might seem especially apposite. Although we would obviously prefer it if civic responsibility were voluntarily displayed, in the absence of such responsibility we might increase the likelihood of its voluntary expression in future if those who have failed to show it are exposed to its human demands.

What about the potential for re-offending if offenders are not locked up? Community-based sanctions appear to be no more likely to result in recidivism than imprisonment. But even if it is thought that a person is inclined to err again, constraints other than imprisonment – such as electronic monitoring, house arrest, and intensive supervision – might be considered before imprisonment. Although confining, these do not amount to imprisonment and, for many offenders, may just as adequately deter as any imprisonment (especially if a repeated failure is accompanied by the threat of imprisonment). These constraints could also be associated with various restitutive or community penalties.[15]

Imprisonment as punishment seems to have most to be said for it when there is a high risk of continuing serious criminal activity, and only incarceration provides an acceptable risk-minimizing penalty. We should remember, however, that judgments of dangerousness are fraught with difficulty. Such judgments are better determined by repeated lawlessness than by some form of psychosocial assessment, though even in the former situation it is important not to overemphasize the need for incarceration. The analysis of crime patterns suggests that for many who engage in criminal activity, criminality represents a phase rather than a settled disposition. Even if, given the social potency that the fear of crime possesses, we might err on the side of caution, our tendency to overestimate the risk of re-offending should give us pause before we determine that incarceration would be justified.

---

[14] For a robust defense of corporal punishment, see Graeme Newman, *Just and Painful: A Case for the Corporal Punishment of Criminals*, 2nd edn. (Albany, NY: Harrow & Heston, 1995).

[15] To advocate a greater use of community-based sanctions is not to suggest that they are without ethical challenges of their own. See, for example, Andrew von Hirsch, "The Ethics of Community-Based Sanctions," *Crime & Delinquency* 36 (1990): 162–73.

Conditions of confinement

Before we reflect on the actual conditions of imprisonment, let us first note some longstanding legal/ethical constraints on punishment, including of course the conditions of confinement. Both the English Bill of Rights (1689) and the eighth amendment (1789) to the US Constitution prohibit punishments that are "cruel and unusual." In more recent documents, such as the United Nations Universal Declaration of Human Rights (1948) and the European Convention for the Protection of Human Rights and Fundamental Freedoms (1953), the prohibition is of "cruel, inhuman or degrading" and "inhuman and degrading" punishment.

The older and more recent formulations come to pretty much the same. What is problematic about cruel and unusual punishment is that it is inhuman and degrading. *Cruelty*, which involves the intentional (or maybe reckless) infliction of physical or mental suffering on a weaker person, disproportionate to whatever suffering might have been justified as punishment, is inhuman because it displays a failure of regard for one of the basic requirements for human interaction. A basic moral requirement for our interactions with others is a recognition of their oneness with ourselves as feeling, perceiving, and reasoning beings, and giving their feelings, perceptions, and reasons the same weight that we give our own. Those who act cruelly assault that connectedness by causing pain and fear. Their infliction shows both a disregard for, as well as a tendency to undermine, the qualities that constitute our human distinctiveness. The pain (of cruelty) threatens to reduce us to the level of what we may characterize as animality (which I here understand as responsiveness primarily to sensations of pain and pleasure). It may even be worse than that, because physical and mental cruelty often exacerbate suffering through an exploitation of the imaginative possibilities of our human consciousness.

The *unusualness* of a punishment is not normally considered apart from its cruelty. It is ordinarily seen as an intensifying characterization ("cruel and unusual"), for to say that a punishment is unusual may otherwise indicate no more than that it falls outside some statistical norm. In the case of punishment, however, its denomination as unusual may also provide something more than an intensification, for "novelty" may constitute an additional affront to human dignity. Although it goes too far to say that "frequency of use furnishes evidence of wide acceptability, and . . . the very fact of regular use diminishes the insult,"[16] many punishments that are characterizable as unusual (say, branding, mutilation, the stocks, and the execution of minors) may also be seen as especially degrading (and degraded).

Human dignity has its foundations in our capacity to frame for ourselves the choices we make, the paths we tread, and the goals we pursue. It also has a behavioral expression as a kind of manifest bearing. To "carry oneself with dignity" is not simply to have a particular standing but also to assert control over the terms of one's self-presentation. The danger of imprisonment is that it will diminish both control and self-presentation. It becomes an engine of degradation.

Against this background of constraints on imprisonment, we can identify a number of prison practices that are often morally, if not legally, questionable. Although these are usually explained as security needs, and in certain circumstances may even be justifiable as such, their practice often reflects less admirable concerns, born of the imbalance of power and the environment of disgrace that characterize prison life. Excessive use of solitary confinement, lockdowns, unnecessary and humiliating strip, body cavity, and pat searches (sometimes exacerbated by being cross-gendered), long delays in processing calls for medical assistance, multiple celling, allowing prison conditions to become squalid, turning a blind eye to prisoner-on-prisoner abuse, chain-gang practices, and even institutional boredom, sometimes individually and often collectively violate ethical – even if not legal – demands that imprisonment not be cruel, inhuman, or degrading.

But we should ask more positively: Under what conditions *should* prisoners be kept? First off, we need to remind ourselves that people are sent to prison *as* punishment and not *for* punishment. Conditions need not be easy, but neither should they be unduly harsh. There is often an unspoken commitment to a doctrine of "penal austerity," that is, to the view that conditions inside prison should be no better than those an inmate would experience on the outside.[17] The doctrine gets what plausibility it has from the idea that punishment is to be seen as an imposition, not a benefit. But the imposition is constituted by the confinement. More significantly, because the choice to imprison gives the state almost total control

---

[16] Laurence H. Tribe, *American Constitutional Law* (Mineola, NY: Foundation Press, 1978), 917.

[17] See Richard Sparks, "Penal 'Austerity': The Doctrine of Less Eligibility Reborn?" in *Prisons 2000: An International Perspective on the Current State and Future of Imprisonment*, ed. R. Matthews and P. Francis (Basingstoke: Macmillan, 1996), 74–93.

over the conditions of a person's life, the state also acquires the obligation to ensure that those conditions are acceptable and do not humiliate
or degrade. A person may have had a socially deprived and harsh existence outside the prison; that is no reason to make the prison experience
even harsher. We should not resent the fact that, despite the discipline of
confinement, people can be better off in prison than outside it. What we
ought to seek is a prison experience that, in addition to confining the person, also prepares that person to function more responsibly than before.
Although advocates of penal austerity have given it potent political form
when they complain of "country clubs" and "vacation spas," the doctrine
of penal austerity uses an inappropriate benchmark for determining prison
conditions.

Consider now how these general ethical constraints might impact on specific conditions and practices. Although the recommendations that follow
may seem obvious, they are frequently breached.

Space and environment

Although prisoners are usually allowed to leave their cells for limited periods
each day, much of their time is spent in cells equipped with basic necessities – bed, toilet, washbasin, and maybe a few other amenities. But cells
may be too small, too exposed, too hazardous, and too uncomfortable to
be humane. There should, therefore, be sufficient space to allow for certain
basic activities – such as standing up, walking round, sitting, lying down –
and, compatible with the need for security and safety, the cell environment
should allow for the retention of dignity and a reasonable degree of well-
being.

Space and environment needs also encompass such matters as the
maintenance of cell space, smoking policies, ambient temperature, noise,
light/darkness, and privacy. Although privacy and security will always be
in tension, the former can often be given greater importance than it currently is. Strip (or even clothed) searches, for example, a staple of prison life,
should be conducted only as necessary and with the same restraint, professionalism, and detachment as gynecological or medical examinations. Given
that a large proportion of women in prison have been abused, cross-gender
searches should normally be prohibited (demands for equal employment
opportunities can be met in other ways).

One of the most serious problems currently confronting penal institutions is that of overcrowding. Although clear legal requirements regarding space allocations for each prisoner often exist on paper, a lack of close court oversight, political intransigence, and reluctance to spend sufficient additional public monies on prison facilities (or, better, on alternatives thereto), have led – in the United States and United Kingdom – to overcrowding in at least half their prisons. In some cases, overcrowding has reached crisis proportions. This has brought with it a set of additional problems – such as severe discontent, an increase in prisoner-on-prisoner abuse, and a greater prevalence of transmissible diseases.

Work and activity

Boredom is the psychic equivalent of lack of space. If it is inhumane to deny people adequate opportunities to exercise their bodies, it is degrading to deny them mental stimuli. Humans realize themselves through activity, and though that activity need not be work, productive activity represents one of the major ways in which we escape internal isolation and are able to influence the world beyond us. The enforced idleness of prison warehousing saps energy, undermines the spirit, and does nothing to assist inmates to reintegrate themselves into the wider community. Although some prisoners might expect to spend the rest of their days behind bars, most are able to anticipate release and, if their prison experience does little to assist (or even impedes) their return to that wider community, recidivism should come as no surprise.

Although some kinds of work and work conditions (such as chain gangs) can themselves be dehumanizing, there is no reason why prison work should dehumanize. Work that is designed to serve the needs of the prison population itself – the provision of food, maintenance, cleaning, and agricultural labor – is meaningful, and it is reasonable to expect prisoners to contribute to the conditions of their well-being. Neither should there be any problem about expecting prisoners to engage in other kinds of productive labor: quite a few prisons have government contracts for computer and appliance repairs, equipment and machine maintenance, clothing production, and so on. No doubt such work assignments will need some measure of individualization and, given the deprived backgrounds of many prisoners, some training may also need to be provided. Although some kinds of work will be inherently challenging and satisfying, part of the satisfaction of productive work often comes from its being recognized and valued by others. In practical terms, this suggests that prisoners should not be expected to work without remuneration, or be treated as cheap or slave labor. Even if their remuneration is discounted to contribute to the costs of their "board and lodging," such work holds out the possibility of greater self-discipline and responsibility and may assist in later social reentry.

Amenities

What kinds of creaturely comforts should be available to prisoners? Should they have color TVs, cable access, DVD players, movies of their choice, coffeemakers, well-equipped gymnasiums, libraries, and so on? Although most of the items mentioned have occasioned "country club" quips from conservative "tough on crime" critics of prisons, few of them have been in a hurry to join. No doubt there have been isolated cases in which prison amenities have been unwisely generous. Usually, though, the so-called luxuries (such as well-equipped gymnasiums) have served important social and psychological purposes that critics have overlooked. Furthermore, they have presumed that the so-called luxury items have been purchased using public monies when in fact they have usually been financed from earnings or phone income. The reality is that most prisons are poorly provided for, given their large inmate populations, and the weight of the argument favors access to additional rather than fewer amenities.

In addition, of course, there are some basic amenities to which every prisoner should have access – such as a disease-free bed, a place to write, and sanitary toilet and washing facilities. These, though, are mostly physical requirements. One of the most serious deficiencies in prison life is the lack of mental stimulation and preparation for life on the outside. And so there is a strong argument for access to current information about the wider social world, library facilities, discussion and learning opportunities, and other stimuli that may help to overcome the nagging sense of worthlessness possessed by many inmates. In addition, given that many prisoners will be engaged in legal activity concerning their cases, they should have reasonable access to essential legal materials.

Medical, psychiatric, and social work amenities should be readily accessible. Prisoners have higher than average medical, psychiatric, and social

needs, and dealing with these is essential if reentry into the wider society is not to be harder than it will in any case be. Fortunately, prisoners
in the United States now have a constitutional right to medical care.[18] But
although the medical resources devoted to prisoners have increased enor-
mously, the vast increase in numbers incarcerated, the generally escalating
cost of medical care, the increasing numbers of aging prisoners and prisoners with expensive healthcare needs, and the difficulty of getting competent
health carers or the outsourcing of medical care to for-profit providers still
leave much prison medical care with a lot to be desired.

"Graying" of the prison population has become a serious matter.[19] With
larger numbers in prison serving longer sentences, with diminished access
to parole, a sizable number of prisoners now die in prison. Most prisons
were not built with that in mind and so they do not usually have hospice
facilities. In some prisons, though, inmates have been trained to be hospice
carers. Compassionate release is one option, but even so the problem is
placing a significant strain on medical resources. As we have noted on more
than one occasion, when the state imprisons, it must assume responsibility
for the basic care of those it incarcerates.

In some prisons, the desire to reduce malingering has resulted in
inmates being charged for medical consultations (usually as a copayment).[20]
Although it is reasonable to be concerned about the misuse of limited
resources that malingering involves, it ought to be considered whether the
malingering itself may reflect a failure in prison administration. Malingering is often a strategy for getting temporary relief from the confines and
boredom of a cell. Rather than using it as a reason to charge all prisoners
for medical calls, might it not be better to charge only those who display a
pattern of frivolous calls?

Although prisoners have no right to expect luxuries (unless as rewards
or individually purchased privileges) during the time of their incarceration,
they do not lose their claim to the basic goods and amenities of life. They
should have access to enough goods and amenities to help them develop as
the citizens we expect them to be.

[18] *Estelle v. Gamble*, 429 US 97 (1976).

[19] See Ronald H. Aday, *Aging Prisoners: Crisis in American Corrections* (Westport, CT: Praeger, 2003).

[20] See Public Law 106–294 Federal Prisoner Health Care Copayment Act of 2000, <http:// thomas.loc.gov/cgibin/bdquery/z?d106:SN00704:@@@L&summ2=m&>.

Visitation and access

Diminished access to valued social contacts is one of the most painful costs of imprisonment. Controlled and limited weekly visits may be permitted, but they are often frustrating or infrequent because of distance or bureaucratic routines. Mail is often censored, and the ability to have phone access to others is constrained by cost (often gouging) and limited phone facilities. Such constraints can be devastating because inmates' identities are often strongly bound up with their preexisting social involvements. What is more, their capacity to stay out of trouble after spending time in prison is likely to be significantly affected by their ability to sustain and benefit from such relationships. Calls to a loved one who may be having his or her own problems are hardly made easier when there is a frustrated line of inmates waiting for their turn to make an expensive phone call.

In determining that imprisonment is an appropriate punishment, we need to factor in the impact that imprisonment will have on valued others. If the person who is imprisoned was significantly responsible for family income or family stability, incarceration will place great strains on those who remain outside. Although this may not count decisively against imprisonment, it may – especially in view of the need for future social reintegration – constitute a strong reason for providing counseling services and for making access easier and more productive than it usually is. In some countries this extends to private conjugal visits. Although they may pose security risks and present other problems (pregnancy, for example), their longer-term benefits should not be ignored. In most cases, though, and in general with issues of visitation and access, the security issues are overplayed. Prisoners are more likely to get contraband from prison officers.

Along with support for ongoing relationships, there is also an argument for establishing mechanisms that will enable victim–offender reconciliation to take place. Where such reconciliation can be achieved, non-recidivist attitudes and dispositions are also likely to be nurtured.

Opportunities

We have noted already that most offenders will eventually be released and will resume their place in the wider society. There is no doubt that reentry can be extremely difficult. The controlled and regimented prison world can atrophy initiative and responsibility (presuming that it was present before-hand), and leave a person unprepared for the multiple choices and unstruc-tured character of life outside. Social skills are lost, and there is the stigma of incarceration to be borne.

If we argue, as we must, that the state's authority to punish derives in part from the overall value that punishment will have in securing a just and peaceable society, then reentry must be prepared for. Recidivism is not just the failure of those who lapse again into crime; it also represents a failure of the criminal justice system. We will pursue this further in Chapter 14.

Because a significant proportion of those who are incarcerated also lack knowledge and skills needed for productive employment, efforts to provide them are incumbent on a liberal democratic system committed to providing conditions for human flourishing. This liberal democratic obligation also extends to the skills that are necessary for satisfactory social negotiation. And therefore we should expect that prisons will make efforts to provide for both the technical and social skilling of those who are as yet ill-equipped to take a productive place in the wider society. It has been the tragedy of prison policy and practice that programs of these kinds are often politically disfavored and therefore targeted when funds are tight.

Abolition

Many – perhaps most – prisons fall far short of the expectations I have been outlining, and the implementation of these expectations is not readily fore-seeable. The cost of maintaining prisons is already high and, were some of the initiatives I have suggested taken up, they would rise even higher – unless, of course, recourse to imprisonment was greatly diminished. But many of the suggestions I have made would be politically unpopular; the courts have shown themselves to be reluctant to impose detailed require-ments on prison services; and there are also structural features of prison life that would impede their implementation. The most potent – but also most intractable – structural impediment is the power differential that often operates within prisons, most critically that between prison officers and pris-oners. Even if individual prison officers move among inmates unarmed, it is known that collectively they are able to exercise a great deal of control. And the old adage about power tending to corrupt may be nowhere truer than in prisons where the differential is at its greatest – even in a liberal democracy.

Although it need not be the case, the abusive expression of power tends to be endemic to differential power relationships. This we have reason to think from the few controlled studies that have been done.[21]

The chronic problem of abusive behavior in prisons raises the issue of prison abolitionism, a movement with strong Quaker roots and a significant presence in Europe. The advocates of decarceration vary in their radicalism. At one extreme are those who see no value and only disvalue in incarceration. At the other extreme are those who accept the necessity of some incapacitative incarceration, but believe that many – and perhaps most – of those currently imprisoned should be subject to alternative social sanctions. Among the radical abolitionists are those who believe that incarceration, along with other punitive responses to "crime," tells a false story about both the punished individual and the nature of criminal offenses – namely, that offenders should bear full responsibility for what they do and that social prohibitions reflect an "objective moral order." We touched on some of these issues in Chapter 2. Other abolitionists, however, are more troubled by what they see as the inappropriateness of an *incarcerative* response to violations of social order. In their view, incarceration tends to leave social relations where they were or worse off. Offenders are not treated in a way that restores them to full social acceptance, and victims and offenders are left unreconciled. Thus, among those who espouse "restorative" approaches to wrongdoing will be some who oppose incarceration altogether (as well, of course, as those who wish only to diminish our dependence on incarceration).

Among the more radical proponents of decarceration, some theorize about preferable alternatives for social control. They advocate positive rather than negative incentives for social conformity, they champion social measures that diminish the temptations and opportunities for crime ("situational crime prevention"), and they often urge a more egalitarian social order, or at least one in which more people will have a reasonable opportunity for developing and realizing humanly dignifying aspirations.

---

[21] See the work of Philip Zimbardo, updated in Craig Haney and Philip G. Zimbardo, "The Past and Future of US Prison Policy: Twenty-Five Years After the Stanford Prison Experiment," *American Psychologist* 53 (1998): 709–27; and of Stanley Milgram, updated in Thomas Blass, "The Milgram Paradigm After 35 Years: Some Things We Now Know About Obedience to Authority," *Journal of Applied Social Psychology* 29 (1999): 955–78.

Unfortunately, as is implicitly recognized in the more radical critiques of prisons, imprisonment is now deeply etched into our way of doing things, and though we might reasonably work, on the one hand, to diminish our dependence on it and, on the other, to improve conditions through increased accountability, imprisonment will not soon become a marginal instrument in our social response to crime. As we will suggest in the next chapter, we should work toward the greater professionalism of those who administer prisons. Ultimately, though, the problems go much deeper than that.

13   The role of correctional officers

But for the grace of God there [go I].[1]

Although we might hope for a diminished reliance on imprisonment, we cannot expect to see prisons vanish from our social landscape. For even were we to devise alternative penalties for many of the offenses and offenders now attracting prison sentences, there would almost certainly be a group of those for whom imprisonment would remain the most appropriate penalty. And so there will need to be people to administer prisons. In this chapter we attempt to provide an account of the correctional officer's role, and to explore some of the tensions created by that role. (Our discussion of the correctional officer's role, however, will not presume the idealized scenario of a prison system that is limited only to those who are justifiably incarcerated.)

Prisons are complex institutions. They usually operate under the umbrella of a government body headed by a commissioner/director and are divided into a variety of units, some focused on the administration of the government office that oversees prisons and others directed to general areas of prison administration, such as training, human relations, internal affairs, health and other support services, finances, and physical plant and related contracting. Individual prisons have their own supervisory structure comprising a prison warden/superintendent or governor (mostly in England) and various deputies, with the extent and depth of the administrative structure of the prison usually reflecting its size in terms of both physical plant and number of inmates. Although our main focus in this chapter will be on prison officers (or guards) – the group that has day-to-day contact with inmates – it is important to remember that the larger structures exist, for prison officers do not work in a vacuum but are significantly affected by

---

[1] Based on words reputedly uttered by John Bradford (c. 1510–55), a sixteenth-century English Protestant martyr, on seeing prisoners led to the scaffold.

factors over which they have only minimal control. The tone of a prison tends to be set by the warden (who may value security but have scant regard for rehabilitation or who may believe that security and rehabilitation are mutually reinforcing). But whatever the warden's beliefs and policies, much of what he is able to achieve in his role as prison warden will be constrained by outside forces to whom he is formally accountable, a situation that often gives rise to complaints, not only from prison officers but also from prison administrators, concerning the stress and role distortion that these constraints impose.

Our procedure in this chapter will be to outline professional goals for prison officers and then to grapple with some of the tensions that occur in attempting to realize these goals – tensions that arise among the goals themselves, between professional ideals and institutional culture, between prison officers and those to whom they are answerable, between officers and inmates, and finally between officers and other professionals who work within the prison setting. We conclude with some suggestions for strengthening the professionalism of prison officers.

Custodial ends and professionalism

Although we have increasingly come to expect that those who occupy public roles will discharge the responsibilities of their role professionally, it is only recently that these expectations have come to be realized, even partially, with respect to the role played by corrections officers. The elements of professionalism (as we outlined them in Chapter 4) have been hard to come by for prison officers, given a variety of disparate factors including the remote siting of many prisons, typical workplace conditions, and the limited training available to those who work in that environment. Professionalism in prison involves the provision of prison services by those who see themselves committed to the ends or purposes of the institution of imprisonment and to enhancing the provision of its services, the latter often requiring the injection of additional resources. Professionalism thus involves far more than doing a job, notwithstanding that research findings indicate that "work satisfaction" for prison officers is often articulated negatively as work periods "without trouble" or in which "troubles" have been surmounted without significant cost. (Later we shall suggest how this negative perspective may tend to compromise a professional outlook.)

What, then, are the ends of imprisonment toward which the profession-alism of prison officers should be directed? Construed broadly (along lines suggested in the last chapter), the end toward which prison institutions must direct themselves is the fulfillment of the larger purposes of the liberal democratic state: they must work to contribute to the protection of citizens' rights and the furtherance of their welfare. And this is achieved in part by their securing us against further predations by those who have violated the constraints of our social life. This is the broader purpose of imprisonment – the punitive incapacitation of violators in ways that we hope are propor-tionate to their offenses – so that they will be deterred and, if possible, rehabilitated. The rehabilitation of offenders is important because almost all who enter prison will eventually leave it. The prison experience should therefore look forward as well as back.

Construed narrowly, the role of prison officers is often expressed via the mantra of "care, custody, and control," a mantra that, unfortunately, tends to obscure the future orientation of imprisonment and focuses instead on custody and control.

I shall now go on to spell this out in greater detail, but the detailed pic-ture should be seen against the following background: because the practice of imprisonment – to the extent that it is justifiable – takes place within the framework of a liberal democratic polity, imprisonment must not deny the dignity of those imprisoned even as it affirms and secures the rights of those it protects. Recognizing the dignity of those imprisoned requires being sensitive to their welfare needs, needs that become all the more important to recognize and meet given that those imprisoned are rendered almost totally dependent on the state for recognition of the prerequisites of their dignity. One should not see imprisonment, imposed in part to protect the welfare of others, as being in tension with the protection, indeed promotion, of the welfare of those imprisoned.

In light of this, added to prison officers' other responsibilities – or, per-haps better, framing those responsibilities – will be a responsibility for the face-to-face affirmation of inmate dignity and the securing or provision of welfare to prisoners. Unfortunately, however, the responsibility of prison offi-cers to secure the dignity of inmates is often undermined by the dehumaniz-ing environment of certain types of prison arrangements. The dehumaniza-tion associated with supermax prisons and even special housing units (SHUs) is often as much a matter of architecture and technological infrastructure

as of decisions by individual prison officers. Nor do individual prison officers have much to do with the dehumanizing effects of the unconscionably
long sentences that some prisoners are expected to serve, as these sentences
are often a function of legislative fiat (as in "three strikes" legislation) or
the implementation of ill-thought-out sentencing guidelines.

Let us turn now to a closer look at "care, custody, and control" as a way
of specifying a prison officer's role obligations. Although care is mentioned
first, the emphasis tends to be on custody and control rather than on care.
I shall begin with a review of custody, followed by accounts of control and
care, and then consider the issue of their integration.

Custody

The custodial function of prisons relates primarily to public safety. One
of the main justifying reasons for imprisonment is to punish in a way that
secures public safety: the restriction of liberty removes (for a time) the threat
of further predations and thus imprisonment serves as both punishment
and incapacitation. Because one of the primary functions of prisons is to
provide protection against public endangerment, prisons should be as secure
as they need to be to prevent escape.[2]

In light of this, prison officers are called upon to act in ways that will
not compromise security and conduce to escape. This helps to explain the
warning against overfamiliarity with inmates, with its potential for compromising security (and probably safety). And – perhaps ironically – the need for
security also helps to explain why prison officers normally move unarmed
among prisoners. They are greatly outnumbered, and their being armed
would present an opportunity for being disarmed and, once the prisoners
were themselves armed, the temptation as well as opportunity for escape or
other undesirable conduct would be heightened.[3]

---

[2] But having the distinction does not guarantee the appropriate classification of prisoners.
There is some evidence that many who are classified as medium-security in private
prisons would be housed in minimum-security public prisons.

[3] There may nevertheless be a potent and important symbolism in the fact that prison
officers are generally unarmed and also confined. It can communicate a "We're in this
together" message, and this can have the potential to translate into a central ethic of
fairness in officer–inmate relations. Where inmates are treated fairly, the likelihood of
hostage-taking is diminished.

In considering custodial care, it might be well to keep in mind that the custodial function now served by prisons can often be adequately achieved through less restrictive means than imprisonment – think of court orders that forbid people to associate with certain others, house arrest, and curfews. This suggests that if imprisonment is to be justified there may need to be reference to some more pressing concern than custodial care. Some marginal recognition of this can be found in the distinction among low-, medium-, and maximum-security prisons. We shall soon return to consider what the more pressing need may be.

Control

Although prisons differ in the level of control they exercise over inmates' activities, for a large majority of prisoners in medium- and maximum-security prisons control predominates over other concerns. In theory, a prison could comprise a large village, fenced off from the world outside, within which inmates could interact at will. In practice that is not the case. Not only are prisoners fenced off from the rest of society, they are also fenced off to varying degrees from each other. Moreover, their activities are highly regimented. It is understandable that some regimentation is required both to ensure that prisoners do not endanger one another or prison officers and to meet the demands of dealing with large numbers of people in a confined space and with limited resources. In addition, some regimentation is necessary to implement the decision (justified or not) to limit outside contacts: for example, phone use may be restricted or regulated, mail may be censored, and visitations may need to be arranged in advance. No doubt, at least in some cases, one may question whether prison life is more regimented than it need or should be or, more critically, one may question whether the restrictions have been *made* necessary by the way in which they have been imposed. For example, some constraints are such that "fighting back" by prisoners is to be understood not only as a natural reaction on their part, but also as an assertion of their dignity in the face of affronts to it. Orders, even those that restrict prisoner activity, should be such that, even when they are not to inmates' liking, they have reasons that can be understood and acknowledged by those whom they affect. This is part of what it means to preserve the dignity of prisoners within a prison environment.

No doubt, being subject to control in a prison environment can be oppressive and degrading. Control may involve, and be seen to involve, the assertion of power for its own sake – a reminder of who is in charge, and/or a breaking of the will of the incarcerated – rather than being exercised for some manifestly justifiable end. It may also be exerted indirectly or through proxies by, say, a deliberate failure to protect prisoners from one another so that, say, sexual predation by some prisoners on others is used as an instrument of management or as retaliation for an offense against an officer. (Inquiries into prison rape have shown that prison officers sometimes knowingly avert their eyes – and ears – thus allowing some prisoners to prey on others.) Of course, sometimes officers are themselves predators, using their control as a tool for manipulation and punishment. Although the problems of abuse on inmates are worst in maximum-security prisons, many prison officers straight out of academy are "broken in" by an initial assignment to a maximum-security prison where abuse is likely to take place. ("Everybody's got to do their time at the bottom of the barrel"[4] is how those assignments are justified.) Needless to say, making inexperienced novices deal with maximum-security prisoners as their initiation into prison work can conduce to their developing crude defenses for themselves and to seeing those in their "care, custody, and control" in a distorted light. The distortion in perspective is not because maximum-security prisoners are more manageable than they appear to be, but rather because most prisoners are not to be viewed as those who need maximum-security treatment. (Clearly, however, some are: in the United States, the growth of predatory and rival urban gangs has created a huge challenge for law enforcement and also for prison and public safety.[5] Gang leaders have been known to seek to run their operations from within the prison, with outside rivalries sometimes played out within the prison environment, a situation that presents law enforcement officials – both within and outside of prisons – with a major managerial challenge.)

[4] See Ted Conover, *Newjack: Guarding Sing Sing* (New York: Random House, 2000), chapters 2–3. Conover describes the ways in which recruits are broken down and then rebuilt, the development of an us–them mentality, the fostering of informal codes and the "gray wall of silence," the reconceptualizing of prisoners as subhuman, the substitution of power relations for those of justice, and so on.
[5] I leave aside here – though it should not be left aside in some larger analysis – how it is that gang members have come to be as they are.

Clearly, control is important, but just as important is why, when, and how control is exercised, matters that need to be both investigated and monitored. Given that vast numbers of those who are imprisoned pose little threat either to officers or to one another, subjecting them to what can only be seen as humiliations runs the risk either of damaging what are probably already fragile personalities or, no better, of breeding aggressive defiance.

It must be remembered that a large number of those who are imprisoned for wrongdoing suffer from significant mental health problems – problems that may well have contributed to their offender status.[6] They need careful, competent, and respectful handling. Psychiatric and other care is often seriously lacking and prison officers are left with the consequences. It is not easy to be firm, fair, and discerning when institutional constraints easily aggravate a precarious mental or emotional condition.[7] Control cannot be divorced from the particulars of those controlled.

Care

As mentioned earlier, when the state incarcerates it assumes responsibility for the care of inmates. First and foremost, that involves both a recognition of and a commitment to the preservation of their dignity. (Some have argued that when we punish wrongdoing we are already acknowledging, at least to some degree, the dignity of those whom we punish, for in punishing wrongdoing we affirm the responsible agency of those who offend.[8]) Dignity should not be compromised during the period of incarceration, but should be reflected in care for prisoners' physical and psychic well-being *as well as* concern for their better flourishing in future.

As noted above, it is unreasonable to expect that prison officers will be able to attend to all the physical and psychological needs of inmates. Often

---

[6] See Paula Ditton, *Mental Health and Treatment of Inmates and Probationers*, Special Report (Washington, DC: US Department of Justice, Office of Justice Programs, Bureau of Justice Statistics, 1999); A. J. Beck and L. M. Maruschak, *Mental Health Treatment in State Prisons, 2000*, Special Report (Washington, DC: US Department of Justice, Office of Justice Programs, Bureau of Justice Statistics, 2001); Jamie Fellner and Sasha Abramsky, *Ill-Equipped: US Prisons and Offenders with Mental Illness* (New York: Human Rights Watch, 2003).

[7] This is not to deny that there is a group for whom the discipline and structure of a prison may enable them to put their lives together.

[8] Here we leave aside the significant possibility that some who are deemed responsible for what they have done should not have been so held.

prison officers must operate more like 911 (or 000) dispatchers – critical mediators of requests for assistance. Although they should be trained to provide basic first aid and CPR, one of their main roles will be to be sensitive to the various needs of inmates and to broker effective responses to these needs from qualified others.[9]

The religious desires of prisoners should be included in care for psychic well-being. Whatever one may think about the epistemic status of religious belief, it is undeniable that for at least a proportion of those who are imprisoned religion constitutes or comes to constitute a source of meaning and purpose, and responsiveness to its requirements – whether in terms of ritual and practices – should be positive, even if, at a time of increasing concern with religiously based terrorism, discerning. Officers (and administrators) need to make such accommodations as they are able.

Unfortunately, both the physical and psychic needs of inmates are vulnerable to exploitation, and may be used to manipulate or punish. By withholding or delaying care, or by preventing or compromising religious observance, officers are able to extend their control in unethical ways.

The three dimensions of care, custody, and control were insightfully combined in the Correctional Officers' Creed (1979) that the late Bob Barrington, a professor of criminal justice at Northern Michigan University, composed for the American (later, International) Association of Correctional Officers. It is as good a general statement as we have of a professional vision for corrections officers.[10]

Correctional Officers' Creed

To speak sparingly . . . to act, not argue . . . to be in authority through personal presence . . . to correct without nagging . . . to speak with the calm voice of certainty . . . to see everything, and to know what is significant and what not to notice . . . to be neither insensitive to distress nor so distracted by pity as to miss what must elsewhere be seen . . .

To do neither that which is unkind nor self-indulgent in its misplaced charity . . . never to obey the impulse to tongue lash that silent insolence

---

[9] For some recent examples of failures, see Christina Jewett and Dorothy Korber, "Questions Persist over Jail Health Care," *Sacramento Bee*, 12/18/2005, A1.

[10] More traditional codes also exist, notably the United Nations (OHCHR) *Standard Minimum Rules for the Treatment of Prisoners* (1955; 1977) and the American Correctional Association's *Code of Ethics* (1975; rev. 1990).

which in time past could receive the lash . . . to be both firm and fair . . . to know I cannot be fair simply by being firm, nor firm simply by being fair . . .

To support the reputations of associates and confront them without anger should they stand short of professional conduct . . . to reach for knowledge of the continuing mysteries of human motivation . . . to think; always to think . . . to be dependable . . . to be dependable first to my charges and associates, and thereafter to my duty as employee and citizen . . . to keep fit . . . to keep forever alert . . . to listen to what is meant as well as what is said with words and with silences.

To expect respect from my charges and my superiors yet never to abuse the one for abuses from the other . . . for eight hours each working day to be an example of the person I could be at all times . . . to acquiesce in no dishonest act . . . to cultivate patience under boredom and calm during confusion . . . to understand the why of every order I take or give . . .

To hold freedom among the highest values though I deny it to those I guard . . . to deny it with dignity that in my example they find no reason to lose their dignity . . . to be prompt . . . to be honest with all who practice deceit that they not find in me excuse for themselves . . . to privately face down my fear that I not signal it . . . to privately cool my anger that I not displace it on others . . . to hold in confidence what I see and hear, which by telling could harm or humiliate to no good purpose . . . to keep my outside problems outside . . . to leave inside that which should stay inside . . . to do my duty.

Although an aspirational document rather than a code of conduct, Barrington's creed helpfully acknowledges and responds to the deep tensions within the custodial role and, though it does not resolve them in some formulaic fashion, it provides a framework for wise and ethical judgment. Insofar as it is deficient, its deficiency lies primarily in the absence of a sufficiently forward-looking dimension: for the most part those who are incarcerated will be released and those who have their care, custody, and control should count preparation for their release among their important concerns.

Confronting tensions

Tensions among custodial goals

The three goals of care, custody, and control are not intended to be pursued in isolation but together and with regard to one another. Care is to be provided in ways and to the extent that custodial and control functions are not compromised; custody is to be ensured in ways that will not breach the requirements of care and control; control is to be exercised in ways that do not undermine the demands of care and custody. Each has a moderating effect on the others.

It is sometimes said – and it appears so in practice – that the security interests of a prison take priority over others. What that sometimes means is that the prison's caring functions are to be sacrificed to its custodial and control functions. But it is better to seek to realize them all and to see their potential for mutual reinforcement rather than to engage in their simple prioritization (a point that is all the more acute given the weak justification that we have for imprisoning many who are currently incarcerated). The suggestion that care, custody, and control should be seen as mutually reinforcing need not be viewed as unrealistic – at least for medium- and minimum-security settings, in which officers are also confined and unarmed for substantial periods of time. Such officers must be expected to have an interest in their joint realization.

Although Barrington's creed understandably (and rightly) refuses to offer an algorithm for calculating appropriate levels of care, custody, and control, it nevertheless affirms the need for an appropriate balancing of goals. The dignity of the incarcerated is affirmed and there is a recognition that the conditions of their incarceration must not be permitted to derogate from that dignity. That is a rock-bottom requirement, one that permeates care, custody, and control. Dignity, however, is also possessed by fellow inmates, prison officers, victims, and the wider public, and this is implicitly recognized by the custodial and control dimensions of Barrington's creed. Thus officers are called to be sensitive to distress and to possess pity but not "to miss what must elsewhere be seen." They are, moreover, to confront fellow officers "without anger should they stand short of professional conduct" at the same time as they support their reputations. Correction is to be offered in a way that does not humiliate or undermine authority.

Tensions between ideals and culture

Students of imprisonment have noted that the realities of much prison life have led to both prison officers and prisoners developing coping mechanisms that come to constitute informal codes of practice. These informal codes – street wisdom – tailor institutional requirements to what is seen as "reality." Although such informal mechanisms may be honored in the breach no less than in their observance, they nevertheless play a strategic role in the practical interplay of prison officers and prisoners. The following two examples capture something of their flavor.

Kelsey Kauffman's study of Massachusetts prisons revealed the following code for prison officers:

1. Always go to the aid of an officer in distress
2. Don't lug drugs
3. Don't rat
4. Never make a fellow officer look bad in front of inmates
5. Always support an officer in a dispute with an inmate
6. Always support officer sanctions against inmates
7. Don't be a white hat
8. Maintain officer solidarity against all outside groups
9. Show positive concern for fellow guards.[11]

Jeffrey Ross and Stephen Richards provide a corresponding code for prisoners:

Do:
Mind your own business
Watch what you say
Be loyal to convicts as a group
Play it cool
Be sharp
Be honorable
Do your own time
Be tough
Be a man
Pay your debts

Don't:
Snitch on another convict
Pressure another convict
Lose your head

---

[11] Kelsey Kauffman, *Prison Officers and Their World* (Cambridge, MA: Harvard University Press, 1988), 86–117.

Attract attention

Exploit other convicts

Break your word.[12]

Both codes reflect and seek to reinforce an adversarial relation between officers and inmates and both advocate a group solidarity that is likely to be corruptive of more nuanced ethical expectations. One of the ethical challenges for prison officers will be to negotiate the expectations of professionalism with these other powerful (but not iron-clad) expectations. The strength of such informal codes will almost certainly depend on the prevailing climate of a prison: to the extent that professionalism by officers is fostered and supported, both officer and prisoner codes are likely to be seen as provisional.

Tensions between officers and those to whom they are accountable

It can be frightening for a person who is unarmed to be locked into an environment in which he or she is outnumbered by many people who have shown themselves to be antisocial and sometimes dangerous, and who may have some reason to resent his or her presence. There is of course backup, but that may offer only limited comfort. Prison officers frequently consider that those who supervise them – and certainly those in managerial positions – fail to appreciate the hazardous or at least unnerving nature of their situation. How stressful the experience is will depend partly on the history of the particular institution. Although Barrington notes that officers should "expect respect from . . . superiors," and not "abuse the one for abuses from the other," where the original abuse might emanate from either inmates or superiors, he does not register as vividly as he might the tension that often exists between supervisors and those supervised. The street cop / management cop divide that exists in policing exists no less in corrections.[13]

---

[12] Jeffrey Ian Ross and Stephen C. Richards, *Behind Bars: Surviving Prison* (Indianapolis, IN: Alpha Books, 2002), 72.

[13] See, in particular, Elizabeth Reuss-Ianni and Francis A. J. Ianni, "Street Cops and Management Cops: The Two Cultures of Policing," in *Control in the Police Organization*, ed. Maurice Punch (Cambridge, MA: MIT Press, 1983), 25–74.

Tensions between officers and prisoners

Barrington recognizes the inherently conflictual relationship that prison officers have to their charges. The officer is expected to act with firmness and authority, to maintain a professional distance, to be alert and vigilant, forthright and strong. At the same time the officer is not to nag or be captious, but to be sensitive, fair, patient, dependable, and understanding.

Many of the ethical problems that arise in custodial institutions arise because a correct balance has not been kept. An important area of concern has been the level of fraternization that should exist between prison officers and inmates. A relationship that is first and foremost a professional one, in which officers and prisoners acknowledge their respective situations, should provide the framework for an appropriate level of familiarity – though the best way to balance a concern for order with a desire for the future well-being of inmates is not provided by a textbook, manual, code, or rules. Overfamiliarity or fraternization can often lead to favoritism, exploitation, corruption, the provision of opportunities for "divide and conquer" games by inmates, and even blackmail. But at the same time as prison officers acknowledge the equal humanity of their charges, they should not forget why (most of) their charges are where they are. They should be alert to the corruptive possibilities inherent in the connection they have with inmates. The giving and receiving of sexual favors has a well-documented history, as has the use of officers as conduits for contraband. Officers strongly desire that their workdays should go smoothly, and the temptation to "purchase" a trouble-free unit through unprofessional fraternization can be a strong one.

Still, exceedingly difficult ethical problems may arise for prison officers. Consider the case of Jason and Eric, two long-term prisoners in a maximum-security prison. In their third year, it appears to David, a prison officer, that Jason and Eric have developed a significant affection for each other and that, if it has not done so already, the relationship is likely to express itself intimately. David, however, suspects that Jason is HIV positive, but since the state does not require mandatory testing of inmates, he is not 100 percent sure; he wonders whether Eric is aware of this and, if so, what risks Eric is prepared to take. State policy outlaws the distribution of condoms, though clearly some make their way into the prison, and prisoners also use makeshift protective devices. The availability of condoms would seem prudent in this particular case. What is David's responsibility? There is a range of options. One would be to do nothing at all – it could be claimed that because sexual activity of this kind is not approved by the prison authorities, concern for the consequences it might have does not belong "on the radar screen." Or, given the general disapproval of such sexual activity, should steps be taken to separate the two? Or might Eric be taken aside and warned about the possibility that a partner might be HIV positive, so that he should make his choices in an informed way? More compassionately, could David refer to signs of their affection and offer to provide condoms "just to be on the safe side," even though to do so would violate prison regulations? Another possibility would be to note their affection and suggest to each of them that they might request testing, leaving it for them to work out a *modus operandi* in the light of the results. There may be other possibilities as well.

Outside the prison context, a harm-reduction approach would seem to be the most appropriate.[14] Condoms would be readily available. Irrespective of the views one has about same-sex relationships, a moralistic refusal to make harm-reducing options available is less ethical than knowingly allowing others to expose themselves to the risk of serious consequences. Moreover, because the state has taken it upon itself a responsibility for inmates' well-being, it must accept some responsibility for what happens (given what David is aware of) and cannot claim that responsibility has been fully assumed by Jason and Eric. David might want to reason that it is only a matter of happenstance that condom distribution is not permitted in his state, and that if he smuggles them in he would not be violating some deeply held moral principle. He would, though, be transgressing state law, and could not claim that that was of only little moment. Alternatively, some measure of harm reduction might be achieved by separating Jason and Eric, transferring one of them to another unit or even to another prison. Being cruel to be kind? But that just deals – unfeelingly and perhaps only temporarily – with a single case. Should we assume that Jason will then remain

---

[14] We should, though, not overlook the fact that harm-reduction approaches are sometimes claimed to condone or encourage conduct that is otherwise unacceptable. This is not the place to debate the issue of acceptability. What can be said, however, is that a strategy of harm reduction need not signal condonation of disapproved-of behavior, and – with respect to the behaviors involved – there is little empirical evidence that it encourages them, even if it does not do much to prevent such behavior from occurring.

celibate, or that this way of dealing with such problems responds adequately to what is almost certainly a wider problem? Such a move could also stir up trouble, if not from Jason or Eric, then from other prisoners who may feel threatened by a strategy of separation. Perhaps Jason and Eric's situation should provide the institution with reason to think through the wisdom of current practice, even if not current policy (which is likely to be highly politicized).[15] It should rethink the matter for prudential no less than moral reasons. For, if Jason is HIV positive and Eric becomes infected, the state will have responsibility for his ongoing care. On the other side, it will be argued – though this would require empirical backing – that condom availability will lead to an increase in prison rape or in the bartering of sex for various benefits.

Although Barrington's creed sets up broad ethical parameters for cases such as this, it needs to be supplemented by a rich understanding of the institutional context. And even the suggestions so far canvassed need to be supplemented by additional discussion. For example, it is all very well for David to think that he should make an exception in this case, but making exception to a general principle – "It is OK to make exceptions to policies whenever I believe it would be right to do so" – is quite problematic. Indeed, as we noted in Chapter 1, when we assume a professional role, we ordinarily give it priority in cases in which our individual judgment would lead us to act otherwise. Probably David's best move is to attempt to initiate an institutional discussion of the issue, possibly leaving the particular case of Jason and Eric out of it. In the meantime, there might be a general announcement about the dangers of unprotected sex. This would hardly constitute an ideal situation; it illustrates, though, the straitened circumstances in which ethical decision-making must sometimes take place.

Tensions between officers and professionals who work in a prison setting

Although prison officers represent the first line of responsibility for what happens "behind bars," they are not the only people to have close contact with prisoners. A variety of health, education, and welfare providers come into the prison on an intermittent basis, bringing their professional

---

[15] It may of course not be at liberty to alter the policy if state law forbids it.

expectations with them. What they expect as professionals who are dispensing services will not always sit comfortably with what prison officers see as requirements for security. The issue was graphically illustrated recently by reports of pregnant prisoners giving birth while shackled to their beds.[16] Since priority was given to security, healthcare personnel were required to provide their assistance under conditions that were significantly less than ideal for them and almost certainly cruel to the women giving birth. It was not a situation that required such measures. Were the women giving birth going to make a run for it? Or were they going to try to use available equipment as a weapon? To what effect? In cases such as this – and one suspects, in many other cases – more reasonable accommodations are possible. Because the state assumes responsibility for the welfare of those it imprisons, it must ensure that those responsible for welfare are given adequate resources and can provide what they should in a manner that is professionally responsible.

Other professionals – social workers, lawyers, chaplains – may wish for greater privacy than prison authorities want to allow. Although US courts have argued that a prisoner has no right to privacy in his cell[17] (which is not quite the same as saying that a prisoner ought not to be accorded any privacy), when a prisoner has dealings with professionals who would ordinarily observe client confidentiality, the privacy of their transactions should also be honored in a prison setting. The professionals involved may be sworn to act in ways that would uphold prison standards for security, such as agreeing not to convey contraband or messages. But in their professional role they ought to have sufficient privacy to be able to dispense their services professionally.[18]

It is an unfortunate fact of many prison systems that these services are often poorly provided – not just from the point of view of prison officers who fail in their responsibility to act as go-betweens or first contacts, but also in respect of the quality of professional services available to inmates. Quite a number of prison scandals have centered round tendered health and

---

[16] See Adam Liptak, "Prisons Often Shackle Inmates in Labor," *New York Times*, March 2, 2006, A1.

[17] *Hudson v. Palmer*, 468 US 517 (1984).

[18] After 9/11, as Lynne Stewart, the lawyer for Sheik Omar Abdel Rahman, found, that supposed privacy was frequently breached. Conversations between lawyers and their clients are now sometimes monitored.

welfare services that have been completely inadequate. It is very difficult for prisons to attract competent personnel who are willing to work at rates and in conditions of the kind that prisons provide.

Whither corrections?

The fact that in some societies (for example, the United States) the prison population has been growing and is disproportionately drawn from both historically disadvantaged minorities and immigrant groups that have been prone to discrimination has helped to aggravate the substandard conditions that are found in many prisons. It has also helped to perpetuate the general lack of concern about them. But, as well, other social facts have contributed to the perpetuation of poor treatment for many. One is the greater likelihood that middle-class and white-collar offenders will receive fines or probation rather than incarceration; another is the likelihood that, if incarcerated, middle-class and white-collar offenders will be assigned to the comparatively better conditions of a minimum-security institution. Both of these contribute to the perception that those who end up in maximum-security prisons are "beyond the pale," a perception that, in turn, tends to remove these groups from the concern of those who, generally speaking, are in a better position to effect changes in public policy generally (and so changes in public policy with respect to prison life in particular). Except for truly outrageous incidents, what happens in prisons does not attract the attention of a large segment of the public, much less ignite their concern. But it is more than public apathy that is responsible here. The single most important factor that counts heavily against improvement in prison life is the social opprobrium felt by the public toward criminal violators. It is not simply that the public is apathetic with respect to what happens in the prisons (except to complain about the cost to taxpayers). It is, rather, that the public seems not to believe that inmates, having been found guilty of wrongdoing, have any rightful claim on their concern. The public's much more direct contact with police officers conduces to a greater interest in them, and in preparing the latter for making ethically sustainable decisions. But this does not flow through to prison officers. Often placed remotely and behind walls to oversee society's outcasts, prison officers are seen as having a job to do that has little to do with ethics or constitutional rights. The prisoners they oversee have forfeited their claims. Or so it seems. (Politicians, too, do not seem to care about the lot of prisoners, usually being only too happy to exploit the nonvoting inmate in order to win votes as those who are tough on crime and so more than ready to reduce it by increasing the prison population.)

These do not exhaust the facts that allow prison conditions to deteriorate. There is also the relatively secretive operations of jails and prisons, the historical reluctance of the courts to involve themselves in the nitty gritty of prison conditions, the low educational expectations of prison officers (and hence the relatively small or selective interest in prison dynamics shown by researchers in higher education); and so on.

Would professionalization (as discussed in Chapter 4) improve the quality of correctional workers' conduct and, as well, the conditions in correctional facilities? A drive for increased professionalization probably would not hurt, though I would also argue that here, as in the case of policing, it is professionalism rather than professionalization that is most needed. Perhaps, though, some modest increase in the latter would help to foster the former. What is clear is that academy training that fails to focus explicitly and pervasively on the ethical dimensions of correctional work also fails in any claim it may have to professionalism.[19]

Although some changes are taking place in the academy in this regard, they are often marginal, and then too often undermined by the realities of prison resources and the way in which the prevailing prison culture works against what is learned in the academy being put into practice "in the field."

One thing is clear: a society that responds as punitively as it does in the United States and incarcerates as readily as does the United States will soon reap the unfortunate consequences of those policies – unless, that is, imprisonment comes to be viewed as an opportunity as well as a punishment. Nevertheless, if English and European[20] – as well as some US – prison initiatives are any indication, possibilities for more productive outcomes exist. Leadership has always been an important factor both in society generally as well as in hierarchical organizations, and where prison policy and prison leadership have looked beyond punitiveness and a narrow understanding of "care, custody, and control" to the reintegration of inmates into the communities to which they will eventually return, it has borne fruit. Of course, the

---

[19] "The Academy seemed to embrace an institutional denial that what we were being taught to do had a moral aspect." Conover, *Newjack*, 42.

[20] See, for example, Vincenzo Ruggiero, Mick Ryan, and Joe Sim (eds.), *Western European Penal Systems: A Critical Anatomy* (London: Sage, 1995).

future-looking vision that should characterize correctional leadership must be accompanied by the ability to communicate that vision supportively to others, along with the resources that are required both to communicate the vision and to put it into practice. This can be a problem within a community that is generally unsympathetic to and pessimistic about prisoners. The link between reformist management and lower recidivism will need to be shown.

In addition to good leaders, there must also be enlightened unions. As officer unions have become stronger, so too has the potential for collective improvement of work conditions and the quality of life within prisons. But unions have always been two-edged swords. To the extent that they are labor organizations rather than professional associations, they can become self-serving in ways that are at variance with the legitimating purposes of their institutions. So, unless both officer unions and management share some sort of unified professional vision, reformist energies are likely to be dissipated by institutional politics.

Ultimately, however, what is most critical is broader social support for more enlightened penal policies. That will require a decreased reliance on imprisonment as a mode of punishment, much greater transparency, and a willingness to invest more wisely in rehabilitative programs. As a number of European countries have already shown, a good deal is achievable, though of course every system has to take into account (without being bound by) the realities of the prevailing social culture.

14 Reentry and collateral consequences

> Even when the sentence has been completely served, the fact that
> a man has been convicted of a felony pursues him like Nemesis.[1]

We have already noted that about 95 percent of those who are sentenced to prison are later released back into the community – several hundred thousand each year in the United States. You might think that once people had served their sentences – had, as it were, paid their debt to society – they could then resume their lives with all the rights and privileges of ordinary citizens. But that would portray the situation inaccurately. For many of those released from prison there are what are spoken of as the "collateral consequences" of their conviction. Some of these consequences, of course, are understandable. Those convicted of corporate fraud might be barred from returning to executive positions; those who have multiple convictions for driving under the influence may have their driving licenses suspended for a long period; and convicted child-molesters may be prohibited from employment that involves working with children. Such people have lost our trust, and, presuming that it can be done, restoration of such trust must be earned.

But the story is not just about risk management. It is also about status. At one time serious felons used to be subject to "attainder," that is, the loss of all their civil rights, including rights to property and possessions, rights to inherit and bequeath, and the right to bring suit. Although we have abandoned such extreme responses, it is still quite common for people who have completed their sentences (or even, sometimes, those who have been placed only on probation) to suffer various consequences to their status beyond the common social opprobrium of having a criminal record.

---

[1] National Council on Crime and Delinquency, "Annulment of a Conviction of Crime: A Model Act," *Crime & Delinquency* 8 (1962): 98.

Consider the following collateral consequences of conviction, drawn mostly from US jurisdictions, though some also hold for other liberal democratic polities. In a number of US states, those convicted of felonies cannot gain public employment or hold public office. Those convicted of drug felonies may be denied federal assistance, including access to federal housing and food stamps. Eligibility for student loans may be suspended for a period. Federal law excludes felons from many government jobs, from receiving federal contracts, and from owning firearms. They may no longer have the right to vote and will not be eligible to serve on a jury. These represent only some of the consequences of criminal conviction. Although laws relating to such disqualifications are constantly changing, particularly in a federal system such as the United States, all of the examples referred to are quite recent. We will refer to others later.[2] Were those accused aware of them beforehand, they might have been more reluctant to accept a plea bargain. In any case, they often add greatly to the problems of reentry.

Several questions arise here. Should we see such disabilities or disqualifications as part of the punishment for crime or as civil penalties? In either case, are they appropriate, and, if so, why?

Roadblocks to reentry

Given that a significant proportion of those who are imprisoned lack marketable skills for the work force or other socially acceptable roles that they may wish to adopt, we might hope that imprisonment would constitute an opportunity as well as a penalty. Incarceration presents the state with the chance to provide alternatives to crime as a career or lifestyle. If nothing else, the skilling that imprisonment might offer should relieve the boredom that often attends it. Unfortunately, basic skilling – literacy and trade skills – is not well provided for in many prisons. And, ironically, some of the other skills that prisoners may be taught in prison cannot be subsequently used in the marketplace.

Ex-prisoners who have developed skills in prison as barbers, cosmetologists, nail technicians, or athletic trainers (to mention a few) while in prison

---

[2] What is and what is not permitted to those who have served prison sentences is constantly changing. Not even local officials can keep up. A good resource on the state of play is The Sentencing Project, <www.sentencingproject.org/>.

often cannot market these skills upon release. Like many forms of employment, those with criminal records will find themselves excluded by statute or the rules of professional/trade associations. A sampling of other types of jobs from which ex-felons may find themselves excluded includes landscape architecture, family therapy, engineering, real estate, electrolysis, land surveying, interior design, and shorthand reporting. In some US states, it is possible to apply for a certificate of relief or certificate of good conduct – but these often take time to qualify for and organize, and though such certificates may not be "costly" in themselves, ex-felons are likely to need formal assistance in applying for them and may not find it easy to scrape together the necessary resources. Moreover, such applications do not necessarily succeed (only about half are successful), and certificates need not carry weight with a potential employer. In other cases, only an executive pardon will enable an ex-felon to resume all his opportunities, but their granting tends to be haphazard.

Except for clear cases of risk or eroded authority, there should be a presumption that, once those who have been incarcerated have done their time, they can resume the life of ordinary citizens. Such presumptions can of course be overridden (for reasons that we will explore), but it is already hard enough for people who have been imprisoned to readjust to the world "outside." If we are seriously interested in diminishing the high rate of recidivism, we should place as few barriers as possible in the way of those who are reentering the wider society.

Civil disqualifications or punishments?

How should we view such disqualifications? Sometimes they are clearly intended as punishments. The recidivist drunken driver who loses his license for a two-year period receives that suspension as part of his sentence, and we can assess it as we do any punitive imposition: Is it appropriate and proportionate to the crime? Does it serve a legitimate social purpose? Except in unusual circumstances, a lifetime suspension would be seen as unreasonably harsh, even if it served to keep the roads a bit safer (assuming that the harshness did not prompt drivers to violate the ban).

Some disqualifications seem to serve more as civil penalties. Those who are responsible for providing the public with services may wish to assure their clientele that the providers of those services can be trusted. And so, as part of that assurance, they may exclude people who have a criminal record from offering the service in question. In such cases, although proportionality in the retributive sense may not be appropriate, we may still ask whether such a ban is reasonable, given the variety of offenses for which people can be convicted. It is likely is that we will want to see some "match" between the disqualification and the offense. It may make some (often minimal) sense to prevent (at least for a time) a person who has been convicted of violent assault from seeking employment as a barber, but why does it make sense to prevent a person who has been convicted of food stamp fraud from being employed as the skilled barber he learned to be while in prison?

Sometimes it is difficult to know whether a disqualification is to be viewed as a punishment or simply as a civil disablement. Perhaps a disqualification can be both. The embezzling company director who is barred from accepting company directorships for five years after serving his sentence is being punished as well as kept from a position that he has abused in the past and may be tempted to abuse again. As well as communicating our censure, we want to see whether he can keep his sheet clean once returned to society.

A serious problem with many disqualifications is that those subject to them do not realize what will be effected by their conviction. Nor could they have been easily discovered, because such disqualifications are often scattered through disparate pieces of legislation. Disqualifications are unlikely to be mentioned at arraignment or sentencing, even though, were they known, they might have made a defendant more reluctant to accept a plea agreement.

Grounds for disqualification

As we noted at the beginning of this chapter, post-conviction disqualifications make most sense when the offense for which a person has been convicted is likely to affect the trust that others could place in that person to deliver services in an appropriate manner. A gynecologist who has taken sexual liberties with patients or an accountant who has fiddled the books has a credibility problem. Many occupations involve a fiduciary relationship between client and provider. That is, the client assumes an environment of trust in which the provider has some kind of privileged access and is entrusted with the responsibility of handling that access with integrity as well as competence. In cases in which a fiduciary relationship has been violated, it may be some time before the assumption of trust can be reestablished. For, once lost, trust takes effort to restore.

The foregoing examples suggest that a major reason for rendering people ineligible for certain opportunities or benefits is risk management. A good deal of social life is based on trust. Although we should not be gullible, our social life cannot function adequately unless we can presume that those who are licensed to provide certain services can be relied upon to deliver them with integrity as well as competence. Competence is not sufficient, given that we are often putting ourselves in the hands of such service-providers. It is of course reasonable that we do some checking of our own, but unless the field is unregulated or known to be problematic, we cannot be expected to cover every possibility. *Caveat emptor* is inadequate to the pressures of contemporary social life.

Several factors might be considered relevant to post-conviction disqualification. Where there is a high presumption of public trust – as in the professions, in which members have often been given the right to be the exclusive providers of a service – it seems fair that those who have criminally violated the terms of that service provision should be prevented from offering such services until they have shown that they can once again be trusted to do so. The privilege of being an exclusive provider is meant to go with a high degree of trust. Coupled with that, there is often a significant vulnerability on the part of those who make use of the services. People who need lawyers or doctors are often in no great position to pick and choose among them or to investigate them, and it is therefore important, as part of the conditions of a satisfactory social life, that we provide assurances that those who are permitted to offer such services can be trusted to deliver them in a way that does not take advantage of others. If it is not a matter of vulnerability, then it is one in which great trust in the provider is required – there is a fiduciary relationship whereby the provider is trusted to act for the other. Another consideration that is likely to be of relevance is where the person is accorded a degree of social authority and a criminal conviction would detract from that. We might not wish to disqualify a judge who had been convicted for driving under the influence; but if the judge threatens or blackmails an ex-lover in order to keep the story from getting out we are likely to wonder about the judge's probity and impartiality, qualities that are important to judicial authority.[3]

However, many existing disqualifications seem to do no more than play to the "tough on crime" approaches of many politicians – and, of course, also to the prejudices of a wider politically vocal public who are or can be persuaded that criminals should not benefit from taxpayer dollars. (They appear to forget that recidivism is probably a bigger drain on those dollars than publicly provided opportunities for breaking out of the cycle that looms.) Making ex-felons ineligible for food stamps, educational loans or grants, and public housing, and keeping them out of forms of employment that are not clearly related to their offenses, seem to be counterproductive responses even if such benefits can be abused. Almost any opportunity can be abused; but to use the possibility of abuse as a reason for denying fairly basic opportunities is surely the wrong way to go. The presumption that benefits and opportunities are likely to be abused reflects not only cynicism but prejudice. Even the convicted drug-user who relapses may simply be stumbling as part of an arduous process of recovery.

A deeper reason for making ex-offenders ineligible lies in a sense of fairness. Access to educational loans or housing is limited, and it is often felt to be unfair that ex-felons should have access to resources that some "good citizens" will not therefore be given. The argument would be stronger were ex-felons privileged in some way; but if they have already served their time, why should they continue to be penalized? Once that has happened, their ability to compete with others is simply leveling the playing field.

In addition to being denied certain opportunities for employment and the wherewithal for everyday needs, ex-felons are often denied important opportunities for participating in civic life. Perhaps understandably, ex-prisoners are disqualified from jury service – they may find it difficult to bury any resentment they feel against the criminal justice system (though in fact few will ever have gone before a jury); and, it may be argued, who are they to judge the guilt of others? Even so, it is not easy to see why this should be a lifetime ban rather than for a set period after release (or the conclusion of parole). Unless we are prepared to say that those who have violated our criminal laws are incapable of redemption, there should be some social

---

[3] See the example given in Chapter 9, note 17.

mechanism that will enable most criminals to regain social rights or privileges that they have had to surrender. After, say, ten years, as in many places, a person might automatically become re-eligible for jury service or be eligible to apply to have jury privileges restored. In quite a number of countries jury privileges are immediately restored at the conclusion of mandated oversight – as a recognition that debts have been paid and that the person is being given an opportunity to start afresh.

The case of voting

A more significant disqualification concerns voting rights. In the USA, prisoners retain their right to vote in just two US states (and Puerto Rico). In many other countries that right is also retained, though it is sometimes suspended in the case of long sentences. Where the right is suspended, it is almost always automatically restored upon completion of the sentence. Although there has been significant change in recent years, a number of US jurisdictions still *permanently* disenfranchise those convicted of crimes or permit voting rights to be restored only after a fairly arduous process has been followed, often after a significant period of ineligibility. Given the significance of voting rights to citizenship in a liberal democratic polity, this is a serious disability.

In February, 1972, Abran Ramirez, a forty-three-year-old farmworker, married, with five children, sought to register to vote in San Luis Obispo County, California. His application was refused because he had a felony conviction and had spent some time in prison. Twenty years before, Ramirez had been convicted in Texas of "robbery by assault," an offense that he said arose out of an argument in a restaurant. Without counsel, and on advice of the judge, he had pleaded guilty. He was paroled after three months and successfully served out a ten-year parole period.

After his application was refused, Ramirez and others petitioned the Supreme Court of California as part of a class action. The court accepted that the exclusion fell foul of the equal protection clause of the US Constitution's fourteenth amendment, which requires that similarly situated people be treated equally by the laws of the state they are in. By being denied the vote they were being denied equal protection of the law that gave Californian residents the right to vote. But on appeal the US Supreme Court reversed this decision, 6:3.[4] Not surprisingly, the argument turned on constitutional issues, in particular whether §1 of the fourteenth amendment (the equal protection clause) trumped §2, which permits an exception to the right to vote in respect of those found guilty of "participation in rebellion, or other crime." The Court argued that §1 could not have been intended to prohibit what is permitted by §2. The only question concerned the meaning of §2. The majority held that the permission allowed states to exclude from voting any who had been convicted of a felony – not just a felony that might have been construed similarly to rebellion (such as piracy and treason). And, because the provision was constitutionally based, it did not require grounding in a "compelling state interest."

Although some have questioned the breadth of the Supreme Court's interpretation of §2, our question here is whether denying Ramirez the vote was morally justified – not only now that he had been released and served out his parole, *but even as he was incarcerated*. In an aside at the conclusion of his opinion, Justice Rehnquist noted the claim by some who had submitted briefs that the rehabilitation of those who had served their sentences was fostered by returning them to full citizenship. (He might have also applied it to those who were currently incarcerated.) He chose not to pass judgment on this claim, but argued that it was for California, and not the Supreme Court, to decide whether restoring the vote to ex-felons would be rehabilitative. Given that §2 of the fourteenth amendment is only a permission, it was open to states such as California to determine that good would be done by re-enfranchising ex-felons. It makes some sense to argue that the more open and welcoming the society to which felons return, the easier it will be for them to find their way in it. It makes even better sense to argue that if prisoners have not only the opportunity to consider the rights and duties of citizenship while they are serving their sentences but also the opportunity (and even encouragement) to act on such matters by voting, the preparation for their return to the community and the transition to it will be made easier. Although this looks like a radical suggestion, it is so only in the United States. Most European countries (Bosnia, Croatia, Cyprus, Denmark, Iceland, Ireland, Finland, Latvia, Lithuania, Macedonia, the Netherlands, Poland, Slovenia, Spain, Sweden, Switzerland, and Ukraine) permit prisoners to vote, and most of those that do not (Armenia, Bulgaria, the

---

[4] *Richardson v. Ramirez et al.*, 418 US 24 (1974).

Czech Republic, Estonia, Hungary, Romania, and Russia) are still emerging from dictatorial pasts.

The suggestion just made does not have any particular application to Abran Ramirez. It was, after all, ten years after his release from parole that he sought to assert his right to vote. But what did it say about him that he was then refused? What does it say about any disenfranchised group of people – whether they constitute an ethnic minority, women, or ex-felons? Basically it says that they are second-class citizens who, though they may have political obligations, can be denied one of its critical rights – the right to vote that, at least in the United States, is thought to be sufficiently important to be given constitutional status.

It is also a denial of a basic moral expectation of a liberal democratic state – namely, that people should generally be permitted and probably are morally obligated to have a measurable say in decisions that affect their interests.[5] Given the extent to which prisoners and even ex-prisoners are affected by social policies, there would seem to be a pressing reason for permitting them to register views on the social decisions that affect them. It is hardly surprising that prison conditions are left off the political radar screen as much as they are when those who have experienced them are given no opportunity to register their voice. Politicians have no need to accommodate ex-felons in their election sales pitches when those who might publicly voice their concern about prison conditions and the collateral consequences of imprisonment cannot register that concern at the ballot box.

The right to vote, though a civil right, taps into even deeper issues than citizenship – into the matter of personhood. For better or worse – though, we trust, better – the liberal democratic state is an attempt to create a social order in which the potentials of personhood can be broadly maximized. As we have already noted, the Lockean state of nature is not a good environment for personal flourishing because our basic human rights cannot be secured. And so a civil order is instituted to ensure not only that they can be secured but also that certain distributive minima can be assured (such as basic education, healthcare, and welfare). The state thus becomes an important element in the realization of our personhood.

---

[5] See David T. Risser, "The Moral Problem of Nonvoting," *Journal of Social Philosophy* 34, no. 3 (Fall, 2003): 348–63.

That is why measurable participative guarantees such as the vote are so important. True, the franchise is not all-important. Free speech, freedom of association and religion, the right to a fair trial, and various rights against intrusions by government agents (such as privacy rights, rights against unreasonable search and seizure, the right against self-incrimination, and the prohibition against cruel and unusual punishment) are also important. But the right to vote has an important symbolic as well as real value as a guarantee of effective participation in public affairs. In denying Ramirez the right to vote, California was telling him not only that he was a second-class citizen but that he did not deserve the right to participate countably in an important aspect of his life as a human being.

Of course, those who oppose giving voting rights to felons or ex-felons have not wished to accept such conclusions. Some, indeed, have employed basic liberal democratic arguments to reach alternative conclusions. They have argued that when people commit crimes they reject the terms of the social contract that is constitutive of a liberal democratic order and have therefore forfeited, or excluded themselves from, its benefits (or at least some of them). The state is no longer bound to them because they have rejected its terms of association. Ramirez, it is argued, morally disenfranchised himself by refusing to accept the conditions of liberal democratic social engagement. Of course he did not lose everything – he was not made an "outlaw" in the sense of one who is denied all his civil rights – but he was put in roughly the same position (in this regard) as a person who has been granted permanent residency but does not (yet) have citizenship. However, whereas the permanent resident may aspire to citizenship as a fuller realization of his rights of personality, Ramirez was – at least at that point – given no opportunity to reassert or recover his right. Although that has now changed in California and in a number of other states (albeit with varying degrees of difficulty), there are, as we noted earlier, still a number of states that permanently disenfranchise ex-felons.

There is, however, a critical weakness in the argument that violation of a law represents a rejection of the terms of the social contract. Who of us can claim that we have never violated any law? True, any violation may subject us to a penalty (if we are found out), but that penalty is part of the contractual understanding. We remain bound by the broad terms of the contract – and bound to accept the penalty – but we do not reject its terms altogether. There is more to a rejection than a violation. Although it is difficult to know the exact original facts in Ramirez's case (since it was plea-bargained), it can hardly be said that what he did put him outside the terms of the social contract, even if he violated one of its mandates.[6] Had Ramirez not accepted the jurisdiction of the court that sentenced him, we might perhaps have had more reason to wonder about his wholeheartedness, but that was not the case and neither is it the case with the vast majority of those who are convicted of crimes.

Even were we to argue that part of Ramirez's penalty for violating the law should have been a suspension of voting rights while in prison or on parole, it is difficult to see why this disqualification should have continued beyond that period. As we noted earlier, issues of public trust may mandate some additional constraints beyond the service of a sentence, but there was no connection between the offense for which Ramirez was convicted and his fitness to vote. One might imagine, perhaps, that conviction of a violent crime might lead to one's being prohibited from owning a firearm or something like that, but the connection with voting is much less obvious.

Nevertheless, an argument that is often used in these contexts appeals to what is known as "the purity of the ballot box." First enunciated in 1884, it articulates a widespread sentiment that those who have committed felonies have morally discredited themselves. It was not used in Ramirez's case – which dealt exclusively with the issue of constitutional provision for states to deny voting privileges to their residents. But it may well have informed the views of those responsible for maintaining what was then California's exclusionary state law, and it has often figured in other cases. In the Alabama case in which it was first invoked, several overlapping considerations were advanced for refusing to permit ex-felons to resume their voting rights:

> The manifest purpose is to preserve the purity of the ballot box, which is the only sure foundation of republican liberty, and which needs protection against the invasion of corruption, just as much as that of ignorance, incapacity or tyranny . . . The presumption is, that one rendered infamous by conviction of felony, or other base offense indicative of great moral turpitude, is unfit for the privilege of suffrage, or to hold office, upon terms

---

[6] Indeed, were the argument to be taken seriously, Ramirez ought to have been no longer legally bound by the criminal law of the State of California.

of equality with freemen who are clothed by the State with the toga of political citizenship. It is proper, therefore, that this class should be denied a right, the exercise of which might sometimes hazard the welfare of communities, if not that of the State itself, at least in close political contests.[7]

Despite the appearance of a single argument here, there are really several: (1) those convicted of felonies are not worthy to vote – either (a) because they are not morally competent, or (b) because they are no longer "one of us"; if they do vote, either (2) their participation will undermine the authority of the voting process because (a) the vote will not reflect the will of those committed to the ends of a republican polity or (b) by acting irresponsibly they have shown their incapacity to vote responsibly, or (3) serious deleterious consequences will flow from such a permission by (a) tainting the results, (b) skewing the results, or (c) inviting electoral fraud. There is a tendency for opponents of voting rights for ex-felons to skip from one supportive consideration to another. However, no one of the claims is strong enough to justify continued disenfranchisement. Nor, collectively, do they add up to a justification for exclusion.

Let us use Ramirez's case to illustrate. (1)(a) Why, for example, should Ramirez's conviction have shown him to be morally incompetent to vote? Morally incompetent, perhaps (though I doubt it), to own a firearm, but why should this also cast doubt on his moral capacity to make sound political judgments? Had Ramirez been guilty of treason or rebellion, we might reasonably have raised the question, but surely not in the case of a relatively simple assault. (1)(b) Perhaps it serves as a convenient affirmation of our identity that we can characterize Ramirez and those like him as "them," though, like almost all "us/them" divisions, it does not withstand much scrutiny. Ramirez has served his time. It is now time for the benefits as well as burdens of his citizenship to be reinstated. (2)(a) The idea that voting by ex-felons will undermine the authority of the voting process by incorporating the votes of those who lack commitment to republican values surely over-interprets the significance of a felony conviction, and most certainly in the case of someone such as Ramirez, who got carried away by a particular incident. A failure to live up to republican values should not *ipso facto* be seen as a lack of commitment to them. (2)(b) Moreover, unlike infants

---

[7] *Washington v. State*, 75 Ala. 582, at 585 (1884).

or the insane, Ramirez had not shown himself to be incapable of voting responsibly. The very fact of his punishment constituted a recognition that he could be held responsible for his acts. Irresponsibility should not be confused with nonresponsibility. (3)(a) Nor can we assume that deleterious consequences will follow from the franchise being given back to ex-felons. Why should we assume, that, like the rotten apple in the barrel, they will taint the whole? Once convicted and punished, do we have any reason to assume an ongoing rottenness? (3)(b) Do we have any reason to think that ex-felons will vote as a bloc to defeat good initiatives or electoral candidates? Even were ex-felons to vote as a bloc, would their doing so be any more problematic than other voting blocs that are currently undisturbed (and even cultivated by the major political parties)? Indeed, were they to do so (though it would be very unlikely), they might well exert valuable pressure for change (to deplorable prison conditions, for example). (3)(c) And, finally, should a failure in one area of an ex-felon's life be taken to indicate a failure in others? Why we should think Ramirez would perpetrate electoral fraud is beyond comprehension. Ironically, those found guilty of electoral fraud usually retain their voting rights, because their offense is not seen as felonious.

There is one other dimension to the voting debate that was not so apparent at the time at which Ramirez's case was heard, but which has become much more prominent as increasing numbers have been disabled from voting. This has been the disparate impact of disqualification. The burden of disqualification has fallen disproportionately on historically deprived minorities, particularly African-American males. Although it is sometimes argued that the chips must be permitted to fall where they do, the argument tends to gloss over the connection between the history and the criminality, and the slow and painful efforts that are needed to reverse this situation. Racial discrimination and the disparities that it has engendered may have been ameliorated, but they have not yet vanished. Moreover, because some communities are much harder hit by deprivation and criminality, and those who are taken from them are not counted in census tallies (but rather as part of the communities in which the prisons are sited), not only has the eligible voting population diminished but members of these communities are also unable to achieve the kind of political representation and economic benefits that can be responsive to their needs. And the cycle of deprivation and criminality is perpetuated. Only recently have court decisions begun to take notice of this fact.[8]

Unblocking reentry

Earlier we noted how the problems of reentering society after a felony conviction are exacerbated by a variety of disqualifications. Nowhere is this problem more critical than in access to housing and employment. Many ex-felons are disentitled from housing eligibilities,[9] they are prohibited from getting a (commercial or, in some cases, private) driver's license (sometimes permanently), and many job opportunities are denied them. These problems have increased since September 11, 2001, ostensibly as a response to the need for greater national security.

As we noted earlier, there may sometimes be precautionary barriers to employment – when, for example, there is a reasonable relation between the trust needed for a particular form of employment and the offense for which the person was convicted. This might be important in cases in which the employment involves a fiduciary relationship (say, law, business) or the client population is especially vulnerable (say, children, and residents in nursing homes). But often – and most critically since September 11, 2001 – the barriers have had little relationship to prior offenses. A criminal record *as such* disqualifies. A major problem area involves disqualifications due to drug possession or use. In the United States, these comprise a substantial proportion of felony convictions and disproportionately affect poor minorities.[10] A major review is needed here. Even if the devastation sometimes caused by drugs is something that we need to address as a society, we may reasonably ask whether current practices of criminalization represent an enlightened

---

[8] See, for example, *Farrakhan v. Washington*, 338 F.3d 1009 (9th Cir. 2003). On the economic effects of current distributional policy, see Eric Lotke and Peter Wagner, "The Modern American Penal System: Prisoners of the Census: Electoral and Financial Consequences of Counting Prisoners Where They Go, Not Where They Come From," *Pace Law Review* 24 (2004): 587–607.

[9] The problem is exacerbated by the fact that private landlords will often do a record check and refuse to rent to people with a criminal record.

[10] It needs to be remembered that poor minorities are no more likely to use drugs than others; they are just more likely to be caught.

social response to the problem. But if, in addition to the imprisonment that is often prescribed for drug possession and use, those who have been released find that their criminal record excludes them from many forms of employment, it is not difficult to anticipate a recidivist effect. It is well established that steady employment, along with access to other social benefits, is an important antidote to recidivism.

The situation is even worse than this. For legislation now allows (and sometimes mandates) retroactive scrutiny of the records of those who are currently employed in certain kinds of position and, despite the fact that they may have given untroubled and faithful service, they can find themselves out of a job. Even when legislation does not exclude employment in a particular occupation, employers have shown themselves unwilling to employ those with criminal records.[11] This creates a catch-22 situation. If a prospective employee is up-front about his past (often a sign of determination to do things differently), his past may be held against him, but if (knowing the way the job market works) he does not disclose his past (and is found out), he may be fired for lying. The increasing accessibility of (sometimes inaccurate) criminal records makes the latter increasingly likely.

Several responses seem to be morally called for. First of all, a substantive relation between a particular disqualification and conviction for a crime (or crime of a particular kind) should have to be demonstrated. Was the offense of a kind to undermine the trust demanded or the authority exercised by this occupational position? Secondly, other than in quite exceptional circumstances, disqualifications should not be permanent. As we know, people sometimes do foolish things when they are young, but over time become much more responsible. Or, just as often, they are rehabilitated, if not by prison then by other events in their lives. In almost any case, it ought to be possible (and easy) for those convicted of a crime to put it behind them. They should not be "marked for life." Thirdly, retrospective background checks should be discouraged, except in cases in which the client population is extremely vulnerable, and even then should be acted upon only with restraint. The case of convicted pedophiles working with children might be a case in point. We should give more weight to what is patently the case (an unblemished work record) than to what is speculatively argued (persisting

---

[11] Though they are formally barred from refusing to employ *solely* because of a criminal record.

dangerousness). Fourthly, people who are offered plea bargains (that is, the vast majority of those who have criminal records) should be informed of the major collateral consequences of their agreeing to plead guilty to particular charges. People do not make judgments about whether or not to go to trial simply on the basis of their guilt or innocence: they also take into account the costs to them of the trial process and, of course, any potential long-term costs (such as collateral consequences).[12] Publicity is an important liberal democratic value, and a failure to disclose the full consequences of a particular course of action (such as, for example, accepting a plea bargain) violates that expectation. And finally, to the extent that criminal records are made publicly available, there should be a strong commitment to ensuring their accuracy (perhaps by penalizing those who post inaccurate records). There should be an undertaking by public agencies that make records available that what is available can be relied on.

It is in the interest of a strong liberal democracy not only that it secures the important rights of its citizens through appropriate means, including the criminal law, but also that, in cases in which people have transgressed its expectations, significant efforts are devoted to ensuring that they become more socially productive members. It is to neither the credit nor the strength of a liberal democracy that its policies create an ever-growing number of people whom it has marginalized.

[12] As it presently stands, however, the large – and problematic – disparity between plea bargained and trial penalties tends to be determinative.

Selected further reading

The items mentioned here supplement any material referred to in notes.

General

Discussions of criminal justice ethics, conceived of as institutional and professional ethics, are relatively recent. A few are single-authored – Cyndi Banks, *Criminal Justice Ethics: Theory and Practice* (Thousand Oaks, CA: Sage, 2004); Joycelyn Pollock, *Ethics in Crime and Justice: Dilemmas and Decisions*, 4th edn. (Belmont, CA: Thomson Wadsworth, 2004); Jay S. Albanese, *Professional Ethics in Criminal Justice: Being Ethical When No One is Looking* (Boston: Pearson, 2006); several others are collections – Paul Leighton and Jeffrey Reiman (eds.), *Criminal Justice Ethics* (Upper Saddle River, NJ: Prentice Hall, 2001); Michael C. Braswell, Belinda R. McCarthy, and Bernard J. McCarthy, *Justice Crime and Ethics*, 5th edn. (Cincinnati, OH: Anderson, 2005). But there also exist more general jurisprudential discussions that are likely to be valuable ethical resources. For the US context, see Joshua Dressler, *Understanding Criminal Law*, 3rd edn. (New York: Matthew Bender / Lexis-Nexis, 2001); for the British discussion, see Andrew Ashworth and Mike Redmayne, *The Criminal Process*, 3rd edn. (Oxford: Oxford University Press, 2005); Lucia Zedner, *Criminal Justice* (Oxford: Clarendon, 2004).

Part I: Criminalization

Broad questions of political theory are canvassed in Leslie Green, *The Authority of the State* (Oxford: Clarendon, 1988); A. John Simmons, *Justification and Legitimacy: Essays on Rights and Obligations* (Cambridge: Cambridge University Press, 2001); and Tom Christiano, "Authority," in *Stanford Encyclopedia of Philosophy*, ed. Edward N. Zalta, <http://plato.stanford.edu/entries/authority>. For a detailed and wide-ranging discussion of criminalization, see Joel Feinberg, *The Moral Limits of Criminal Law* (New York: Oxford University Press, 1984–8), 4 vols.

Chapter 1

Critical discussions of major social contract theorists can be found in Christopher W. Morris (ed.), *The Social Contract Theorists: Critical Essays on Hobbes, Locke, and Rousseau* (Lanham, MD: Rowman & Littlefield, 1999). On role morality, see Alan Gewirth, "Professional Ethics: The Separatist Thesis," *Ethics* 96 (January, 1986): 282–300; Michael O. Hardimon, "Role Obligations," *Journal of Philosophy* 91 (1994): 333–63; and David Luban, *Lawyers and Justice* (Princeton, NJ: Princeton University Press, 1988), Chs. 6–7.

Chapter 2

Apart from Feinberg (above), see H. L. A. Hart, *The Concept of Law*, 2nd edn. (Oxford: Clarendon, 1997); R. A. Duff and Stuart Green (eds.), *Defining Crimes: Essays on the Special Part of Criminal Law* (Oxford: Oxford University Press, 2005); Alan Norrie, *Crime, Reason and History: A Critical Introduction to Criminal Law*, 2nd edn. (London: Butterworths, 2001).

Chapter 3

An influential recent discussion of dirty hands can be found in Michael Walzer, "Political Action: The Problem of Dirty Hands," *Philosophy & Public Affairs* 2 (Winter, 1973): 160–80. A good deal of material is collected in Paul Rynard and David P. Shugarman (eds.), *Cruelty and Deception: The Controversy over Dirty Hands in Politics* (Ontario: Broadview Press, 2000). A more general discussion of ends and means is Giuliano Pontara, *Does the End Justify the Means?* Filosofiska Studier, no. 20 (Stockholm: Filosofiska Institutionen vid Stockholms Universitet, 1967). A good discussion of the "ticking bomb" scenario can be found in David Luban, "Liberalism, Torture, and the Ticking Bomb," *Virginia Law Review* 91 (2005), 1425–61.

Part II: Policing

General discussions of police ethics include Edwin Delattre, *Character and Cops: Ethics in Policing*, 5th edn. (Washington, DC: AEI Press, 2005); John Kleinig, *The Ethics of Policing* (Cambridge: Cambridge University Press, 1996); Tim Newburn (ed.), *Policing: Key Readings* (Cullompton: Willan Publishing, 2004); Seumas Miller, John Blackler, and Andrew Alexandra, *Police Ethics*, 2nd edn. (Sydney: Allen & Unwin, 2006); Seumas Miller and John Blackler, *Ethical Issues in Policing* (Aldershot: Ashgate, 2005); and Seumas Miller (ed.), *Police Ethics* (Aldershot: Ashgate, 2007). A collection of international documents can be found in Ralph Crawshaw and

Leif Holmström, *Essential Texts on Human Rights for the Police: A Compilation of International Instruments* (Leiden: Brill, 2001).

Chapter 4

On the police role, most influential has been Egon Bittner, *The Functions of Police in Modern Society* (Washington, DC: National Institute of Mental Health, 1970). But see also William Ker Muir, Jr., *Police: Streetcorner Politicians* (Chicago: University of Chicago Press, 1977); Carl Klockars, *The Idea of Police* (Beverly Hills, CA: Sage, 1985); and Peter Manning, *Policing Contingencies* (Chicago: University of Chicago Press, 2003).

Chapter 5

Police discretion is surveyed in Samuel Walker, *Taming the System: The Control of Discretion in Criminal Justice* (New York: Oxford University Press, 1993). A valuable corrective on discretion is George P. Fletcher, "Some Unwise Reflections about Discretion," *Law & Contemporary Problems* 47 (Autumn, 1984): 269–86. A standard work on selective enforcement is Kenneth Culp Davis, *Police Discretion* (St. Paul, MN: West, 1975). For additional material, see John Kleinig (ed.), *Handled with Discretion: Ethical Issues in Police Decision Making* (Lanham, MD: Rowman & Littlefield, 1996).

Chapter 6

On coercion generally, see Scott Anderson, "Coercion," *Stanford Encyclopedia of Philosophy*, ed. Edward N. Zalta, <http://plato.stanford.edu/entries/coercion>. A valuable compendium of documents and European cases is Ralph Crawshaw and Leif Holmström, *Essential Cases on Human Rights for the Police: Reviews and Summaries of International Cases* (Leiden: Martinus Nijhoff, 2006). For discussions of chokeholds and high-speed pursuits, see James J. Fyfe, "The Los Angeles Chokehold Controversy," *Criminal Law Bulletin* 19, no. 1 (1983): 61–7; Dennis Kenney and Geoff Alpert, *Police Pursuits: What We Know* (Washington, DC: PERF, 2000); Geoffrey P. Alpert and L. A. Fridell, *Police Vehicles and Firearms: Instruments Of Deadly Force* (Prospect Heights, IL: Waveland Press, 1992). Additional material on the police use of force can be found in Jerome H. Skolnick and James J. Fyfe, *Above the Law: Police and the Excessive Use of Force* (New York: Free Press, 1993). Sissela Bok, *Lying: Moral Choices in Public and Private Life* (New York: Pantheon, 1978), is a major resource for discussions of deception.

Part III: Courts

Broad-ranging philosophically oriented discussions can be found in Antony Duff, Lindsay Farmer, Sandra Marshall, and Victor Tadros, *The Trial on Trial: Truth and Due Process* (Oxford: Hart Publishing, 2004); and Larry Laudan, *Truth, Error, and Criminal Law: An Essay in Legal Epistemology* (Cambridge: Cambridge University Press, 2006). For a review of the criminal courts of England and Wales, see Lord Justice Auld, *A Review of the Criminal Courts of England and Wales* (September, 2001), www.criminal-courts-review.org.uk/index.htm>.

Chapter 7

On prosecutors generally, see William McDonald (ed.), *The Prosecutor* (Beverly Hills, CA: Sage, 1979); Bennett L. Gershman, *Prosecutorial Misconduct*, rev. edn. (St. Paul, MN: Clark Boardman Callaghan / Thomson West, 2005); Stanley Z. Fisher, "In Search of the Virtuous Prosecutor: A Conceptual Framework," *American Journal of Criminal Law* 15 (1988): 197–261; Bruce A. Green, "Why Should Prosecutors Seek Justice?" *Fordham Urban Law Journal* 26 (March, 1999): 607–43; Leslie C. Griffin, "The Prudent Prosecutor," *Georgetown Journal of Legal Ethics* 14 (Winter, 2001): 259–307; Abbe Smith, "Can You Be a Good Person and a Good Prosecutor?" *Georgetown Journal of Legal Ethics* 14 (Winter, 2001): 355–400. The rise of plea-bargaining is detailed in George Fisher, *Plea Bargaining's Triumph: A History of Plea Bargaining in America* (Stanford, CA: Stanford University Press, 2004). For good examples of prosecutorial codes, see *The Code for Crown Prosecutors* (London: Crown Prosecution Service, 2004), <www.cps.gov.uk>; International Association of Prosecutors, *Standards of Professional Responsibility and Statement of the Essential Duties and Rights of Prosecutors* <www.iap.nl.com/stand2.htm>. Effects of pressures to win are detailed in Catherine Ferguson-Gilbert, "It is Not Whether You Win or Lose, It is How You Play the Game: Is the Win–Loss Scorekeeping Mentality Doing Justice for Prosecutors?" *California Western Law Review* 38 (Fall, 2001): 283–309. On excesses in closing arguments, see Rosemary Nidiry, "Restraining Adversarial Excess in Closing Argument," *Columbia Law Review* 96 (1996): 1299–334. Recent discussion of Lord Brougham's position can be found in Albert W. Alschuler, "How to Win the Trial of the Century: The Ethics of Lord Brougham and the O. J. Simpson Defense Team," *McGeorge Law Review* 291 (1998): 291–321.

Chapter 8

See generally, Monroe H. Freedman, *Lawyers' Ethics in an Adversary System* (Indianapolis: Bobbs-Merrill, 1975); David Luban, *Lawyers and Justice* (Princeton,

NJ: Princeton University Press, 1988); William Simon, *The Practice of Justice: A Theory of Lawyers' Ethics* (Cambridge, MA: Harvard University Press, 1998); Rodney J. Uphoff (ed.), *Ethical Problems Facing the Criminal Defense Lawyer: Practical Answers to Tough Questions* (Chicago, IL: Criminal Justice Section, American Bar Association, 1995). Arthur Applbaum raises probing questions about the morality of professionalism in "Professional Detachment: The Executioner of Paris," and "Are Lawyers Liars? The Argument of Redescription," in *Ethics for Adversaries: The Morality of Roles in Public and Professional Life* (Princeton, NJ: Princeton University Press, 2000), 15–42, 76–110. On the relativities of prosecutorial and defense power, see David Luban, "Are Criminal Defenders Different?" *Michigan Law Review* 91 (1993): 1729–66. On defending those who appear to be undefendable, see Abbe Smith, "Defending Defending: The Case for Unmitigated Zeal on Behalf of People Who Do Terrible Things," *Hofstra Law Review* 28 (Summer, 2000): 925–61.

Chapter 9

See, generally, John T. Noonan, Jr., and Kenneth I. Winston (eds.), *The Responsible Judge: Readings in Judicial Ethics* (Westport, CT: Praeger, 1993). For examples of detailed codes of judicial conduct, see American Bar Association, *Model Code of Judicial Conduct* (Chicago, IL: ABA, 2003); Council of Chief Justices of Australia, *Guide to Judicial Conduct* (Carlton, VIC: Australian Institute of Judicial Administration, Inc., 2002). For discussions of particular judicial values, see Shimon Shetreet and Jules Deschenes (eds.), *Judicial Independence: The Contemporary Debate* (Dordrecht: Martinus Nijhoff, 1985); Ofer Raban, *Modern Legal Theory and Judicial Impartiality* (London: Glasshouse Press, 2003). On conflicts of interest, see David Luban, "Law's Blindfold," in *Conflict of Interest in the Professions*, ed. Michael Davis and Andrew Stark (New York: Oxford University Press, 2001), 23–48.

Chapter 10

See, generally, Jeffrey Abramson, *We, the Jury: The Jury System and the Ideal of Democracy*, with a new preface (Cambridge, MA: Harvard University Press, 2000); John Kleinig and James P. Levine (eds), *Jury Ethics: Juror Conduct and Jury Dynamics* (Boulder, CO: Paradigm Publishers, 2006); Valerie P. Hans, *The Jury System: Contemporary Scholarship* (Aldershot: Ashgate, 2006). The seminal discussion of juries is found in Harry Kalven, Jr., and Hans Zeisel, *The American Jury* (Boston: Little, Brown, & Co., 1966). A useful historical discussion can be found in Albert W. Alschuler and Andrew G. Deiss, "A Brief History of the Criminal Jury in the United States," *University of Chicago Law Review* 61 (1994): 867–928. Jury unanimity is defended in Richard A. Primus, "When Democracy is Not Self-Government: Toward a Defense of the Unanimity Rule for Criminal Juries," *Cardozo Law Review* 18 (1997): 1417–57.

Part IV: Corrections

See, generally, John Kleinig (ed.), *Correctional Ethics* (Aldershot: Ashgate, 2006); John Kleinig and Margaret Leland Smith (eds.), *Community, Discretion, and Correctional Ethics* (Lanham, MD: Rowman & Littlefield, 2001).

Chapter 11

On the general theory of punishment, see John Kleinig, *Punishment and Desert* (The Hague: Martinus Nijhoff, 1973); R. A. Duff, *Trials and Punishments* (Cambridge: Cambridge University Press, 1986); Nicola Lacey, *State Punishment: Political Principles and Community Values* (London: Routledge, 1988); Igor Primoratz, *Justifying Legal Punishment*, 2nd edn. (Atlantic Highlands, NJ: Humanities Press, 1999); R. A. Duff, *Punishment, Communication, and Community* (New York: Oxford University Press, 2000); Jeffrie G. Murphy, *Getting Even: Forgiveness and Its Limits* (New York: Oxford University Press, 2003). A useful compendium of materials on capital punishment is Evan J. Mandery (ed.), *Capital Punishment in America: A Balanced Examination* (Boston, MA: Jones & Bartlett, 2004). Restorative alternatives are discussed in John Braithwaite, *Crime, Shame and Reintegration* (Cambridge: Cambridge University Press, 1989); Gerry Johnston (ed.), *A Restorative Justice Reader: Text, Sources, Context* (Cullompton: Willan Publishing, 2003); Andrew von Hirsch, *et al.*, *Restorative Justice and Criminal Justice: Competing or Reconcilable Paradigms?* (Oxford: Hart Publishing, 2003).

Chapter 12

For discussions of imprisonment, see Michel Foucault, *Discipline and Punish: The Birth of the Prison* (New York: Pantheon, 1977); Norval Morris, *The Future of Imprisonment* (Chicago: University of Chicago Press, 1974); Alison Liebling (with Helen Arnold), *Prisons and Their Moral Performance* (Oxford: Clarendon, 2004); and Richard L. Lippke, *Rethinking Imprisonment* (New York: Oxford University Press, 2007). More focused discussions can be found in Richard Harding, "Private Prisons," in *Crime and Justice: A Review of Research*, ed. Michael Tonry, vol. 28 (Chicago: University of Chicago Press, 2001), 265–346; Douglas C. McDonald, "Medical Care in Prisons," in *Crime and Justice: A Review of Research*, ed. Michael Tonry and Joan

Petersilia, vol. 26: *Prisons* (Chicago: University of Chicago Press, 1999), 427–78; Richard L. Lippke, "Against Supermax," *Journal of Applied Philosophy* 21, no. 2 (2004): 109–24; Richard L. Lippke, "Prison Labor: Its Control, Facilitation, and Terms," *Law and Philosophy* 17 (1998), 533–57. Broad critiques of imprisonment can be found in Nils Christie, *Limits to Pain* (London: Martin Robertson, 1981); W. de Haan, *The Politics of Redress: Crime, Punishment and Penal Abolition* (London: Unwin Hyman, 1990).

Chapter 13

On the role of correctional officers, see Alison Liebling, David Price, and Guy Schefer, *The Prison Officer*, 2nd edn. (Cullompton: Willan Publishing, 2007); Elaine Crawley, *Doing Prison Work: The Public and Private Lives of Prison Officers* (Cullompton: Willan Publishing, 2004); Robert Johnson and Shelley Price, "The Complete Correctional Officer: Human Service and the Human Environment of Prison," *Criminal Justice and Behavior* 8, no. 3 (1981): 343–73; John Kleinig, "Professionalizing Incarceration," in *Community, Discretion, and Correctional Ethics* ed. John Kleinig and Margaret Leland Smith (Lanham, MD: Rowman & Littlefield, 2001), 1–15. Various codes for prison officers might also be consulted, e.g., United Nations, Standard Minimum Rules for the Treatment of Prisoners, <www.unhchr.ch/html/menu3/b/h_comp34.htm>; American Probation and Parole Association, Code of Ethics, <www.appa-net.org/about% 20appa/codeof. htm>; United Nations, Basic Principles on the Use of Restorative Justice Programmes in Criminal Matters (UN), 2000, <www.restorativejustice.org/ rj3/UNdocuments/UNDecBasicPrinciplesofRJ.html>.

Chapter 14

Detailed discussion of collateral consequences can be found in Marc Mauer and Meda Chesney-Lind (eds.), *Invisible Punishment: The Collateral Consequences of Mass Imprisonment* (New York: The New Press / W. W. Norton, 2002); Joan Petersilia, *When Prisoners Come Home: Parole and Prisoner Reentry* (New York: Oxford University Press, 2003); Jeremy Travis, *But They All Come Back: Facing the Challenges of Prisoner Reentry* (Washington, DC: Urban Institute Press, 2005). On voting, see Jeffrey Reiman, "Liberal and Republican Arguments against Felon Disenfranchisement," *Criminal Justice Ethics* 24, no. 1 (Winter/Spring, 2005): 3–18.

Index